# KEY CONCEPTS IN BILINGUALISM

# Palgrave Key Concepts

**Palgrave Key Concepts** provide an accessible and comprehensive range of subject glossaries at undergraduate level. They are the ideal companion to a standard textbook making them invaluable reading to students throughout their course of study and especially useful as a revision aid.

Palgrave Key Concepts
Key Concepts in Accounting and Finance
Key Concepts in Bilingualism
Key Concepts in Business and Management Research Methods
Key Concepts in Business Practice
Key Concepts in Criminology and Criminal Justice
Key Concepts in Cultural Studies
Key Concepts in Drama and Performance (second edition)
Key Concepts in e-Commerce
Key Concepts in Human Resource Management
Key Concepts in Information and Communication Technology
Key Concepts in Innovation
Key Concepts in International Business
Key Concepts in Language and Linguistics (second edition)
Key Concepts in Law (second edition)
Key Concepts in Leisure
Key Concepts in Management
Key Concepts in Marketing
Key Concepts in Operations Management
Key Concepts in Philosophy
Key Concepts in Politics
Key Concepts in Public Relations
Key Concepts in Psychology
Key Concepts in Second Language Acquisition
Key Concepts in Social Research Methods
Key Concepts in Sociology
Key Concepts in Strategic Management
Key Concepts in Tourism

**Palgrave Key Concepts: Literature**
*General Editor: Martin Coyle*
Key Concepts in Contemporary Literature
Key Concepts in Creative Writing
Key Concepts in Crime Fiction
Key Concepts in Medieval Literature
Key Concepts in Modernist Literature
Key Concepts in Postcolonial Literature
Key Concepts in Renaissance Literature
Key Concepts in Romantic Literature
Key Concepts in Victorian Literature
Literary Terms and Criticism (third edition)
*Further titles are in preparation*

**Palgrave Key Concepts**
Series Standing Order
ISBN 978-1-4039-3210-5
(*outside North America only*)

You can receive future titles in this series as they are published by placing a standing order. Please contact your bookseller or, in the case of difficulty, write to us at the address below with your name and address, the title of the series and the ISBN quoted above.

Customer Services Department, Macmillan Distribution Ltd, Houndmills, Basingstoke, Hampshire RG21 6XS, England

# Key Concepts in Bilingualism

Fredric W. Field

© Fredric W. Field 2011

All rights reserved. No reproduction, copy or transmission of this publication may be made without written permission.

No portion of this publication may be reproduced, copied or transmitted save with written permission or in accordance with the provisions of the Copyright, Designs and Patents Act 1988, or under the terms of any licence permitting limited copying issued by the Copyright Licensing Agency, Saffron House, 6-10 Kirby Street, London EC1N 8TS.

Any person who does any unauthorized act in relation to this publication may be liable to criminal prosecution and civil claims for damages.

The author has asserted his right to be identified as the author of this work in accordance with the Copyright, Designs and Patents Act 1988.

First published 2011 by
PALGRAVE MACMILLAN

Palgrave Macmillan in the UK is an imprint of Macmillan Publishers Limited, registered in England, company number 785998, of Houndmills, Basingstoke, Hampshire RG21 6XS.

Palgrave Macmillan in the US is a division of St Martin's Press LLC, 175 Fifth Avenue, New York, NY 10010.

Palgrave Macmillan is the global academic imprint of the above companies and has companies and representatives throughout the world.

Palgrave® and Macmillan® are registered trademarks in the United States, the United Kingdom, Europe and other countries.

ISBN 978-0-230-23233-4    ISBN 978-0-230-34446-4 (eBook)
DOI 10.1007/978-0-230-34446-4

This book is printed on paper suitable for recycling and made from fully managed and sustained forest sources. Logging, pulping and manufacturing processes are expected to conform to the environmental regulations of the country of origin.

A catalogue record for this book is available from the British Library.

A catalog record for this book is available from the Library of Congress.

10  9  8  7  6  5  4  3  2  1
20 19 18 17 16 15 14 13 12 11

# Contents

Preface vi

**The Key Concepts** 1

References 192

Index 200

# Preface

In view of the amazing proliferation of terms in studies of bilingualism, it seemed like a good idea to provide a brief, concise, and easy-to-read glossary of some of the most basic concepts a student might encounter in an introductory course. Given the rapid development of technology (and our ability to peer into the human mind/brain), some facets of recent research are quite new and controversial, particularly as long-held beliefs come under intense scrutiny. Researchers want to know what really happens when a child grows up with two languages (good or bad?), how entire communities are shaped by their collective bilingual abilities, and how bilingualism impacts society in general. New terms capture fresh insights, expressing ever greater degrees of specificity, especially as links between language specialists (researchers) and educators (practitioners) continue to grow.

**Purpose and scope**
The world has changed in the last 50 years, and it is not likely to stop changing in the foreseeable future. There is no question that today's teachers will encounter an increasingly multilingual and multicultural classroom. And, this is not just for those who find themselves in urban settings where hundreds of languages are spoken. Twenty-first-century London may very well be a microcosm of the former British Empire, but the same can be said of Los Angeles, California—with a portion of the former Spanish Empire thrown in. Even so, there is a constant flow of migration into remote rural areas, as well, as in-migrants seeking jobs and security travel further and further into the heartland of nations for whom English is the predominant and socially preferred language.

It is also apparent that today's school teachers are being pressed by political forces to improve the lot of their students. Standardized national testing in the United States and the relentless pressure to improve test scores in such basic skills areas as mathematics and the language arts also demand that teachers become experts—or near experts—with an almost global knowledge of learning processes and teaching methods, in addition to a well-developed sensitivity to the host of cultural issues today's students bring with them into a school setting. It is simply not possible to know *every* language that may be heard in the classroom and on the schoolyard or that may be spoken by students with their parents in the home. Nevertheless, educators must serve each and every student.

Consequently, this little book is intended for future and present-day educators, to help them navigate the vocabulary of bilingualism, specifically as it pertains to the concerns of classroom teachers. It is not exhaustive by any stretch of the imagination. But, it is hoped that it covers enough specialized vocabulary to help those who may get stalled in a sea of often conflicting terms. It is designed to be a quick reference for the generalist and those new to areas of research and practice, from a nontheoretical point of view. It is one thing to develop intuitions regarding our students' needs via experience; it is another to learn from others whose areas of expertise may differ substantially from our own. We all need to increase our knowledge and ability to cope with the growing challenges of education in the 21st century.

## Plan of this book

The book lists entries alphabetically so that various terms can be located easily and quickly. All entries are cross-referenced with other concepts and issues that are closely related and, therefore, likely to appear in similar contexts. Definitions are reasonably brief, except, perhaps, in cases when longer explanations seem necessary. At times, some background information is necessary for the reader to comprehend more fully long-standing controversies. Even then, additional reading may be necessary (the entries in this book should provide a sufficient number of keywords to enable a thorough search for more details). In addition, there is a conscious attempt to give illustrations and examples in layman's terms (for the nonspecialist). It is assumed, however, that the typical reader has at least the command of the English language sufficient to handle undergraduate university courses in general. Some overlap among entries is inevitable, but needless repetition is avoided. For example, the terms *bilingualism* and *multilingualism* are typically linked by specialists because in either case, a person speaks more than one language (e.g., see Myers-Scotton 2006: 2). These terms are often used interchangeably, despite the fact that many people might find a semantic difference. To be multilingual might mean to know several languages, and bilingual, only two. Consequently, as the term *bilingualism* is defined, the reader is advised to *see* **multilingualism**.

The field of bilingualism is both multidisciplinary and interdisciplinary, involving autonomous academic fields of study in which lines of separation are becoming increasingly blurred. Therefore, terminology covers several large areas of study. For example, the typical course in bilingualism covers the social and linguistic causes and effects of individual bilingualism and societal bilingualism that encompass interrelated areas of sociology and linguistics (e.g., sociolinguistics). Such courses also cover psychological and neural facets of bilingualism involving knowledge of both psychology and neurology (psycholinguistics and neurolinguistics), especially regarding how the human brain comprehends and produces bilingual speech. There are the psychological and social aspects of specific bilingual language phenomena, the consequences of intense language and cultural contact (e.g., linguistic borrowing, when speakers of one language use words from another); these concepts are traditionally treated by branches of linguistics, sociology, and anthropology. Importantly, for educators, there are a host of terms commonly associated with bilingual education, many of which imply familiarity with educational psychology and current pedagogical practices that, in turn, presuppose some knowledge of all of the above.

With respect to individual bilingualism, this book places an emphasis on terms related to the bilingual child. A bilingual is not merely a person with some knowledge of two languages, and he or she is certainly not two monolinguals (a person who speaks only one language) inside of one body. We are thus quickly drawn to the controversy of how speaking multiple languages influences the way we think, communicate, behave, and interpret the world around us. In addition, a person *becomes* bi- or multilingual whenever he or she learns a new language (as a child or adult); so, a number of terms and concepts related to the acquisition and development of language typical of texts on bilingualism are included. Definitions, consequently, focus on the *processes* of bilingualism and what it means for a person to become bi- or multilingual.

Societal bilingualism is that specific area that covers the social and linguistic issues that crop up when entire communities become multilingual, for example, among immigrant groups that become language minorities as a consequence of in-migration. For instance, within a bilingual community, members will show a wide range of abilities in each language, from (a) full proficiency in one and limited proficiency in the other to (b) native-speaker abilities in both, and (c), all degrees in between. Typically, such a community shifts from a traditional, ancestral, or heritage language to the socially dominant language of society, in a sense, trading in the old language for a new one. However, some groups hold on to their ancestral tongues quite tenaciously. This brings up the fact that younger generations often go through a kind of emotional tug-of-war over language loyalties and adherence to deeply felt cultural beliefs and religious customs, matters that define our views of ourselves and our position in the universe and in society.

Another important set of terms are used to describe the bilingual mind/brain and what is currently known about the way our brains process language—how it is acquired, stored, and used in everyday life. They describe how the individual deals with stronger (psychologically dominant) and weaker languages, where specific functions of language may be located inside the head, and what brain injuries (lesions) reveal about the ways our brains are organized. Language specialists have long discussed how our linguistic abilities differ from general intelligence, but controversies still persist. We can and do "think" without language. We can mention just two activities requiring mental skills: (1) participating in sports in which players must calculate distance, speed, and trajectory of objects while trying to strike or kick them, and (2) playing a musical instrument with some precision and skill. In neither activity do the participants consciously talk to themselves online (so to speak) about what their brains and bodies are doing. It is safe to say that nearly every person who reads this preface will stop from time to time to engage in those inner conversations whereby we put our thoughts (hence, thinking) into words (language). Therefore, measures of linguistic abilities are not necessarily measures of intelligence, our cognitive abilities, or our individual abilities to think. Then, of course, there is the age-old debate of Nature v. Nurture, and what the language faculty (the mental ability to acquire language) says about human nature. The terminology specifically addresses mental aspects of bilingualism and how the brain accommodates multiple language systems.

Regarding the consequences of individual and societal bilingualism, other terms are particularly relevant to all people living in a multilingual world, terms that refer to bilingual language phenomena—which necessitates discussion of cultural and linguistic contact. Many of us have seen adults in stores and markets speaking a "foreign" language to a child, while the child responds (quite capably) *in English*— two people, speaking two different languages, yet somehow communicating and understanding each other. We have all probably witnessed bilinguals using both languages at the same time, moving seamlessly from one to the other in casual conversation (the phenomenon known as "code-switching"). This may be a sign of high degrees of proficiency in both the languages, not necessarily a lack of ability, though it is often thought of that way. Code-switching is one of the normal consequences of long-term societal bilingualism; borrowing of various sorts is another that can lead to language change. Terminology in this area may be particularly helpful to educators who deal with such things on a daily basis.

The final set of associated terms pertains to bilingual education. They cover classroom beliefs and practices and how profoundly they can affect bilingual children. Perhaps, many of today's educators are most concerned that their students attain maximum proficiency in English, and as soon as possible. However, much research indicates that the most efficient path for most language learners to attain full proficiency in English is a bilingual one. It is not necessarily true that adding more intense English instruction (at the expense of a child's native-heritage language) will produce greater ability in English, or that it is the quickest and most effective path to an *educated* form of English. One must respect the bilingual child's social and cultural background or risk provoking negative reactions of the community from which the child originates. This is illustrated time and again by the persistence of indigenous languages in the Americas, which, despite centuries of concerted efforts to obliterate them by colonial powers, are once again thriving as a result of revitalization efforts and the official recognition of their status. Moreover, there are practical and logistical concerns that educators may wish to consider. There are only so many hours in a child's school day: increase the amount of language instruction, and you must decrease the amount of time allotted for academics. Finding the right balance may be the key. Controversial, highly politicized topics concerning the nature of bilingual programs have polarized entire communities for or against bilingual education.

Studies of bilingualism and multilingualism are obviously multidisciplinary, involving large areas of studies that once may have seemed exclusive. However, for the student and academic, it has become increasingly clear that many topics of discussion are necessarily interdisciplinary. The field of bilingualism encompasses appropriately a wide range of topics from how the human mind/brain works to the realm of national and international politics, where theories of language learning and the societal effects of bilingualism are continuous sources of controversy.

## 4-M model

A recent model of code-switching that states there are four kinds of morphemes involved based on their level of activation in language production (Myers-Scotton 2002: 16–18, 2006: 267–271).

As evidenced in research of the Matrix Language Frame (MLF) model, it was clear that all morphemes are not equal with respect to their distribution in bilingual speech (i.e., in conversational, intra code-switching). In essence, these morphemes are divided into content (including the abstract representations of the roots of nouns, verbs, etc.) and system morphemes. The 4-M model is a refinement of the MLF model in that it makes finer distinctions among system morphemes. They are comprised of two types, early-system morphemes (such as plural markers and determiners—e.g., *the* and *a/an*) and late-system morphemes. Late-system morphemes are further divided into bridge (such as conjunctions and particular prepositions) and outsider morphemes, for example, agreement markers that cross phrasal boundaries. (For detailed discussion, read Myers-Scotton 2002: 16–25.) *See* **code-switching, Matrix Language Frame (MLF) model, system morpheme**.

## Access

Access refers to the mental ability to comprehend or retrieve a particular word in the online processing of speech.

In psycholinguistic studies, access involves how the mind/brain organizes the mental lexicon. In general, words can be located in our mental "dictionaries" by their forms (their outward appearances—spoken, written, or signed) or their meanings (each with a number of potential definitions/denotations and implied meanings/connotations). For example, when a person sees an object that he or she recognizes as a chair or desires to use that word in speech, the word "chair" becomes accessible for usage. The speaker, therefore, retrieves the correct word form from her/his mental lexicon for that object. Likewise, when a person sees or hears a word that looks or sounds like the word *chair*, he or she will have access to its meaning. In the case of tangible objects such as chairs, a mental image of the object (according to basic physical or perceptual features—has four legs, a back, seat, etc.). *See* **lemma, lexicon, perception, productive knowledge, receptive knowledge**.

## Acculturation Model

A model of language acquisition that featured cultural factors as causes for the relative speed of development in second/subsequent language acquisition (SLA).

The key study involved six adult learners of English in the oft-cited Harvard Project. One, Alberto, was consistently behind the others in the development of English (Cazden *et al.* 1975; Schumann 1975, 1978). Searching for reasons, Schumann developed the Acculturation Model from an analysis of Alberto's background.

The model was based on the concept of social distance (how far apart groups felt from each other socially and culturally). This was seen as a group-level phenomenon consisting of eight factors: (1) social dominance, (2) integration pattern, (3) enclosure, (4) cohesiveness, (5) size, (6) cultural congruence, (7), attitude, and (8) intended length of residence. Alberto was a member of a subordinate group, a language and ethnic minority that had created a social distance from the target-language group.

The group to which Alberto belonged (Latin American immigrants in Cambridge, Massachusetts) were not socially or culturally dominant, and they maintained their own unique cultural identity. So, their desire to integrate into the surrounding culture was moderate. The group was enclosed, with its own churches, newspapers, and support groups. They were also a cohesive unit, precluding contact with the majority group. Regarding size, the group was large enough to remain culturally separate, maximizing intragroup contact, thus minimizing intergroup contact. As to congruence, significant cultural differences existed between minority and majority ethnic groups. Concerning attitudes, intergroup attitudes ranged from neutral to hostile. Finally, the intended length of stay was not permanent. Thus, motivation to learn the target language and culture was hindered because it was built on utilitarian/instrumental motivation (Larsen-Freeman and Long 1991: 251–266).

The model, though certainly groundbreaking, has been criticized for various reasons, one being that it is not testable; valid measures of social distance have yet to be developed. *See* **attitude, dominant, instrumental, integrative, motivation, Pidginization Hypothesis, recessive**.

### Accuracy

Refers to how well a language learner approximates the speech norms of native or highly proficient speakers of a language variety. It is often implicit that accuracy includes knowledge of a standard language because of the prevalence of personal and institutional biases against nonstandard varieties. Strictly speaking, however, accuracy is relative to the norms of a specific community regardless of how standard their speech might be.

For instance, an English language learner (ELL) may make repeated and systematic mistakes when speaking English. She or he needs to increase her or his accuracy by learning to avoid those mistakes and to exhibit the same kind of production/performance a native speaker shows under normal circumstances according to the tacit "rules" of the language variety. Accuracy is one part of overall proficiency (the ability to use a language successfully or well). The other is *fluency*, which implies the ability to speak quickly (flowingly). *See* **competence, fluent/fluency, performance, proficiency, standard, vernacular**.

### Achievement

Typically refers to the outcome of schooling, the relative success of individual or groups of students.

In many studies of the academic achievement of bilingual students, there is mention of an "achievement gap," meaning that certain language minority students lag behind their monolingual English counterparts. This also suggests that bilinguals appear to have trouble with academic language. Such notions began fairly early on in the literature on bilingualism. For example, the work of Cummins (1976, 1984) made observations that children still learning a second or subsequent language often struggle in school settings, and it was implied that their lack of proficiency in the second language was the cause. Critics of such research over the years have pointed out that the causes most likely lie in socioeconomic factors. Poor academic performance may correlate with low socioeconomic status, but, they do not exist in a cause-and-effect relationship. Being poor does not cause a child to do poorly in school.

In other words, children without a lot of the resources that middle-class (mainstream) students apparently have may not fare as well as their more privileged classmates. Children from lower socioeconomic levels are often speakers of minority languages or nonstandard dialects of English, giving the impression that *language* influences academic success. However, language acquisition and academic progress are two separate issues, though they do appear to be interrelated. For instance, language proficiency refers to factors that include the typically unconscious acquisition of language. Academic performance is often linked to the effects of schooling and various social and economic factors, for example, access to literate forms of (any) language, cultural attitudes to the educational process, and prior experience with the institutions of education. As a term, *achievement* may also refer to progress made in language proficiency as measured by standardized tests. *See* **achievement gap, testing**.

## Achievement gap

The apparent discrepancy on standardized test scores between mainstream students and those from various minority or seemingly impoverished groups. The gap is typically in specific academic skills (e.g., literacy and mathematics), and other content areas such as the sciences. Underlying causes, however, are most likely linked to numerous social issues that act in concert to affect performance in the classroom.

While it is expected that one would find gaps in the academic performances of individuals, and perhaps even groups, there exist large gaps among groups that appear to be based on ethnicity, language proficiency, and socioeconomic status (SES). Extensive national testing in the United States, for instance, shows that these gaps exist. That is, mainstream students seem to do better in standardized tests than do ethnic, language minority, and lower SES children. It is evident that standardized tests are modeled after the values and behaviors of mainstream students, and that various minorities must learn those values and behaviors (and not the reverse).

A lot of research has been devoted to this topic, particularly following the early work of Cummins (1976, 1984) (with language-minority students in the US and Canada), and Skutnabb-Kangas and Toukomaa (1976) and Toukomaa and Skutnabb-Kangas (1977) (with Finnish immigrant children in Sweden) that suggested that poor performance in schools by immigrant children was traceable to their bilingualism despite the fact that they might appear to be proficient in the language of instruction. *See* **BICS, bilingualism, CALP, functional literacy, literacy, multilingualism, testing**.

## Acoustic phonetics

The science of the physical characteristics of language sounds (phones), particularly how it relates to the ways human beings may perceive those sounds according to specific acoustic properties.

For example, differences between sounds that are pronounced roughly in the same place in the vocal tract and in the same manner (/t/ and /d/) can be very subtle. But careful spectrographic analysis can demonstrate differences that the human brain can detect that are, then, interpreted as meaningful contrasts in the specific language to which they belong (as part of its phonetic inventory). *See* **articulatory phonetics, categorical perception**.

## Acquisition

Refers, in general, to the ways knowledge is gained through unconscious observation; it is typically associated with the ways children acquire (or "get") their native languages. It is more like acquiring a skill (e.g., playing a musical instrument or playing a sport).

Acquisition is typically contrasted with *learning* and the ways adults pick up second or subsequent languages. Learning includes types of knowledge that can be memorized or consciously grasped through study and memorization (e.g., an introductory course in linguistics). Many researchers find this distinction useful because children do not receive explicit language instruction but acquire their first languages easily and effortlessly. Second-language (SL) learners often study intensively with various degrees of success. Questions are raised concerning whether or not aspects of a native language are *learned* later in life, and whether (or how much) aspects of a second or subsequent language can be acquired by adults unconsciously through exposure and interaction with native speakers. *See* **Acquisition-Learning Hypothesis, learning**.

## Acquisition-Learning Hypothesis

A hypothesis proposed by Stephen Krashen that creates a distinction between acquiring and learning a human language.

According to the hypothesis, the process of *acquisition* is a result of meaningful interaction (through *comprehensible input*). In contrast, *learning* comes through conscious study (with accompanying attention to form or error correction, e.g., in a formal, classroom situation). In essence, acquisition is a type of learning, and it captures the ways that children "get" their language(s). The term *learning* (or language learning) typically refers to the ways that people learn languages later in life, for example, as adults. The distinction has been useful, particularly for teachers and administrators.

There is much controversy, however, about where the boundaries between acquisition and learning might be, and whether adults can master languages the ways children do. For example, researchers ask if this uniquely human ability to naturally acquire language stops. If so, is it lost suddenly or gradually, completely or partially, permanently or temporarily? Is this loss also biological/developmental? How much of it is based on other social or psychological factors? Do adult learners acquire the *grammar* of the target language in the same or similar developmental steps as those acquiring their first or native language, and what does this tell us about language and the language faculty? What about a critical or optimal age? Other questions are raised concerning the similarities and differences between the two processes, native-language acquisition (NLA) and second/subsequent language acquisition (SLA). Can SL learners *acquire* their new language in the same ways that children acquire their first (native) language? *See* **acquisition, Affective Filter, Critical Period, and Input Hypothesis, Monitor Theory,** **native-language acquisition, Natural Order Hypothesis, and second language acquisition**.

## Activation

The spreading of electro-chemical activity (mental processes) in the brain, detectable by such technological means as magnetic resonance imaging (MRI) and computer-assisted tomography (CT scans).

A language is activated when it is in use. Forms and structures become mentally available for recall and usage. Neurological research has shown that a multilingual person's languages can be activated selectively (individually) or in relative strengths. According to current psycholinguistic research, levels of activation can also be inferred from linguistic evidence, for example, in code-switching (the alternation of languages in conversation) and in other bilingual language tasks such as translation. Such studies shed light on how a bilingual accesses vocabulary items (words and expressions) in each of her/his languages, how degrees of proficiency can affect differential access to a bilingual's languages, and how languages may influence one another. For example, bilinguals typically favor one language over another, and find it easier (or quicker) to translate from a second language to their native (so-called backward translation) language (Michael and Gollan 2005: 391).

The concept of activation is also critical to connectionist models of language processing that have been based on the early work of James McClelland (e.g., McClelland and Rumelhart 1981; McClelland and Elman 1986; Rumelhart and McClelland 1986). *See* **computer-assisted tomography (CT), connectionism/connectionist models, language modes, magnetic resonance imaging (MRI, fMRI), parallel distributed processing (PDP)**.

## Active knowledge

Refers to the type of knowledge or awareness that a speaker requires to produce a form (word or phrase) correctly and in appropriate contexts according to the ways native and proficient speakers produce them. The term *active* is therefore often used interchangeably with *productive*, which is the type of knowledge required for the selection of grammatically correct and appropriate forms (Nation 1990: 30–49). *See* **passive knowledge, productive knowledge, receptive knowledge**.

## Additive bilingualism

A bilingual learning situation in which competence in a second or subsequent language is added to competence in a native language.

For example, those who are proficient speakers of at least one language before emigrating to the United States, the United Kingdom, or other nation in which English is the predominant or official language may learn English as a second language while actively maintaining their native language(s). As they do, they are adding to their existing linguistic repertoire. It is often associated with *sequential* (or consecutive) bilingual acquisition in which languages are learned one after the other. The term is also used in contrast to *subtractive* bilingualism, in which a new language is learned at the expense of a native language. While there are many assumed disadvantages to subtractive bilingualism, for example, losing the ability to read, write, and converse fluently in a heritage language, there are obvious advantages to additive forms of bilingualism. A speaker increases his or her linguistic repertoire while losing nothing. See **language maintenance, sequential bilingual acquisition, subtractive bilingualism**.

### Affective Filter Hypothesis

Refers to an imaginary barrier that goes up when language learners are inhibited in some way due to various emotional states, for example, when they are tense, angry, anxious, upset, or bored.

This hypothesis suggests that, for proper acquisition to take place, teachers should take steps to lower the affective filter for successful acquisition. They should help their students to become comfortable and to relax, therefore, becoming maximally receptive for acquisition processes (which depend on interaction and comprehensible input). Critics point out that it is problematic (though it might appeal to the intuitions of teachers) to measure when a student is comfortable enough to acquire language, or truly how much difference relaxation might make. Students experience some pressure on academic tasks and do quite well. There are two additional objections: First, it is not necessary to hypothesize a specific mental barrier or filter to explain why an upset student is not receptive to a teacher's input or method; and second, the theory fails to distinguish between child acquisition of a native language and acquisition of a second or subsequent language (cf. Cook 1993: 65) NB: *affect*, the root of "affective," includes motives, needs, attitudes, and other emotional states of the learner. See **Acquisition-Learning Hypothesis, comprehensible input, motivation**.

### Age

A significant factor to consider in language acquisition, specifically, the age at which a person begins acquiring/learning a language.

In studies of second/subsequent acquisition, there is a saying that "older is faster, but younger is better." In the short-term, older learners appear to be able to take advantage of their previous knowledge. They can use dictionaries (when literate), ask questions, and speed up the process, at least in the beginning stages of acquisition. Younger children may outperform adults in the long run, and younger adolescents will eventually catch or pass older ones. Ultimate attainment is the key. That is, the final outcome of learning, the degree of knowledge and proficiency in a second or subsequent language is more likely to be better when one starts young in the acquisition process, and the younger the better. As far as age cutoffs, research suggests that one to six seems to be the optimum age for acquisition of native-like pronunciation (Larsen-Freeman and Long 1991). The age factor does not appear to restrict or inhibit acquisition of other areas of grammar such as syntax or morphology, or the growth of vocabulary as much as it does native-like pronunciation. See **age of arrival, aptitude, learning strategies, motivation**.

## Age of arrival (AO)

The age at which a learner arrives at a location where a language is spoken natively. It is often contrasted with *length of residence*, how long a person has lived in a country where the target language is spoken.

Much research seems to indicate that age of arrival is much more critical to language mastery than the actual length of time a person is exposed to a second or subsequent language and its speakers (Larsen-Freeman and Long 1991: 154–163). And, it seems to match the experience of many people that a child seems to pick up a new language rather naturally and easily while adults find it considerably more difficult (or time consuming) to acquire a new language relatively late in life. For instance, a child who came to the United Kingdom and had her or his initial exposure to English at age 2 will most likely be much more proficient by age 12 (10 years later) than an adult who arrived in the United Kingdom at age 40 and has spent the next 20 years there. Obviously, there are many other social factors at work in addition to the amount of exposure and experience that the learner has to English. See **age, attitude, motivation**.

## Ambilingual

An ambilingual is a bi- or multilingual person who can use each of his or her languages interchangeably. The term is patterned after *ambidextrous* (being able to use either hand in writing or in sport). In some senses, this may be the rare *ideal* bilingual. As a term, it appears to be useful in referring to proficient bilinguals, but there is much discussion about definition. For example, there is considerable difficulty in measuring degrees of bilingualism and placing individuals into categories as one type of bilingual or another. This is a particularly sensitive issue for teachers and school administrators who often must label a child who does not appear to be proficient in both or all of his/her languages. Instead of classifying children according to the specific set of language skills they do possess, an institution may classify them according to what they do not possess (i.e., lacks proficiency or specific language skills). See **bilingual, placement**.

## Amerindian

A blend of American and Indian to refer to the indigenous (autochthonous) peoples of the Americas and their languages. Alternative terms are First Nation peoples and Native American preferred in the United States and Canada, respectively. However, the term "Native American" also occurs in political discourse to refer to European-origin Americans born in the United States (therefore, native-born), being co-opted by pro-Americanization groups in opposition to immigrants or naturalized American citizens.

## Aphasia

A group of diverse disorders affecting the ability to communicate by oral and/or written language following an injury (lesion) to the brain (e.g., a stroke).

There has been some conflict on how numerous aphasias should be classified, mainly as a result of different approaches to classification, one that focuses strictly on the affected areas of the brain, and the other on the specific linguistic symptoms. The neurolinguist links specific language abilities to the physical, linking language to the functions of the brain. Linguists of various specialties pay careful attention to the linguistic symptoms that manifest themselves after an injury to the brain. (The symptomatology may suggest where the lesion occurred.) So, the focus of each viewpoint is slightly different.

Information of such events or disabilities gathered from the laboratory of nature have given neurologists, pathologists, psychologists, and linguists a great deal of information about how the healthy human brain may be organized. Specific injuries, in many cases, can be associated with particular regions of the brain, for example, Broca's area and Wernicke's area, areas of the brain named after the neurologists who first investigated them. Nowadays, most work on the mapping of brain functions is done through neuroimaging techniques such as CT scans and fMRIs. It is hoped that the more that is known about brain organization, the more that can be done to prevent or reduce damage and aid recovery. (See Paradis (2004: 63–95) for work on bilingual aphasias.) *See* **Broca's aphasia, CT, fMRI, neuroimaging, Wernicke's aphasia**.

## Approach

A way of handling or solving a problem.

In second-language teaching, specific approaches are typically based on assumptions of the nature of language, the nature of the learner or acquirer, and views of the roles of teachers. Some approaches are determined by the nature of the learning task. Approaches to language teaching draw on psychological assumptions of the nature of language. Hence, an approach reflects a particular model or research paradigm. For instance, an approach based on Cartesian principles will assume the innate knowledge of grammar, while those associated with empiricism will not. While many theorists in second-language teaching try to remain somewhat neutral regarding philosophical views (suggesting eclectic methodologies and appealing to the personal convictions of individual teachers), one's approach will define both the methods and teaching activities one uses in a classroom.

There are two other related terms: *method* and *technique*. Various methods that are derived from identifiable approaches characteristically dominate the textbook market. For instance, in the 1970s, the Natural Approach of Krashen and Terrell reflected the tremendous impact of Chomsky and his colleagues. At that time, the preferred methods were often determined by a general view that favored innateness and the belief that all the language learner needed was exposure to the target of acquisition. Therefore, many specific school districts or programs (as a result of a leadership decision) mandated Whole Language instruction and particular teaching methodologies. Its counterpart on the behaviorist side is Audiolingualism (the audio-lingual method or ALM). This was the dominant teaching method for decades. Students memorized scripts and responded to drills to establish good habit patterns in the target language. They were discouraged from free-flowing conversation because they would inevitably make mistakes, and those mistakes might become entrenched and have to be unlearned.

*Technique* usually refers to the formal way things are done properly (e.g., technique on the oboe). In language pedagogy, it refers to a specific classroom activity or lesson (one practices technique). For example, a particular method known as Total Physical Response (TPR) involves acting out and pointing to individual body parts and objects (e.g., via the parlor game "Simon Says"). Activities such as these avoid translation. (When so-called natural approaches were in vogue, any translation was believed to promote monitoring, and thought to actually slow down the acquisition process.) Some techniques are used widely in many methods, for example, drill, practice with worksheets, reading aloud (Celce-Murcia 1991: 1–10). *See* **audio-lingual method (ALM), behaviorism, method, native-language acquisition (NLA), Natural Approach, second/subsequent language acquisition (SLA), technique, whole language**.

## Aptitude

Concerns mental capacity. It is one of many multidimensional cognitive factors in language acquisition; it implies a special knack for language.

For instance, in a relatively homogeneous student group, where individuals may be from the same socioeconomic background and have other similar personal traits, some students will do better than others. It is hypothesized, as a consequence, that intrinsic ability can account for the differences, for example, that an individual's aptitude for language may relate to a complex collection of personal characteristics, for example, the ability to distinguish sounds, learn new words, and infer grammatical patterns in the target language.

Critics of such a view typically bring up the fact that a child's experience at home can greatly shape such personal and individual factors as personality, aptitude, cognitive style, learning strategies, and other social–psychological factors such as motivation and attitude. Another important issue for teachers and administrators is to what degree assessing aptitude is an attempt to measure intelligence. (The ability to do well in academic subjects such as chemistry has little to do with the knack for language learning that some children have.) In addition, some may be tempted to blur the distinctions between academic progress (e.g., grade point averages which rely more on other social and personal characteristics) and actual language acquisition/learning. *See* **age, cognitive style, learning strategies, motivation**.

## Articulatory phonetics

The study of how individual speech sounds (phones) are pronounced (or articulated) according to the physical aspects of speech.

Articulatory phonetics, therefore, is the formal study and analysis of speech sounds according to such characteristics as the configuration of tongue and lips regarding individual (discrete) vowel sounds, and where in the vocal tract (place of articulation) and how the airflow is altered (manner of articulation) regarding individual consonant sounds. The main principle behind this is that every word in every language consists of individual or groups of sounds that are strung together (assembled in strings), which can, therefore, be divided into discrete sound units and described according to sets of linguistic properties. For example, the word *cat* is represented by the string [k + æ + t]. *See* **acoustic phonetics, phonics, phonological awareness**.

## Assessment

A measurement of language or academic abilities.

Often, formal testing is used at the beginning of a school year to put children into the appropriate grade level, class, or program. When testing is *normative*, it helps an institution place students of similar language backgrounds and proficiency levels into similar classroom situations. However, as obvious as it may seem, assessment is usually only in English in such nations as Australia, the United Kingdom, and the United States, where it is the socially and culturally dominant language. Abilities in a native or heritage language are usually not measured, although they are part of a child's linguistic competence. Consequently, typical school placement tests are not measurements of *bilingual abilities*, only relative proficiency in Standard English. This can also be somewhat misleading. Many children may be very proficient, even native speakers, of English, albeit nonstandard regional or social varieties.

Unfortunately, by virtue of a particular surname or physical appearance, some children may be placed into English language development (ELD) programs and lumped together with speakers of other, "foreign" languages even though they may not speak a language other than English. Thus, a student who is quite fluent in a nonstandard variety of English may be grouped with speakers of foreign languages and enrolled into basic English classes. Conversely, a student who speaks an English-lexicon-based Creole variety (e.g., Jamaican) may be categorized as English-speaking for political (not academic) reasons. Consequently, while assessment is undoubtedly well-intentioned, accurate placement of bilingual children into appropriate classes and programs may require more than a simple mass test. Moreover, children's performance can be affected adversely for social reasons, as well, for example, unfamiliar surroundings, "strange-looking" people, and lack of experience in test-taking techniques. *See* **formative testing, normative testing, self assessment, testing**.

## Assimilation

To become like another, more similar, to blend in. It also implies socializing a child into the dominant culture's ways and values. Cultural assimilation, especially in the United States and the United Kingdom, entails adopting majority behaviors, cultural patterns like dress, physical appearance, attitudes to social institutions (education, the economy, government, and religion), and, of course, the usage of Standard forms of English.

This type of assimilation is often referred to in the United States as the *Americanization* process. In the current political milieu in the United States, Americanization is directly opposed to native language maintenance and the preservation of heritage languages and culture. Nevertheless, there is a long history of conflict between indigenous peoples (American Indians) and the Anglo Saxon culture that lies at the base of nearly all national institutions (political, economic, and educational). While the spread of American forms of English has been relatively thorough, there are linguistic and cultural islands where indigenous languages still flourish. And, with increasing migration from Spanish-speaking countries of Latin America, Spanish has become the second most-used language of North America as the supply of first-generation immigrants and numbers of native speakers of Spanish is constantly replenished.

The term is also used in phonology, the study of articulatory rules or patterns involved in speech, as a process whereby one sound becomes like a neighboring one in online speech. For example, when a vowel occurs before a nasal consonant (e.g., /m/ or /n/) in the same syllable, it will be nasalized (air is diverted from the oral cavity into the nasal cavity, and then through the nostrils). Contrast the vowel sounds of the words *cat* and *can* (pronounce them very slowly). The quality of the vowel in *can* is influenced by its neighboring sound; nasalization, a type of assimilation, occurs in anticipation of the nasal consonant /n/. *See* **phonological awareness**.

## Asymmetry

Refers to the typically unequal relationships between languages (and their speakers), of a socially dominant language and, in contrast, a nondominant (or recessive) language variety.

In the vast majority of language contact situations, one language (or dialect) is usually dominant socially, and politically. As a result, it may be the "official" language of government, commerce, and education. That is, it will be the preferred language in all governmental agencies, the courts, law enforcement, and international diplomacy. It will be the language of banking and finance, and all major transactions regarding the regulation of taxes, the exchange of stocks and bonds, and other operations of financial institutions. And, it is typically the medium of education. As a consequence, other, less powerful languages take lesser roles in society in general. In the United Kingdom and former colonial possessions, English is obviously the language of political and socioeconomic power, typically a majority or prestige language. *See* **dialect, dominant, hegemony, language contact, phenomena, recessive, Standard English**.

## Attainment

Reaching a measure of success; the level or degree of proficiency a language learner reaches.

For example, much of the literature on SLA focuses on the extent to which an adult learner can master a new language. *Ultimate* attainment is, therefore, the degree of proficiency that an SL learner finally reaches (in the long run). This proficiency, of course, can be minimal and only at a beginner's level, or it can be quite extensive and native-like (approximately the same as a native speaker). All analogies to "full," "complete," and similar terms seem to break down, mainly because there is nothing to which one can compare attainment in a second language other than the complete mastery of a language that typically accompanies NLA under normal circumstances—that is, with continual exposure to a language and its speakers. There are unusual circumstances under which the acquisition of a majority or culturally dominant language such as English is interrupted or stopped, for example, when children return to their ancestral homeland and are no longer exposed to English and its native speakers. See **achievement, age, age of arrival, fossilization**.

## Attitude

Mental disposition toward something or someone. For example, it may manifest itself in habitual behaviors toward the speakers of a socially dominant language and culture based on feelings or opinion, in the way one speaks of or treats members of that social group.

Studies have been conducted on how attitude and motivation work in bilingual situations. One pioneering effort was done by Gardner and Lambert (1972) which investigated the attitudes of native English-speaking high school students who were learning French in Canada. They found that test subjects with a higher integrative orientation also performed better in French. The study was conducted using direct surveys (how they felt about French) and so-called "matched guise" experiments. In this procedure, recordings of voices speaking French and English were presented to the subjects who were then asked to rate the personality traits of those voices. For example, they were asked if the speakers were trustworthy or not, intelligent or stupid. What they did not know was that the recordings were made by fluent bilinguals in only one of their languages, so they were reacting to a French or English "version" of the same person (see also Hakuta 1986: 157–160; Wardhaugh 2006: 111–113).

Some bilingual programs can increase a child's positive attitude of himself or herself and his or her linguistic and cultural heritage (building self-confidence), and, thereby increase motivation to learn a new language (Baker 2006: 275; 279–280). However, a person's attitude can be relatively negative, while different forms of *motivation* are strong. For instance, there may be culturally held attitudes of an ethnic or linguistic minority toward members of an ethnic or linguistic majority, of a recessive and relatively powerless social group toward a dominant and powerful social group. The colonial nature of English and its native speakers has left marks on those who were brought under domination. For example, in the United States, a lot of antagonism developed as a result of enforced English-only policies among Native Americans (Crawford 1995: 176–186). Consequently, many people still hold deep-seated animosity toward Anglo Americans. Similarly, in-migrants from Latin America may see the United States and the English language as representing an imperialistic foe known for exploitation. While instrumental motivation may be high to learn English, negative attitudes may inhibit acquisition. See **Acculturation Model, instrumental motivation, integrative motivation, motivation**.

## Attrition

The gradual loss of a population due to death, migration, or other incremental causes.

When applied to languages and processes of language death, it is the gradual disappearance of a language as members of its community die out or move away and are not replaced by new, native speakers. In this manner, the natural transmission of the language is halted. The pool of speakers gradually shrinks until the language is essentially abandoned (it fades from existence) because there are no more speakers. The term may also refer to the gradual loss of forms and structures of the language itself during processes of shift (Campbell and Muntzel 1989; Dorian 1989). *See* **language attrition, language death, shift**.

## Audio-lingual method (ALM)

An approach to second/subsequent language instruction based on a behaviorist view (a la B. F. Skinner) of learning. It stresses habit formation via the memorization of scripts or scenarios (e.g., "¿Dónde está la biblioteca?" in Spanish), constant grammar drill and practice. It focuses on form and the avoidance of mistakes, which are seen as potentially causing bad habits in the performance of the second language. It does not stress fluent, interactive conversations.

This approach has given way in much of the world to more interactive approaches which stress the interaction of learner with various speakers of the target language. Communicative tasks (e.g., gathering information) replace rote memorization and drill. Many current approaches were influenced a great deal by the work of Noam Chomsky that emphasized the unconscious ways that children go about the task of NLA. They essentially recreate their native languages from the ground up, from individual sounds to words, and from words to sentences. The work of Krashen and Terrell (1983), the *Natural Approach*, broke new ground by applying Chomskyan principles to language learning. However, many more recent approaches have come to embrace a blend of the two approaches, according to constructivist views and neo-Piagetian views of biological development which incorporate some practice and drill and error correction with more naturalistic approaches. Current approaches appear to occupy middle ground between the ALM and the Natural Approach. *See* **behaviorism/behaviorist, Chomsky, Natural Approach, interactionist, constructivism**.

## Autobiographical memory

One's own personal remembrances of past experiences as an example of language as a medium of thought (and personal narrative).

Most of us can't remember what happened when we were very young; most such early childhood memories, when they do occur, are of isolated, perhaps traumatic events. Continuous memories usually begin when we are around 4 and a half years old (Hoff 2009: 284). There is little consensus on why that is, other than to suggest that language is somehow involved, and that culturally influenced ways of recounting our pasts may also affect the ways memories are stored.

Regarding bilingual autobiographical memory, it appears that memories are recorded in a language-specific manner. That is, memories are tied to the original language of encoding (memory storage). For example, pre-immigration memories were recalled in the bilingual's original first language, even when given specific language cues in the second (Heredia and Brown 2006: 230–232). *See* **encode**.

### Babbling
The beginning stages of childhood speech, particularly as syllables begin to emerge in regular patterns.

Even before infants learn their first words, they assemble individual speech sounds into utterances that contain sound clusters or syllables (e.g., ba-ba). They typically learn to produce sounds (phones and phonemes), put them together in combinations of sounds, and apply the intonation patterns that they have acquired to these utterances. This is the first step in the emergence of the spoken language. Eventually, of course, they hit proverbial pay dirt with sound combinations such as "ma-ma" and "pa-pa" and discover the wonders of spoken language. Bilingual infants (in BLFA) show the ability to perceive separate phonological systems for their languages, and early babbling progresses as with monolingual children of each language (Yip and Matthews 2007: 9). It remains to be seen how sociolinguistic factors affect bilingual babbling (De Houwer 2009: 169–171), particularly, regarding the dominance of one language (and the influence of the mother tongue/maternal language).

Apparently, there is no direct connection to the famed biblical account of the Tower of Babel where the languages of the world were confounded and people could no longer understand each other. However, the sense of the word "babble" is similar—baby seems to be happily saying something rather important, but listeners fail to comprehend. *See* **Bilingual First Language Acquisition (BFLA), canonical babbling, nonreduplicated babbling**.

### Babbling drift
When a child's babbling gradually drifts in the direction of the language being learned (the target). *See* **babbling**.

### Balanced bilingual
A person who is, in principle, highly proficient in both (all) the languages that he or she possesses. It is implicit that he/she is both fluent and accurate (able to speak according to native-speaker norms) in either language.

Balance seems to entail the bilingual's being adept in a wide range of registers in both languages, from the informal registers of speech used with family and close friends to the formal, academic (typically written) language used in institutional settings such as school. It is also assumed that degrees of literacy are equal in both languages so that the bilingual can read and write in either with equal ease. However, such terms as "ideal bilingual," "full bilingualism," and "balanced bilingual" have been criticized because they imply that other types of bilingualism are less than ideal, a consideration especially for educators in modern multilingual societies (Romaine 1995: 6). The fact that the truly ambilingual person is a relative rarity points to the need to see other types of bilingualism more as the norm, rather than lesser states of bilingualism. See **ambilingual, bilingual, biliteracy, registers, semilingualism**.

## Behaviorism/behaviorist

Looking at the actions and psychological events of human beings (organisms) as behaviors. As a philosophical doctrine or school, it sees psychology as the science of behavior, and not of mind *per se*. Conceived in this way, there can be no innate thoughts or "thought" apart from the physical impulses that govern human action.

It also includes the theoretical view of some philosophers and psychologists that all knowledge, including the knowledge of language, is a product of experience, or conditioned response, and that behavior can be explained as the effects of factors outside of the mind/brain. A behaviorist perspective is that the brain starts out as a blank slate, or *tabula rasa* upon which all human abilities and knowledge are etched by experience alone. It is typically associated with the psychologist B. F. Skinner and behaviorist approaches to language instruction (e.g., *ALM*) that stress grammar drill and practice, repetition, and memorization. See **Audio-lingual method, empiricism, Locke, Skinner**.

## BICS (basic interpersonal communication skills)

According to James Cummins, the elementary type of speech necessary for basic communication, for example, for children to form relationships with peers or for adults to function relatively successfully in society.

As an outgrowth of the Threshold Hypothesis were claims by Cummins in the early 1980s of two different kinds of language skills, BICS (basic interpersonal communication skills) and CALP (cognitive/academic language proficiency), the first obviously associated with informal, spoken language (which, according to Cummins, takes from one to three years to master), and the other with highly literate, written forms. This distinction has appealed to the intuitions of teachers, who see their bilingual students struggle with an English-based curriculum.

Such theories, however, are open to criticism, particularly from language specialists who see them as somewhat simplistic. They apparently (1) fail to consider a child's semantic and pragmatic competence while looking only at surface grammatical performance (e.g., on standardized tests); (2) they lack empirical evidence based on well-constructed research; (3) they are full of implicit, subjective judgments about language and supposed links to intelligence, and oversimplifications of the true nature of language acquisition; and (4) they typically understate the complex relationships among a child's language development, cognitive development, social environment, and experience in the classroom (Hoffman 1991: 130–135; Larsen-Freeman and Long 1991: 62–63, 88–92; Romaine 1995: 265–273; Baker 2006: 170–180). See **CALP, Cummins, elaborated code, pragmatic knowledge, restricted code, Thresholds Theory**.

## Bidialectal

A person who is relatively proficient in more than one dialect of a language. Obviously, this term can be controversial, particularly in view of the difficulties that professional linguists have in defining the words *language* and *dialect*.

For example, one problem encountered in the United States is with African American Vernacular English (AAVE), also known as Ebonics. Is it a dialect of English, or is it a separate language with African roots? While its status has been debated quite vigorously on social and ethnic grounds for a number of years, the vast majority of linguists see AAVE as a legitimate dialect of American English. Perhaps part of the debate harkens back to a time when AAVE, previously known by names such as Black English (BE) and Black English Vernacular (BEV), was considered merely "bad" or "broken" English, and when it was considered inferior to or below standard (substandard) (Dillard 1972). Today, linguists refer to such social varieties as *nonstandard* in that they are simply not standard. In view of the fact that AAVE functions like any language or dialect, with all the expressive and informational functions as any so-called standard, it should not be referred to substandard. *See* **dialect, nonstandard, standard.**

## Bilingual

A term used to refer to persons who possess or can speak two languages. It is often used interchangeably with *multilingual*. In either case, a person speaks more than one language (see Myers-Scotton 2006: 2). In addition, it is used as an adjective to designate types of educational or government programs, for example, bilingual education, bilingual services, and so on.

Definitions are notoriously problematic. There are questions of how proficient one must be in both languages, for example, if one year of high-school French counts as "knowing" a language and qualifies a person, say an English speaker, as bilingual. Therefore, because proficiencies can vary considerably, all definitions of *bilingual* will be relative and perhaps subjective. It may be a bit like "beauty is in the eye of the beholder." For example, the so-called *balanced bilingual* is one who is equally adept at both; however, balanced bilinguals are relatively rare. In contrast, a *functional bilingual* may be fully proficient in a native or ancestral language, but only be able to get by in a second or subsequent language. (The reverse is also a possibility in cases of *language attrition*.) Many otherwise proficient bilinguals lie somewhere between extremes in either or both languages. *See* **ambilingual, assessment, balanced bilingual, communicative competence, dominant, functional bilingual, language attrition**.

## Bilingual contact languages

*See* **contact languages**.

## Bilingual education

In principle, bilingual education is academic instruction in more than one language, specifically designed and intended for language-minority (bilingual) children.

For economic and political reasons, however, bilingual education is not always available. In nations where one language is overwhelmingly dominant socially, minority-language children face little opportunity for education in their native languages. For example, in many nations where English is the predominant language, English-only instruction is substituted for true bilingual education under the guise of enabling language-minority students to achieve sufficient proficiency in English to be placed in mainstream classrooms—academic instruction is always in English, with little or no support for those who speak a minority language. In this sense, students are placed into ESL (English as a second language) classrooms in which language instruction is first and foremost.

As a consequence, many educators rank types of programs according to their sensitivity to language-minority students, for example, whether they are strong or weak. Names can be deceiving because some programs are ostensibly aimed at the bilingual student, but they are essentially monolingual programs. For example, the purpose of *structured immersion*, *sheltered English*, and *content-based ESL* is to transition students as quickly as possible into mainstream classrooms. Weak bilingual programs involve limited minority-language instruction, for example, so-called transitional programs. The goals and outcomes of both monolingual and weak forms of bilingual education are monolingualism and subtractive bilingualism. In contrast, strong forms aim for additive bilingualism and biliteracy, that is, the ability to read and write both languages at advanced levels. For example, two-way and dual immersion programs feature a balance of English and heritage language instruction (see Baker 2006; Field 2011). It is important to distinguish ESL in essentially monolingual programs from true bilingual education. *See* **bilingual programs, dual immersion, immersion, mainstream/mainstreaming, SDAIE, sheltered, structured immersion, submersion, subtractive bilingualism, tracks**.

## Bilingual families

Families in which two languages are used.

Romaine (1995) identifies bilingual families according to a set of types that point to the possible complexity of a single household. For example, living under the same roof, there may be more than one type because of the nature of the extended family (several generations living together), with speakers showing various degrees of proficiency in their languages, and who have learned their languages sequentially or simultaneously. The following is a summary:

*Type 1: One person—One language.* In this scenario, the native language of one parent is the dominant language of the community and each parent speaks his or her own language to the child (with competence in each other's language).

*Type 2: One Language—One Environment.* Again, the native language of one parent is the dominant language of the community. However, the parents choose to speak the nondominant language to the child at home, possibly with the idea of maintaining a heritage language and transmitting cultural values through membership in the minority language community.

*Type 3: Nondominant Home Language without Community Support.* This scenario involves some subtle differences. Parents share *the same* native language, for example, Spanish or Punjabi, a culturally recessive language; they speak their native language with their children. Both parents are nonnative speakers of the dominant language; perhaps one or both are English learners. In Type 1 and Type 2 families, it is likely that at least one parent is familiar with Anglo-Saxon culture. The Type 3 family is quite common, particularly for first-generation in-migrants. They are essentially without the support of extended family members because they are still establishing residence, new communication networks, and employment for themselves, and for their children.

*Type 4: Double Nondominant Home Language without Community Support.* In this type of family, parents have *different* native languages, and neither language is the dominant one. Each parent speaks his/her native language to the child from birth (producing a multilingual child). In urban environments, this is not uncommon, especially in communities where ESL programs are offered for adults of many language backgrounds. People meet and form unions to raise families. The child is left to learn English in school (or in day care) or from SL-learners in the home (e.g., from older siblings).

*Type 5: Nonnative Parents.* This situation is relatively rare. Both parents are native speakers of the dominant language. However, one of the parents addresses the child in a nonnative language. For example, both the father and mother speak English, but the father uses another language such as French or German with the child (Romaine 1995: 185). With an increased interest in American Sign Language (ASL) and the knowledge that learning a language natively will have a long-lasting impact, some parents teach ASL to their children. An interesting fact of ASL is that the majority of its speakers (signers) are nonnatives, a consequence of the numbers of deaf and hard-of-hearing children born to hearing parents. Of course, parents who are deaf or hard of hearing will teach their children to be native signers. In the event that their children are able to hear, deaf parents may seek ways to provide an oral language environment for the child, with grandparents and/or other family members. In any case, a child who knows ASL and an oral language is bilingual.

*Type 6: Mixed languages.* This scenario is probably best understood in second- and third-generation households in which both parents are proficient bilinguals and large segments of the community are proficient bilinguals, as well. Individual behaviors have spread throughout the community to the extent that the social conditions for bilingual behaviors and language mixing are almost always present. The existence of bilingual phenomena is accepted and perhaps even encouraged in particular social contexts. There is no patterned bilingualism like that of the Type 1 family, one language—one person, nor in the Type 2 family, one language—one environment. In Type 6 families, both parents mix languages in various ways through rapid conversational code-switching and different levels of borrowing. So, conversational CS occurs irrespective of participants, setting, and topic. Children will engage in intrasentential CS with parents, even grandparents, with most caregivers, and particularly among themselves (among siblings and close friends). *See* **bilingual, bilingual modes, bilingualism.**

## Bilingual First Language Acquisition (BFLA)

Cases of simultaneous language acquisition in which exposure to both languages begins before age three (Yip and Matthews 2007: 25–27). The term refers to native bilingualism, or the acquisition of two (bilingual) first languages.

Establishing which of a bilinguals' languages is her/his native language is obviously important when trying to establish fair comparisons with monolingual children (Romaine 1995: 181). Additional questions follow: For example, does the native bilingual have one language system (that includes both languages—which may account for various types of language mixing in children's speech), or does he/she have two independent systems? This controversy is between those who hold to one, unitary language system in early bilingual development, and those who propose separate development.

Native-language acquisition (NLA) starts at an early age, perhaps even at or before birth. It is evident that this capacity to acquire a native language is influenced by age. While this ability doesn't exactly stop, there is surely something different about learning a language as an adult. However, it is not so clear what the differences are—which particular language skills are diminished. Among the attempts at fixing an age after which processes of NLA may be affected, McLaughlin (1978) proposed the age of three, admittedly somewhat arbitrarily. For lack of a better alternative, McLaughlin's proposal has proved as good a place as any to start. (One also must face the fact that children show evidence of language acquisition at different ages, although all seem to go through the various stages in nearly the same order.) *See* **Acquisition-Learning Hypothesis, Critical Period Hypothesis, native-language acquisition (NLA), one system (or two), second/subsequent language acquisition, Separate Development Hypothesis, sequential bilingual acquisition, simultaneous bilingual acquisition**.

## Bilingual interactive activation (BIA)

An influential connectionist model or theoretical conceptualization of the bilingual lexicon—how a bilingual's vocabulary in her/his respective languages may be structured in the brain (Dijkstra and Van Heuven 1998; Dijkstra 2005: 188v–191; Murre 2005: 164).

It involves written word recognition on different levels, letter characteristics, letters, words (more frequent letter combinations are easier to access), and language nodes (the ability to recognize which language a word comes from). It asserts that words from different languages are represented in a single, unified, or integrated lexicon at the word level (words from both languages in one mental lexicon), and accessed via a language node (a theoretical neural connection). During the initial stages of written word recognition, for example, the selection possibilities that become activated along a particular language node or pathway will be favored. They will be more easily retrieved by virtue of the activation level along their neural connections (influenced by frequency of occurrence of the word). Context, then, acts to disambiguate word choice. The BIA, however, has no model for language acquisition (how that bilingual lexicon becomes organized). *See* **access, activation, bilingual interactive model of lexical access (BIMOLA), bilingual lexicon, connectionism, lexicon, parallel distributed processing (PDP)**.

### Bilingual interactive model of lexical access (BIMOLA)

An influential connectionist model or theoretical conceptualization of the bilingual lexicon that focuses on spoken word recognition (Grosjean 1998; Dijkstra 2005: 188–191; Murre 2005: 164–165).

It emphasizes separate mental lexicons (or modules) for each language, and consists of separate levels, a phoneme level and a word level. Words are, therefore, activated (accessed and retrieved) at progressive levels (or modules) according to word features (that either language may have), individual sounds (phonemes), and whole (phonological) words. The activation of a single phoneme, for example, activates ("lights up") candidates with similar initial phonemes, but inhibits all possibilities with other phonemes. Activation then moves on to the next level, where phoneme combinations (phonological words) light up, and less likely candidates are inhibited (screened out or blocked). See **access, activation, bilingual interactive activation (BIA), bilingual lexicon, connectionism, lexicon**.

### Bilingual language phenomena

Linguistic phenomena such as *code-switching* (the alternation of languages in conversation), *diglossia* (assignment of languages into domains of usage), and linguistic *borrowing* (using words from one language in another) that are typical of situations of intimate and long-lasting cultural contact.

Such situations are typically asymmetrical in that one language (X) is *dominant*. It may be the language of a prestigious, majority, or culturally (hence, politically and economically) influential group. The other language (Y) is often referred to *recessive* (according to a genetics model) because it is not culturally or socially dominant. Its speakers may belong to an ethnic minority, and their language may be socially disfavored within society at large. As a consequence of contact and the pressures of adapting to a new culture and/or language, speakers of Y will become conversant in the new language (X); they will become bilingual to varying degrees. In such situations, it is quite normal for bilinguals to borrow words from the dominant language, assign languages to particular social domains (at home, in school), or alternate usage of the languages in daily, conversational usage. See **borrowing, language contact phenomena, code-switching, diglossia, dominant, recessive**.

### Bilingual lexicon

The mental store of vocabulary items of the bilingual's languages.

According to research on what it means to "know" a word, the mental lexicon includes (a) all the forms a particular word may take (e.g., *go/goes-went-gone-going*), (b) its grammatical function (e.g., verb), (c) its core meaning, and (d) all the possible meanings it can have according to the speaker's knowledge of the world (idioms, specialized usages in a wide variety of discourse contexts). For instance, the word *red* expresses a particular color, but it can be made into a verb (*redden*) and can be used to apply to political views and even military entities (the *Red Army*). In the case of the *bilingual lexicon*, it remains to be seen to what degree the lexicon of one language (a stronger or native language) influences the other (one learned as an adult), or if a native bilingual has two entirely independent lexicons or one, unified bank or store of words that are all interconnected. See **lemma, lexicon**.

## Bilingual programs

Various educational individual programs ostensibly designed for bilingual students. There are significant differences, however, regarding the goals of such programs.

In that the term *bilingual education* can mean many things to many people, any use of the term *bilingual* can be problematic. It can mean almost anything from (a) the education of a child in two (or more) languages with the goal of a bilingual and biliterate student to (b) a systematic program of language instruction designed to eliminate a child's native language. Therefore, different bilingual programs may reflect conflicting goals and contrary anticipated outcomes. For example, English-only programs (e.g., mainstreaming/submersion, structured immersion, Sheltered English, and Content-based ESL) aim to assimilate language-minority children into the majority language and culture by using only the politically predominant language as the medium of instruction. They are essentially monolingual programs for bilinguals.

Weak forms of bilingual education can be thought of as compromises of sorts. They allow for some instruction in the child's native language to alleviate concerns of drastic submersion programs. The prevailing type of program in the United States is *transitional bilingual education* (TBE). Overall, its goal is assimilation, so transitional programs are still subtractive in nature. But, because there is some attention spent to the children's L1, there may be some language maintenance, and strict unilingualism (monolingualism) is not necessarily an outcome. Another weak form is *mainstreaming with foreign language* teaching. It involves elementary schools composed mostly of native speakers of the majority language in which a few foreign languages are introduced ostensibly for enrichment as part of a "well-rounded" education.

Strong forms of bilingual education all share the desired outcome of bilingualism and biliteracy. Minority languages are given equal status with the majority language. Programs are built on an additive, enrichment model, rather than on a compensatory model (temporarily making up for the pressure to lose a heritage language and culture) that weak forms are patterned after. They are also designed to last longer than TBE, going for at least four or five years, ideally from kindergarten until the sixth grade and beyond. In two-way/dual language programs, sometimes referred to as *developmental bilingual education* (DBE), both languages are used as media of instruction. Because there are two targets for acquisition, this has the effect of emphasizing the languages. In *heritage language bilingual education*, the children's home language is used as the medium of instruction, for example, in specific programs used for indigenous languages such as Navajo, Ojibwa, Cherokee, Dakota, Inuit (Eskimo), native Hawai'ian, and also for Spanish in areas where it is a common home language and where it is the majority vernacular in the community. (*See* Baker 2006: 213–225, for detailed discussion.) *See* **bilingual education, immersion, mainstream/mainstreaming, structured immersion, submersion, two-way/dual language programs.**

### Bilingual Syntax Measure (BSM)

One of a number of bilingual language assessment tests that were developed in the late 1960s that were designed to measure the average length of a child learner's utterances in terms of morphemes (word roots and affixes). While it has had its critics, it is still used by some to estimate a child's language development.

Many such assessment instruments were created as a result of *Lau v. Nichols* and an upswing in government-funded bilingual education programs. The BSM primarily focuses on oral language proficiency using a question-answer format (Burt, Dulay, and Hernández-Chavez 1976). In a well-known study, Dulay and Burt (1973) asked ELLs 33 questions about a series of seven colored cartoon drawings. The questions elicited responses that contained a range of grammatical structures, for example, particular word endings that were obligatory in their contexts. They adapted a list of grammatical morphemes from Roger Brown's landmark study of the native acquisition of grammatical morphemes (Brown 1973). Brown's study made no claims about the nature of the order of morphemes. However, the intent of Dulay and Burt was to assess L2 acquisition of English. The list included the noun plural –s, progressive verbal suffix –ing, the copula be, auxiliary be, articles a and the, irregular past verb forms, verbal third-person (present tense) –s, and noun possessive –s (a list similar to but not identical with those of Brown's study). The results showed a pattern that provided evidence of a common order, linking NLA with second-language learning, and a supposed "natural order." Dulay and Burt's findings intrigued SLA researchers because it begged the question of why such an order could be found and implied that grammatical morphemes were acquired according to a scale of difficulty or complexity. In fact, their work spawned an entire genre of morpheme-order studies, each improving on the basic premise.

In spite of its intuitive appeal, subsequent research has demonstrated that the order of morphemes in SLA differ from that of NLA. L2 learners, however, irrespective of native language background, showed significant similarities with each other (Larsen-Freeman and Long 1991: 88–92), which is certainly interesting in itself. Criticisms of the findings and methodology have been many. Among them is the rather simple observation that the items on the list are heterogeneous, at best. The term *grammatical morphemes* (used in the original Brown study), for example, was underdefined, referring to both free (function words) and bound morphemes (inflections). While some affixes represented grammatical categories applied to nouns, others represented those applied to verbs. The morphemes are also language specific, and findings cannot be applied to languages such as Chinese (or Vietnamese) that have no inflectional morphology. Children who acquire languages rich in inflectional morphology appear to learn these systems easily and with little error. Thus, the specific results of Dulay and Burt may have been a consequence of language-specific difficulties in the acquisition of English, influenced by the age of the subjects, their native language (Spanish), or as a direct result of the circumstances of acquisition (tutored vs. untutored settings) (Cook 1993: 25–36). See **assessment, Lau v. Nichols, MLU, Natural Order Hypothesis**.

### Bilingualism

In general, the state of being bilingual, speaking or possessing two languages. As with the terms *bilingual* and *multilingual*, it is often used interchangeably with *multilingualism*. Essentially, bilingualism is an instance of multilingualism (knowing more than one language). The term can also refer to such things as language policies (e.g., the planned bilingualism of Canada). *See* **bilingual, multilingual**.

## Bilinguality

The term specifically denotes "bilingualness," the quality or personal characteristics of being bilingual. It is generally synonymous with *bilingualism*, but excludes political ("planned bilingualism") and educational usages ("bilingual programs"). *See* **bilingualism, multilingualism**.

## Biliterate/biliteracy

The ability to read and write in two languages.

Similar to the problematic definitions of bilingual/bilingualism, biliteracy is a gradient or relative notion, particularly in view of the range of literacy types that are possible in each language. However, any definition of biliteracy must include all the types of literacy in either or both languages, especially those types of literacy that are required for language minority students (both indigenous and in-migrant) required for institutional (academic) settings. Simple functional definitions do not do justice to how formidable the obstacles are for particular language minorities when attempting to acquire literacy in English.

In nations where English is the predominant language, literacy in languages other than English is typically not measured. Wiley (2005: 16–17) points out, literacy is often equated with literacy only in English. All possibilities within a bilingual community, however, exist, ranging from biliteracy to literacy (in one or other language), to nonliteracy. That is, many bilinguals are literate in their native languages; hence, if there is any cognitive advantage to literacy, *per se*, then this should be apparent by their first-language literacy skills. Based on what is known of transfer, language learners can successfully transfer skills from their native language to the target of SLA (so-called "positive transfer"). Consequently, educational practices that systematically deny access to school materials which promote native-language literacy are a disservice to language minority students.

Though no causal relationship has been firmly established between employment and literacy, lower socioeconomic status (SES) does seem to correlate with both lack of academic achievement and low rates of literacy. English proficiency is often linked to getting jobs and having educational opportunities, and rightfully so. For example, data from the National Chicano Survey (1979) (which was designed to measure attitudes toward bilingualism and biliteracy in Chicano-Latino homes) suggested that there was a strong correlation between literacy in English and family income. By comparison, those who were nonliterate (not literate in either language) showed significantly lower family income. But, Spanish literacy was also important. Biliterates had higher rates of employment than those literate only in English, even though family income was slightly lower than those literate in English only (Wiley 2005: 103). *See* **language ideology, literacy, literacy myth, transfer**.

## Biologically transmitted (biological transmission)

Refers to the way particular genetic traits are passed from one generation of organisms to the next generation of offspring or descendants. The faculty of language, and not specific languages, is genetically transmitted from biological parents to their individual offspring. Specific languages are culturally transmitted typically from one generation to the next through interactions among parents, children, and various members of the community. See **culturally transmitted.**

## Bootstrapping

Patterned after the expression, "to lift oneself by your one's bootstraps" (meaning figuratively, to succeed with the help of existing resources). Thus, bootstrapping in language acquisition is using knowledge of one aspect of language to succeed in another.

For instance, the *semantic bootstrapping* hypothesis asserts that a learner uses the meaning of a word to help figure out its syntactic functions in a sentence. For example, in a child's view, semantic *agents* usually are grammatical *subjects* (people do things) in languages like English. Conversely, *syntactic bootstrapping* occurs when a learner uses syntactic knowledge (of word order or inflection) to pinpoint the meaning of a word. For example, there is the oft-cited example of the nonsense word *blick*. *Show me the blick*. Its position (after *the*) is a clear indication that it is a noun or name word. Shown a picture, children will search for an unfamiliar object—the *blick*. Some theorists feel that the two, semantic bootstrapping and syntactic bootstrapping, go together and are vital for child language acquisition (see, e.g., Karmiloff-Smith 1992: 45–47). See **mutual exclusivity, taxonomic assumption, whole-object assumption**.

## Borderlands

Areas near political boundaries where there is a great deal of social and cultural contact, hence language contact.

For example, the entire border that stretches from Texas westward into California that separates the United States from Mexico is a borderlands area. It contains communities and cities that straddle the political boundary that were sometimes almost arbitrarily established—that is, not always along a prominent river like the Rio Grande or along any other kind of natural barrier. Communities depend on the exchange of workers and international shipping routes that typically pass through border crossings and the like. For example, in California, the cities of San Diego and Tijuana, Mexico, sit almost adjacent to each other. People on either side travel across the border on a daily basis to go to work or school, or to engage in all sorts of commercial activities. All along this border, Spanish and English are in continuous contact, and bilingual language phenomena of all kinds occur on a daily, moment-by-moment basis. There are similar situations along the US border with Canada, where French and English are in contact.

Europe has changed considerably with the emergence of the European Union. Shared highways that were once international trade routes marked by border crossings now facilitate trade throughout Western Europe, not to mention one type of currency (the Euro) and laws encourage the exchange of goods and ideas. Nevertheless, nation-states still have what amounts to borderlands areas where political boundaries separated allies, competitors, and foes. A long history of cultural and linguistic contact flourishes despite the (near) disappearance of borders. See **bilingual language phenomena, contact**.

## Borrowing

The use of a word from one language in the usage of another.

For example, the word *tortilla* is a common word in American English, especially in the American Southwest. It is used to refer to a round type of flat bread used in Mexican food dishes. It has been borrowed into English basically for convenience (there is no English word for such a thing). The word, however, originates in Mexican Spanish, and is an adaptation of the Spanish word meaning *omelet* (made from eggs). Many words from Mexican Spanish have been borrowed into US English for the same type of purpose, to fill holes in the lexicon, to represent novel cultural items (like tortillas or tacos).

Borrowing can involve words from any class, though content words are preferred in every borrowing situation. Among content items, there is a hierarchy of sorts, with classes of noun borrowed more frequently and before verbs (chronologically) in the vast majority of cases (see Field 2002). Languages can also borrow meanings (without the form), for example, in *loanshifts*, including *loan translations* (*calques*), in which a meaning is borrowed and represented (morpheme by morpheme) by a native form (e.g., the English *Superman* from German *Übermensch*), and *semantic loans* (or extensions), in which an already existing native word adds (or expands to include) a novel meaning, for example, the Spanish word *grados* ("degrees") to include *grades* (Spanish *notas*) (Field 2002: 9). Thomason and Kaufman (1988) also suggest that the types of words and structures that are borrowed increase with the length and intensity of contact. The longer and more intense the contact is, the deeper the borrowing, including grammatical traits of the donor language. See **contact, bilingual language phenomena, donor, recipient**.

## Bottom-up

Approaches to language teaching that feature attention to form, and the construction of language knowledge from the basic building blocks of language (sounds and words) up to the "higher realms" of meaning in discourse (cf. Morley 1991: 87–88).

Bottom-up approaches feature direct and overt instruction on grammatical structures and the rudiments (e.g., phonics-based approaches to reading). Critics point out that this is unlike the unconscious process of language acquisition in which children acquire language naturally and through observation, with little attention to grammatical correctness. The concepts of top-down or bottom-up approaches are based on the observation that language consists of a hierarchy of forms. Sentences consist of words; words consist of morphemes; morphemes consist of phonemes. Bottom-up approaches are contrasted with *top-down* approaches, in which meaning is considered the driving force of acquisition—that is, the need to interact and communicate with speakers of the target language of acquisition. In some teaching methodologies, bottom-up approaches have been criticized as missing the point of natural acquisition, and were seen as counterproductive in that they apparently promote monitoring (inhibiting acquisition). See **Acquisition-Learning Hypothesis, Monitor Theory, phonics, top-down**.

## Brain-imaging technique

Any of a number of techniques or tests showing relative levels of brain activity in various parts of the brain when performing different tasks. *See* **CT (Roentgen-ray computed tomography, functional magnetic resonance imaging (fMRI), neuroimaging, Positron emission tomography (PET)) scans**.

## Broca's aphasia (also known as motor aphasia, efferent motor aphasia, and verbal aphasia)

A type of aphasia that has characteristic effects on language.

Patients with Broca's aphasia are characterized by a reduction or loss of the ability to speak, but with relatively little restriction to the ability to comprehend speech. Speech production is labored, with relatively short word groupings of around three words (content words like nouns and verbs with no grammatical morphemes). Certain formulaic and frequently used expressions may be uttered with ease, while uncommon words may be distorted. The severity of impairment will range from mild awkwardness to the complete inability to pronounce words. Word order may be affected, and there is limited access to vocabulary items (lexical access is impaired). Comprehension on the one-word level may be normal, while processing of longer utterances is usually poor (Goodglass 1993: 209–210). In addition, Broca's patients are usually very aware of the difficulty they have in speaking, increasing their level of frustration. *See* **aphasia, Wernicke's aphasia**.

## Broca's area

A specific area of the brain located in the left hemisphere at the foot (anterior portion) of the frontal gyrus (fold or bump). It controls facial neurons, physical (movement) aspects of speech production, and language understanding. It is involved with movements of the tongue, lips, and vocal cords.

The region was named after Pierre Paul Broca, a French surgeon, who in 1861 noted specific language impairments in two of his patients after damage to this area. Since then, the region of the brain that he pinpointed is known as Broca's area, and the speech deficit that results from injury is called Broca's aphasia. In recent work in brain scans, various language functions have been located there by fMRI (cf. Thomas 1989: 18–19, 249). *See* **aphasia, Broca's aphasia, connectionism/connectionist models, fMRI, MRI, Wernicke's aphasia, Wernicke's area**.

## CALP (Cognitive/academic language proficiency)

According to Cummins and others, the type of bilingual proficiency (in two languages) necessary to comprehend academic texts in an additional language; used in contrast to *BICS*, or basic interpersonal communication skills.

As an outgrowth of work on a *Threshold Hypothesis*—and the debate concerning so-called *semilinguals* (Cummins 1984)—James Cummins and others noted that immigrant children can acquire informal communicative skills (called BICS—basic interpersonal communication skills) in a new language in a relatively short time, within one to three years, but lag behind their monolingual peers in other kinds of proficiency, for example, the formal, written language of academics. According to Cummins, it can take seven to ten years to master the types of language necessary for high-level academic performance. In response, Cummins proposed that there are types of language that proficiency tests do no always measure. It certainly seems evident (not to mention intuitive) to educators that an SL learner (e.g., a student who is an ELL/EAL) can learn basic speaking and socialization skills rather quickly, depending on attitude and motivation. However, it is equally evident that they will need a considerable amount time to catch up to their monolingual peers in vocabulary (lexicon).

One should be able to anticipate (without creating a new set of terms) that the monolingual English speaker's lexicon will be considerably larger than that of an incipient bilingual. It will contain thousands of words that the bilingual is yet to learn. In cases where the child has been educated in his/her heritage language, perhaps in the country of origin (or in a bilingual classroom), and has obtained age- and grade-appropriate levels of literacy in that language, then academic concepts may have already been learned. All that is needed is to acquire the English vocabulary (labels) to match and augment native-language terms. So, rather than cognitive ability, the problem seems to be semantic development.

Definition is key. In Cummins' view, CALP is equated with the ability to think in a language and use it as a learning tool (to acquire real-world knowledge via the target language of SLA), and the ability to use abstract language in a sophisticated manner. The trouble that emerging bilinguals have with formal registers of academic language is most likely linked to literacy (and biliteracy), the effects of schooling, and, even, perhaps, age or maturity. The connection between language and thought processes is a difficult one to make. It is most likely more complex than a simple dichotomy of language into BICS and CALP (Romaine 1995: 265–273). Further, lack of academic achievement is most likely due to a constellation of factors, the least of which is socioeconomic status. *See* **achievement, assessment, BICS, bilingual, Cummins, elaborated code, literacy, restricted code, semilingual**.

## Calque

In linguistic borrowing, when a meaning or concept is borrowed from one language and represented by forms in the *host* language (Field 2002: 8). It is also known as a *semantic loan* because only the meaning is borrowed without the form. The typical example is the English word *superman* which was taken from the German *Übermensch*. In situations of intensive bilingualism, this is a relatively common occurrence. It maintains the appearance of a native-language form while introducing novel or foreign concepts to the borrowing language. *See* **borrowing, host, loanwords**.

## Canonical babbling

As a baby gets along in her ability to make linguistic sounds, she reaches a point or stage when she utters the same consonant–vowel combination (in a series of clear syllables) over and over in a reduplicated manner (e.g., *da-da*, *ga-ga*). *See* **babbling, nonreduplicated babbling**.

## Caretaker speech

The type of speech associated with parents and other caregivers that is directed to infants at various stages of language development. In English, it has specific characteristics that can be linked to characteristics like exaggerated intonation contours, otherwise excessively careful pronunciation, various kinds of simplification, special words, and so on. It is sometimes referred to as infant-directed speech, motherese, or babytalk. (Adults may also use caretaker speech to address household pets.) *See* **infant-directed speech, motherese**.

## Cartesian linguistics

An approach to linguistics espoused by Noam Chomsky and his colleagues that is loosely based on the philosophy of Rene Descartes. It includes the philosophical view that the knowledge of language is part of human nature. It is, therefore, considered a biological gift or endowment that is part of human DNA. There are direct links with *generative* approaches to language and the language faculty that assume that human beings are born with innate types of knowledge. For example, we are born with the ability to walk, though this ability takes time to manifest itself (or develop). All human beings are likewise born with the ability to talk—except those born with specific genetic impairments or who may have lost it as a result of a physical trauma or illness. This approach stands in direct contrast with *behaviorist* approaches. *See* **behaviorist, Chomsky, generative**.

## Categorical perception

In phonetics, the ability to recognize language sounds (phones and phonemes) as discrete units. It involves a gradual or continuous change along a continuum that is not perceived as gradual but as instances of individually distinct categories of sounds.

For instance, a particular phoneme may be pronounced in slightly different ways depending on its environment (e.g., the /k/ of *ki*, *ko*, *ku*, or *ka*), but each instance is perceived as the prototypical phoneme /k/. Work with infants has found that they can be presented with a range of signals (sounds) that may differ slightly (manipulated electronically) regarding the degree of voicing (the use of the vocal cords), but they will perceive them categorically as either one or the other, for example, /p/ or /b/, /k/ or /g/. No sounds are perceived as being in the middle. This discovery seems to demonstrate a child's innate preparedness for language, though the precise nature of categorical perception is controversial in some approaches (Hoff 2009: 153). See **phonemic awareness, phonological awareness**.

### Census surveys

Typically, questionnaires (surveys) that are distributed by various organizations to determine the number of speakers of particular (foreign) languages and their patterns of usage, the contexts in which languages are used, for example, at home, with family, at work, and in institutional settings, for instance, surveys conducted in Belgium, Canada, Ireland, and formerly in the United States (Baker 2006: 35–39).

Before the 2010 decennial Census, the U Census Bureau sought such information as it gathered other census data. From the results, researchers estimated the number and distribution of speakers of minority languages in a particular locale, thereby measuring the vitality of languages within language minority communities. There are, however, concerns about the reliability of the responses (language usage is typically unconscious) and concerning methodology, in that the answers are not the result of careful linguistic testing. They are, instead, the subjective responses to particular questions that can be interpreted in a variety of ways. Such surveys rely on self-assessment measures of proficiency which are typically a person's opinion of his/her own language skills that are notoriously variable. See **assessment, language use surveys, self-assessment/rating, testing**.

### Cerebral cortex

The external layer of the brain that apparently controls higher mental functions of reasoning. See **brain-imaging technique, Broca's area, Wernicke's area**.

### Charter school

A type of school (primary and secondary) that receives government funding (in addition to donations or grants), but are not encumbered by the restrictions placed on public schools. They are accountable only for student performance that is specified in the school's charter agreement—a performance contract. The popularity of such schools has created long waiting lists, so admission is sometimes done by lottery.

Charter schools offer an alternative to public schools; for example, some may specialize in the arts, sciences, or in sports. In general, they do not charge tuition, have no selective admission requirements, and no religious affiliation. Some have been established by universities or other nonprofit organizations in response to the restrictive atmosphere of state-run schools that strictly require standardized testing in content areas (reflecting federal policies). According to some policies, teachers and administrators of public schools are held accountable for student progress on such standardized testing. Educators face fines, salary reductions, and loss of jobs if their students do not show satisfactory progress, thus creating an atmosphere of competition and, as many report, approaches to education that "teach to the test." Educators find themselves stressing academic performance for their own survival, rather than providing a rounded education that includes such things as the arts, sciences (particularly, the social sciences), and sports/physical education. *See* **bilingual education**.

### Child-directed speech
Speech specifically addressed to a child by adults and other caregivers. *See* **infant-directed speech and motherese**.

### CHILDES (Child Language Data Exchange System)
A large computerized database containing extensive archives of recordings and transcripts of the actual speech of children (of different ages) in a variety of languages. It was established by researchers Catherine Snow and Brian MacWhinney to establish a central source for NLA data. It allows public access to a large corpus of transcripts and actual audio and video recordings from various research programs. Since its establishment in 1984, countless studies have cited CHILDES data. *See* **qualitative research**.

### Chomsky, Noam
A professor at the Massachusetts Institute of Technology (MIT) who is credited with the "Chomskyan," or *cognitive* revolution in linguistics and one of the founders of the so-called cognitive sciences. His view marked a complete change—a paradigm shift—away from the behaviorist model of language learning to a cognitive model. He basically challenged prevailing views of the mind as a blank slate, arguing that all human beings are genetically endowed with the knowledge of language, the cognitive ability to acquire and do language. *See* **cognitivism and behaviorism**.

### Code
An alternative term for language variety (mental aspects of speech) that originated in the fields of *semiotics* and communication theory (referring to signaling systems). Thus, a linguistic code can be a language, dialect, register, or vernacular, or to language as a symbolic system. The term has been adopted into sociolinguistics to refer to language varieties involved in *code-switching*. Some of the controversies over the term relate to distinctions between *elaborated* and *restricted* codes in some approaches to the nature of social systems. These distinctions have been modified and reworded in more current approaches. *See* **code-switching, decode, elaborated code, encode, restricted code**.

### Code-switching
The alternate use of language varieties in bilingual speech, sometimes spelled *code-switching* and abbreviated as *CS* (Myers-Scotton 1993a: 3–5). For example, an individual may go back and forth from one language to another, say, from Spanish to English and back (cf. Myers-Scotton 1993b).

There are principally two types of code-switching: *intersentential* and *intrasentential*. In the former, the switch occurs between sentences, or example, when the conversation changes as a result of a change in participants or a change in topic. A speaker may change languages to accommodate the other participant(s) or for ease of expression (because speakers are more accustomed to discussing particular topics in a particular language due to diglossia). Discussion of a particular academic topic may call forth the language most commonly associated and expected with that particular register of speech (e.g., English in an English-language university environment). The second kind of code-switching, intrasentential, occurs when the alternation of languages is within sentence boundaries. This type of switching implies a kind of language mixing: both languages are in use at the same time. It can become the equivalent of a conversational style in informal circumstances. Both are very common occurrences in bilingual communities as a result of intensive and extensive language contact. *See* **contact, conversational code-switching, diglossia, intersentential code-switching, intrasentential code-switching, language mixing**.

### Code-switching constraints

Apparent restrictions (constraints) on where in an utterance a switch can occur (Myers-Scotton 1993a: 19ff).

There have been many proposed solutions to the problem of constraints. Some of the more influential proposals were generated in pioneering work on language contact, and provided starting points for further research. A few are listed here: for example, one proposed constraint prohibits switching between a pronominal subject and verb (both subject and verb must be in the same language) (Timm 1975). Another suggests that the longer the switched material is, the more natural (hence frequent) it appears to be (Gumperz 1982). The *equivalence constraint* states that the word order of switched elements must be the same or equivalent, for example, the position of the adjective relative to its noun (Pfaff 1979). According to this proposal, any violations are inhibited or blocked. The *free morpheme* constraint suggests that switches cannot occur after a bound morpheme (Poplack 1982). Clyne (1967 and elsewhere) suggests that the usage of an embedded language form may "trigger" the occurrence of longer stretches of EL material, which appears to complement a proposal by Shaffer (1977) that boundaries between switches correspond mostly to phrasal boundaries (e.g., between VP and NP).

However, nearly all of these proposals have been questioned in the literature, and many counter examples have been presented to dispute them. The main criticism has been of their methodology. Most have focused on only one bilingual contact situation, inferring constraints from particular data sets. In contrast, the MLF model (and subsequent 4-M model) and other recent approaches have investigated much larger corpora and cross-linguistic data to examine the underlying, general (mental) processes that may be at work. *See* **4-M model, code-switching, embedded language (EL), Matrix Language Frame (MLF) model**.

### Cognition

The ability to know; how we know how to do things; processes of knowing. It involves perception (seeing and recognizing facts), memory (storing and recalling individual facts and experiences, and connecting them into a coherent system), and judgment (acting upon our "knowledge" of the universe). *See* **Chomsky, cognitive science, domain, Locke, Piaget, Thresholds Theory**.

### Cognitive revolution
The change or shift away from behaviorism to cognitivism in the 1950s in the field of psychology, and the creation of the cognitive sciences (Miller 2003: 141).

Among the most prominent figures in this shift were psychologists George A. Miller and Jerome Bruner; a pioneer of artificial intelligence, Marvin Minsky; and the linguist Noam Chomsky. Chomsky wrote a scathing review of B. F. Skinner's book *Verbal Behavior* that may have served as a catalyst for the development of cognitive linguistics. The aim of this emerging school of thought was to investigate the mental processes that underlie human behavior and to restore concepts of mind (perception and memory). See **Chomsky, cognitive science, cognitivism, mentalism/mentalist**.

### Cognitive science(s)
The interdisciplinary study of human cognition broadly defined, including branches of linguistics, psychology, computer science (e.g., artificial intelligence—finding ways to represent cognitive processes of human perception, reasoning, and language and constructing their counterparts in machines), philosophy, anthropology, and neuroscience.

As a school of thought, it proposes that all mental processes can be reduced to rules and the manipulation (algorithms) of mental symbols in the acquisition of knowledge. It replaced behaviorism as the dominant view in psychology. Its beginnings are associated with the groundbreaking work of psychologist George Miller, linguist Noam Chomsky, among others, who asserted that children couldn't possibly learn language as effortlessly, efficiently, and quickly as they do merely from the evidence they receive from their parents or caregivers, by conditioned response. Thus, in line with Chomsky's version of Cartesian philosophy, all children are born with the innate knowledge of language, or the cognitive faculty of how to "do" language. See **Chomsky, cognition, cognitive revolution, generative linguistics, Locke**.

### Cognitive style
Refers to links between cognition and personality. Though somewhat controversial, it includes an individual's preferred thinking or learning style, how he or she uses information to solve problems. It is one of several mental factors said to influence language acquisition. Cognitive style includes individual abilities such as being able to isolate (abstract out) particular elements from a context (selective attention); being able to categorize and connect elements; and being reflective versus impulsive, aural versus visual, analytical versus synthetic (or a "gestalt" type of thinking that sees the whole picture from the parts). See **age, aptitude, learning strategies, motivation**.

### Cognitivism
A theoretical approach to psychology and linguistics that attempts to explain behavior in terms of processes that occur inside the mind. In the history of linguistics and the cognitive sciences, cognitive approaches came to revolutionize views of the human brain, displacing (perhaps, only partially or temporarily) the entrenched behaviorist approaches that had dominated psychology and learning

theory. The chief competitors with the cognitive school of thought now come from various connectionist models and those approaches to linguistics that are data-driven, rather than driven by a particular theory of the human mind. *See* **behaviorism, Chomsky, cognitive science, connectionism, constructivism**.

## Cohort model

A theoretical model of word retrieval proposed by William Marslen-Wilson that attempts to describe how input (the incoming speech signal) may be linked to or mapped onto a meaning/concept in the hearer's mental lexicon.

It is based on the idea that auditory or visual input stimulates neurons as it first enters the brain rather than at the end of a completed word. As the initial sound segments are recognized, all words that begin with those segments are "on;" other possible word matches (competitors) gradually fall away as each additional segment is identified until or before a "uniqueness" or "recognition" point is reached at which the word is different from all other words in the language. At this point (when the competitors are deactivated and disappear), the correct meaning is thus selected. The fact that words are identified before their uniqueness points suggests that semantic context facilitates word recognition (Marslen-Wilson and Tyler 1980; Marlsen-Wilson 1989: 4–6; Hawkins 1994: 4; Field 2002: 90).

Given the rapidity of the input coming from the speech stream and the sheer number of possible meanings (in principle, infinite), there must be an equally rapid and efficient mapping procedure that identifies forms based on initial sound sequences. *See* **activation, connectionism/connectionist models**.

## Communicative competence

Includes the ability to use sentences in appropriate contexts, therefore, going beyond the mere ability to compose grammatically well-formed sentences. Despite much of the theoretical emphasis on the acquisition of grammar in early studies of child NLA, those who take a more interactionist (or sociological) view of the acquisition of language have looked to other areas of communication that shed light on the tremendous task that children face when acquiring a language—or, in some cases, learning a new language, that reflect the depth and breadth of knowledge they must gain. Hence, communicative competence involves the ability to communicate effectively within a speech community. It can be divided into a number of areas of knowledge, for example, discourse knowledge (how to form larger units of discourse beyond the sentence), pragmatic knowledge (knowing the functions of language within a community), and sociolinguistic knowledge (how usage varies depending on social variables such as status and age). *See* **discourse knowledge, linguistic competence, pragmatic knowledge, sociolinguistic knowledge**.

## Communicative language testing

Testing that involves attempts to measure a person's proficiency in a language in normal communicative contexts (authentic speech situations). As with all communicative approaches, specific linguistic competence is only part of the task required of the acquirer/learner of a language. There are many other facets of language and communication that need to be mastered. *See* **communicative competence**.

## Communication theory
The multidisciplinary study of human communication by various means (through gestures, language, the mass media, etc.).

It deals with how information is transferred from one point to another (e.g., from one group, person, or cell to another). It includes research in a wide variety of fields like sociology, anthropology, psychology, semiotics, and journalism. It is also associated with information theory, which proposes mathematical models that measure the exchange of information among systems, for example, in processes by which information is passed from cell to cell in living such organisms as bacteria and more complex species (biocommunication). With respect to human communication, it focuses on the construction of meaning and the sharing/transmission of knowledge from one person to another. See **communicative competence**.

## Community
In the social sciences, it generally refers to a group of people living together as a social unit within larger societal units, having shared interests, culture, and/or languages. For example, a university community is an identifiable social group that may live in a particular city or town, but within that university community, there may be smaller communities of researchers, professors, students, and so on. See **community bilingualism, speech community**.

## Community bilingualism
The term pertains to the types of bilingualism that develop within an entire community. It is often contrasted with *individual bilingualism*.

In the event that a language minority begins to adopt the language of a social or cultural majority, one by one, members adopt the new language. As their numbers increase, so does the amount of community-wide bilingualism. If members of the community begin to neglect their original (traditional or heritage language or dialect) in favor of the new one, a process known as *shift*, they will show degrees of proficiency in each language. For example, an individual may be fluent/proficient in one language (the heritage language) and a learner of the second. In other cases (e.g., with second-generation bilinguals), speakers may be relatively proficient in both. Later generations may gradually lose the language of their parents and grandparents, so they may be proficient only in the new language. As a consequence, degrees of proficiency in each language variety can manifest themselves within the community at large. See **bilingual language phenomena, individual bilingualism, shift, spread, three-generation rule**.

## Community of practice (CoP)
A group of people (practitioners) who engage in a common activity or passion, and, therefore, work together to develop common strategies to improve the efficiency of their efforts.

Individual members of the group learn to practice their shared activity better simply by interacting on a regular basis. The learning of new and improved methods and techniques for problem solving, information gathering/sharing, and collaboration is a byproduct of interaction and collective learning, not necessarily a conscious goal of the community. CoPs are found in such areas as business, government, and education. For example, there are CoPs dedicated to the implementation of online courses (distance education) from various perspectives, from the technological standpoint (the development of specific educational software), course and program design (set-up of online courses), and training (equipping faculty to engage in interactive, online coursework). As distance education expands, so does the need for CoPs relevant to language teaching (e.g., TESOL courses specifically offered online). *See* **community**.

## Competence

A speaker's overall knowledge of a language, including passive/receptive and active/production knowledge. The term is usually contrasted with *performance*, which is what a person actually produces from the knowledge of grammar, that typically occur interspersed with performance errors; even the most skilled language users make mistakes such as slips of the tongue. But, these slip ups do not take away from the underlying competence that a proficient/native speaker may possess.

This distinction is usually associated with generative approaches, the work of Noam Chomsky and his colleagues, and concepts of the ideal speaker and native-speaker intuitions. Some linguists assert, however, that the only real knowledge a user has of a language is the kind that they can realize in real, online performance. Passive knowledge (and native speaker's intuition) is notoriously difficult to measure, often allowing much greater latitude in usage than a narrow set of prescriptivist rules. *See* **active knowledge, ideal speaker, native-speaker intuition, passive knowledge, performance, prescriptivist, proficiency**.

## Compound bilingual (Type B)

According to a classification scheme by Uriel Weinreich, a bilingual who essentially has only one set of meanings for vocabulary items in two languages.

A significant contributor to the study of language contact, Weinreich defined language contact in terms of the psychological and sociocultural setting of the speakers, thereby bringing to the fore the roles of individual bilinguals in various bilingual phenomena (Weinreich 1953: 3–5, 9–11; Field 2002: 10). He divided bilinguals into three types: A, B, and C. Type B (or compound) bilinguals are those who have acquired their languages in such a way that only one set of concepts underlies two (or more) sets of forms. This type of bilingualism was thought to occur when both languages are acquired in the same environment. Consequently, it implies simultaneous acquisition, in which languages are learned at the same time.

While the work of Weinreich was certainly groundbreaking, inspiring generations of linguists to look into mental processes of bilingual language acquisition and language processing, current psycholinguistic research has found little actual evidence to support three distinct types of bilinguals. Most likely, there is a continuum of types and stages in the process of bilingual language acquisition. *See also* **coordinate bilingual (Type A), one system (or two), Separate Development Hypothesis, simultaneous acquisition, subordinate bilingual (Type C)**.

## Comprehensible input
Language input that is easily understood according to a learner's prior knowledge or experience.

The term is associated with the work of Stephen Krashen and is part of his general Input Hypothesis. It makes a distinction between the kind of input (experience or exposure to language forms) that a person needs for the acquisition process to occur and the kind necessary just for basic comprehension. While many of Krashen's hypotheses have been contested over the years, several of his terms (such as input) seem to accord with the intuitions of teachers. Consequently, they have become part of the vocabulary of language acquisition in the field of education. See **Input Hypothesis, intake, Stephen Krashen**.

## Compressed speech
In languages like English, fluent speech in which forms (sounds) are omitted or changed via phonological processes and the speed of which appears to be accelerated in informal situations (e.g., in forms such as *gonna, cudja*, and various contractions). The apparent rapidity is not necessarily a result of actual speed, though that is certainly a factor. It is at least partly the result of coarticulation processes, the consequent compression (squeezing together and shortening) of forms, and the systematic deletion of *phonemes* and *syllables*. See **informal, registers, speech**.

## Computational modeling
A method of testing hypotheses by creating a computer model of that process and investigating whether the computer can copy (or mimic) that process. Examples are programs that test connectionist models of past-tense formation (attaching the *–ed* ending to the appropriate verb stems), and other programs related to learning words and phonological processes.

At the risk of oversimplification, experts are trying to create programs that mimic learning by helping the computer focus on a specific task, for example, attending to particular sequences of sound, to see if the computer can "learn" words the way a child does (to explain how a child apparently acquires parts of a lexicon). The evidence suggests that children keep some kind of statistical mental record of particular sequences, for example, how often they hear them (Hoff 2009: 21–22). Eventually, the child will be able to map a particular sequence (or label) onto a referent (object or other entity). Computer models have shed much light on the enormity of the task that children take part in on their own, with little/no prodding. See **activation, connectionism/connectionist models, mapping**.

## Connectionism/connectionist models
Computer (mathematical) models of language and artificial intelligence that attempt to link language processing with the anatomical structures of the human brain.

Circuits and pathways are assembled in these models according to current theories of brain organization. For instance, the brain consists of expansive networks of cells called *neurons* that share information (electro-chemical messages) via connections (hence, connectionism), or synapses. The intensity or strength of a signal apparently indicates the relative importance of a message. Similarly, practice and repetition increase the likelihood that a language form or structure will be remembered. Although this resembles behaviorism, it is an attempt to link what is currently known of brain anatomy with machine operation (cf. Gee 1992: 24–49). Humans do get better at things they do repeatedly—practice makes perfect.

Connectionist approaches are typically contrasted with *modular* approaches (*modularity*) associated with early work of Chomsky and others, which view the brain as interlocking sections, or autonomous brain regions. While it was thought that a sequential process that linked auditory (listening) mechanisms to cognitive functions such as word recognition was a logical necessity, no strictly autonomous region has been located in the brain—only series of pathways and a maze of interconnected neurons. Connectionist models are an attempt to solve the problem of modules in accord with biology. But, progress in putting together a machine that can do what every human brain seems to do naturally has been slow. See **activation, bilingual interactive activation (BIA), bilingual interactive model of lexical access (BIMOLA), modular, parallel distributed processing (PDP)**.

## Consecutive language acquisition

An alternate term for *sequential acquisition*, when a bilingual learns her languages one after the other. See **additive bilingualism, sequential acquisition, simultaneous bilingual acquisition, subtractive bilingualism**.

## Constructivism

The philosophy of learning which asserts that all meaning is constructed from experience and developing knowledge structures. It is associated with the Swiss Philosopher Jean Piaget, who suggested that children are active participants in the construction of meaning in language acquisition, and that levels of maturation correspond with stages in acquisition.

Constructivism is typically described in the context of behaviorism and cognitivism, as a philosophical and psychological middle ground that acknowledges to an extent that children have basic innate abilities (though undefined and domain general—not linked to specific neurological architecture) while preserving some principles of behaviorism, specifically that children learn language via an interaction of experience and processes of biological maturation. See **behaviorism, cognitive science, domain, interactionism**.

## Contact

When two (or more) groups of people share the same geographical space, or engage in common activities (e.g., for trade and cultural exchange).

Language contact occurs when one community uses two (or more) languages. For example, in urban societies today, people who speak different languages enter into various kinds of relationships. When these relationships are intensive and extensive enough, speakers of one language may learn the language of another group, becoming bi- or multilingual. This can be the result of immigration as speakers of a minority language learn/acquire a majority language, or when a particular geographical area is colonized or incorporated into a larger state and required to learn a new language. In the United States, for example, speakers of Korean and those of English are in close cultural contact, so Korean and English are in contact as a result. This is not so to the same extent in Korea. See **contact languages, contact phenomena**.

### Contact language (or variety)

A language that has emerged in bi- or multilingual settings, "as a direct result of language contact and that comprises linguistic material which cannot be traced back primarily to a single source language" (Thomason 1997: 3). In other words, a contact language is a single language variety with two (or more) ingredient languages.

Though sometimes controversial, traditional definitions often portray mixed languages as the grammatical infrastructure (morphosyntactic matrix) of one language with the vast majority of its lexicon from another (Bakker 1997: 192–213; Bakker and Mous 1994: 4–5; Field: 2002: 11–15). There is even little consensus among traditionalists that such things as mixed languages exist; while all languages show some degree of admixture for other, "foreign" sources via borrowing, it is very rare to find languages that have equal amounts of grammatical or lexical material from more than one source. However, in most discussions of contact languages, mixed languages are divided into pidgins, creoles, and other bilingual mixtures (e.g., Thomason 1997: 4; Myers-Scotton 2002: 271–293). On the one hand, languages will show extensive lexical and grammatical borrowing, for example, Modern Mexicano (Hill and Hill 1986; Field 2002), while language contact specialists hesitate to call them "true" mixed languages. (There must be some kind of even split between ingredient languages.) On the other hand, languages such as pidgins and creoles may not show much overt mixture between superstrate and substrate; mixture must be inferred, mainly from historical information and the circumstances in which the pidgin or creole has emerged. Nevertheless, in a very broad sense, any language that arises from a situation of intensive and extensive contact can fall into the general category of contact language. See **contact, creole, mixed language, pidgin**.

### Contact linguistics

The study of languages in contact, how they influence each other, and so on. It includes the study of contact phenomena such as borrowing, code-switching, diglossia, and various kinds of language mixing. In recent years, it has also included studies of pidgins, creoles, and other types of mixed languages (called variously bilingual mixes, mixed or split languages). See **contact, contact language, mixed/spit language**.

### Contact phenomena

Language phenomena such as code-switching, borrowing, and diglossia that occur in situations of intensive and extensive language contact. One of the most obvious results of contact is bi- and multilingualism. Consequently, people in contact will acquire each other's languages, alternate usage from one to the other (or keep them separate according to situations of usage), and mix them in various ways. See **borrowing, code-switching, diglossia, language mixing**.

## Content word/item
In traditional classifications of word classes, content items in languages like English are associated with classes of noun (by far, the largest word class of any language), verb, adjective, and adverb.

Content words form the basic building blocks of language (whether called nouns, verbs, and adjectives, or not). They have content because their forms carry identifiable meanings—definitions that can be represented by pictures or verbal descriptions. Consequently, they are relatively easy to translate from one language to another. In addition, they typically belong to open classes of words, classes that may lose old forms and gain new ones in a relatively short period of time via borrowing and other morphological strategies (e.g., suffixation, compounding, etc.). They can also be described as "name" words, because they name (or label) the participants (people, animals, plants, things, and concepts), places, processes, and qualities of daily life. As a group, they are significant in child language acquisition for their naming function, one of the driving forces of the acquisition of vocabulary. Content items are typically contrasted with *function items*, words that basically link, augment, or stand in the place of various content items. See **function word/item**.

## Content-based ESL
Teaching English as a second/subsequent language through instruction in content areas; typically linked to *sheltered* or *SDAIE* programs. Consequently, the students are not taught the English language only; they also receive instruction in such subjects as social studies, literature, math, and science.

Criticisms center mainly on the effects of classifying and segregating ESL/ELL students from other students, with whom they need to interact to reach a more complete mastery of English. Students who are ELLs are isolated from native speakers and thereby lack the interaction that may be necessary for acquisition. While certainly well-intentioned, this may also result in a caste-like system, where language-minority students in such programs are looked down upon by mainstream students. When language-minority status is associated with so-called *visible* ethnic minority status (that can be linked to race or other physical characteristics), this may also foster the impression that minority children are "second-class" citizens. See **ESL, mainstream, sheltered programs (SDAIE), TESL, visible minority**.

## Continuity assumption
States that the emergence of syntax in a child's grammar is gradual and continuous as a result of a biological endowment (innate knowledge). According to Pinker (1996: 6–9), one must assume that development is continuous unless there is strong evidence to suggest otherwise. A child's abilities only need to change in slight increments as his or her syntax develops over time. There is no dramatic "metamorphosis" to explain or account for. See **continuity-discontinuity, discontinuous, tadpole-frog problem**.

## Continuity-discontinuity
Deals with issues of a child's native grammatical system, whether development is smooth, seamless, and continuous, or whether it goes through some kind of abrupt, qualitative change.

Many researchers believe that a baby's first representation of grammar is a semantic one, based on the meaningful relationships among words, for example, the doers (semantic agents) and receivers (patients) of the actions and activities in which they take part or see unfold. Adult grammars are primarily syntactically based. That is, they are abstract grammatical systems based on subjects and predicates and relationships among word classes such as noun, verb, adjective, and determiner (e.g., the articles *a* and *the*). The question is, in language acquisition, how baby's inner theories of the grammar of their target language develop from a semantically based conceptual system to one that is syntactically based, whether language development is continuous (a steady, incremental flow) or discontinuous (abrupt syntactic development).

Researchers such as Pinker (1996) assume that it is continuous, and that there is no dramatic or qualitative change that needs explanation. The child is born with innate categories and she possesses an innate knowledge of the hierarchical organization of language (e.g., of words, phrases, and clauses). The argument for discontinuity is slightly different. It states that syntactic categories of noun, verb, and so on emerge as a result of biological maturation. A child's language system goes through a qualitative change from semantic-based to a syntactic base as his or her syntax emerges. Theoretically, this occurs sometime after age two, showing up more clearly from age three to age four. Both views rely on innate abilities to some extent (Clark 2003: 410–411; Hoff 2009: 264–265). *See* **continuity assumption, discontinuous, tadpole-frog problem**.

## Continuum

As a principle, it is defined as a series of points along a line at which various properties cluster; a spectrum of sorts distinguished by a gradual transition of characteristics (e.g., the color spectrum).

Linguistic phenomena are often best seen as lying along continua of sorts, rather than falling into neat, mutually exclusive categories. For instance, one language may have a high number of inflections for tense and other grammatical categories (e.g., Russian or Spanish), while another has none (e.g., Vietnamese, Mandarin). As it happens, English is situated somewhere between the two with regard to morphological possibilities. This lies at the heart of *linguistic typology*, the ways languages are categorized according to various grammatical characteristics. It is relevant to studies of second-language learning. *See* **order of acquisition, registers, language typology, typological classification**.

## Contralateral connections

The primary connections from the brain to the body go from one hemisphere of the brain to the opposite side of the body. So, what the left ear hears (or left eye sees) goes to the right side of the brain and the reverse, what the right ear hears (or right eye sees) goes to the left side of the brain. *See* **corpus callosum, dichotic listening tasks, hemispheric specialization, ipsilateral**.

## Contrastive analysis (CA)

A method of analyzing second-language performance based on the intuition that where a target language in acquisition is similar to the native (first) language of the learner, SLA will be facilitated. Where they differ, SLA is expected to be more difficult.

Before the emergence of SLA studies, contrastive analysis was used by philologists and linguists to compare language varieties. There are two types. The first is synchronic, that is, two languages are contrasted at the same stage in their development, as contemporaries. The other is the diachronic (across or over time) comparison of separate states in the history of an individual language. For example, work has been done in contrasting Elizabethan English with various national varieties of 21st century English. This type of study, however, is generally known today in historical linguistics as the comparative method. With respect to SLA, methodologies may be similar, but the goals are quite distinct. On the one hand, the comparative method is used to study the course of language change, while CA in language learning is used to point out assumed problematic areas of grammar for a language learner (cf. Cook 1993: 10–11).

The application of CA to language learning has a relatively long history. When structural approaches to language description were prevalent, it was thought that intelligent pedagogical approaches should be based on scientific description (Larsen-Freeman and Long 1991: 52–53). Nevertheless, CA took on a new character in the late 1950s when applied to foreign language teaching and the development of the *Contrastive Analysis Hypothesis* (CAH). Consequently, CA gradually evolved from the analysis of grammatical features, for example, differences in word order, inflectional morphology (and the inflectional categories that may exist in either language), and phonological type (e.g., tonal languages versus intonational languages), to second-language learning. As an example, a Spanish speaker learning English has prior linguistic experience with the notions of tense (present and past) and number (singular and plural), so acquisition of the tense system of English should not be too difficult. However, because of the morphological nature of Spanish, subject pronouns are usually omitted. Therefore, it is hypothesized that a Spanish speaker learning English may have difficulty remembering to put in the subject pronouns. *See* **Contrastive Analysis Hypothesis (CAH), error, error analysis, interlanguage (IL), performance analysis, transfer.**

## Contrastive Analysis Hypothesis (CAH)

Basically, the hypothesis states that where similarities in the native language and target of acquisition exist, acquisition will be easy, and where differences are evident, learning would be labored and difficult.

The application of contrastive analysis to language learning was originally derived from a series of propositions made by Lado (1957) to predict difficulties a learner might encounter when learning a second language. The main insight was that an L1 (first language) influences the learning of a second or subsequent language (L2), via a process called *transfer*. Using the contrastive analysis of the respective languages as a blueprint, researchers felt that they would be able to predict where problems might occur. For example, when a Vietnamese speaker learns English, a contrastive analysis would identify native-language properties that might account for aspects of Vietnamese that are typically transferred into English. Vietnamese does not have tense. That is, it has no present or past tense markers on verbs. The English tense system is notoriously difficult for Vietnamese speakers to learn because tense simply does not exist in their prior linguistic experience. Time reference is possible in Vietnamese, but it is done with adverbs. Thus, a learner's variety of English may refer to past time and the event indicated by a verb with an adverb, rather than a tense marker. For example, "I see you yesterday" obviously refers to past time. Despite one's English (or Standard European) bias, tense endings are not required for time reference in all of the world's languages.

The hypothesis, in its so-called strong form, has been refuted because it routinely fails to predict precisely where these areas of difficulty and ease may be. Where languages differ greatly, SL learners may find few difficulties. In fact, specific differences between languages may be so prominent that learners become acutely aware of them and avoid making mistakes. In that same vein, when SL learners assume that the TL is similar to their native language, subtle differences may go undetected and, therefore, unheeded. In other words, the CAH predicted problems that do not occur; it overpredicted. And, it does not predict areas where difficulties do occur; it underpredicted (Larsen-Freeman and Long 1991: 55–56). Despite its apparent limitations, CA is still seen to offer insights into potential areas of difficulty, or errors that are likely to occur. Wardhaugh (1970) proposed strong and weak versions. The strong version stressed CAH's power to predict—predictions that failed to materialize in the literature. The weak version, however, proposed that a broader interpretation of the hypothesis could still be useful (in retrospect) in finding the source of patterned errors, explainable by transfer (Larsen-Freeman and Long 1991: 56). See **contrastive analysis (CA), error, error analysis, interlanguage (IL), performance analysis, transfer**.

## Contrastive rhetoric (CR)

An extension of Contrastive Analysis Theory to the writing of SL learners, including how language influences the ways information is structured in larger units of discourse (e.g., in the presentation of knowledge in academic settings).

The first major piece in CR, Kaplan's (1966) "Cultural thought patterns in intercultural education" brought an insight to the field of applied linguistics: "Writing is culturally influenced in interesting and complex ways" (Connor 1996: 495). It arose from the evaluations of student essays in English courses written by speakers of other languages (ESL and EFL students). Nonnative writers may have near-native-like control of the lexical and syntactic devices of English available to proficient speakers and writers, yet fail to demonstrate the *pragmatic* skills necessary to compose coherent papers or narratives according to native-writer norms and patterns of usage. Instead, they typically rely on the rhetorical patterns of their native languages and cultures in fairly predictable ways. "A large body of earlier work has established that L2 written discourse and text are invariably affected by [non-native speakers'] first language (L1) discourse norms and paradigms" (Hinkel 2002: 1). Connor (2002) points out that this insight is based on the idea that "language [usage] and writing are cultural phenomena" (494).

One of the criticisms of contrastive rhetoric is that it creates stereotypes because it tends to associate *group behaviors* with that of *individuals*. Nevertheless, it reveals patterns that are also consistent with current ideas of transfer in perception and performance (Gass and Selinker 1993a, 1993b; Eubank, Selinker, and Sharwood Smith 1995). Another criticism is that it relies on a traditional view of culture, that, it is monolithic and static, and based on clear geographical, national, and perhaps ethnic lines (*British*, *Japanese*, or *American culture*). Such a view sees cultures as entities of some sort that act in uniform ways to condition the thought patterns of their members (Connor 2002: 503–504). This leads to an oversimplification of concepts of society, and the multifaceted ways that culture manifests itself in human behavior. An alternative view suggests that culture is not as homogeneous as one might think. In modern urban societies, there is a dynamic interaction among subcultures, socioeconomic strata, ethnicity, sex/gender, and views of morality and ethics. *See* **contrastive analysis, linguistic determinism, linguistic relativity, Sapir–Whorf Hypothesis**.

## Conversational code-switching

The rapid, fluid, online alternation of languages among members of a bi- or multilingual community. In general, this type of code-switching is intrasentential; that is, it sounds like two languages are being spoken at the same time, with words from each language occurring in rapid-fire succession. It is typically insertional (elements of one language embedded in another), and remarkable because of the rapidity in which the switches occur. *See* **code-switching, intersentential, intrasentential**.

## Cooing

Mostly vowel-like sounds uttered by babies as they begin to produce the sounds of language, for example, when they appear to be happy and contented. Cooing typically begins around six months of age and soon develops into different types of babbling. *See* **babbling**.

## Coordinate bilingual (Type A)

Bilinguals who have acquired their languages in such a way that they appear to have two independent linguistic systems (Weinreich 1953: 3–5, 9–11; Field 2002: 10).

According to a classification scheme proposed by Uriel Weinreich, a Type A (or coordinate) bilingual is one who acquires languages in separate environments (e.g., one at home and another in school); this, therefore, implies sequential or consecutive acquisition. Nevertheless, the child may be a native speaker in either or both languages. The obvious problem that linguists have today with such a term is the inherent difficulty language experts have with the measurement and assessment of bilingual proficiencies. Bilinguals usually favor one language over the other, and entire communities assign languages to particular domains of usage (the phenomenon known as diglossia). However, the term *coordinate* may still be useful to describe those bilinguals who are strong in both of their languages. *See also* **assessment, balanced bilingual, Bilingual First Language Acquisition (BFLA), bilingualism, compound bilingual (Type B), Separate Development Hypothesis, subordinate bilingual (Type C)**.

## Corpus callosum

The band of fibrous neurons (commissure) that connects the left and right hemispheres of the cerebrum. It acts to connect the functions of the hemispheres, as the conduit of signals between hemispheres and, thus, among various regions of the brain.

Research in the ways that the corpus callosum works has proved to be important to neurolinguists and the cognitive sciences in the investigation of the brain because of its role in so-called "split-brain" patients. In extreme cases of epilepsy, the corpus callosum may be severed to a degree, relieving the severity of symptoms caused by *grand mal* seizures and lessening the risk of accidental injury. Symptoms of epilepsy are usually controlled by medication, but, as a last resort, this type of procedure may be performed (Gur, Levy, and Gur 1977: 125–129). Significantly, scientists got their first glimpses of the functional architecture of the brain through so-called dichotic listening tasks, for example, and locating various functions of the brain in one hemisphere or the other. Recent work in brain imaging has built upon early work with aphasics and split-brain patients. *See* **aphasia, brain imaging technique, dichotic listening tasks, functional architecture, lateralization, split-brain studies**.

## Creole

A language variety that typically emerges under the austere conditions of forced servitude or labor. It may or may not have a pidgin in its ancestry, though the early literature assumed that all creoles arise from pidgin languages. The term *creole* originally referred to Europeans born on colonial soil; the term was then extended to include the communities in which they lived. It was later used to describe the language varieties spoken in those communities that have become national varieties. In contrast to pidgins, creoles have native speakers, and they fulfill all the natural communicative and expressive functions of language. *See* **creolization, language evolution, language mixing, pidgin**.

## Creolistics

Generally, the study of the origins of creole languages, but often extended to various processes of creolization, including but not restricted to nativization (when a creole or pidgin acquires native speakers), pidginization (the emergence and evolution of pidgin varieties), stabilization (the development of a stable pidgin or creole variety), and various kinds of language mixing (e.g., the emergence of mixed languages).

In some respects, the development of pidgins, creoles, and other bilingual mixtures parallels the linguistic processes of bilingual language acquisition and the development of learner's varieties (interlanguages). In fact, the term *interlanguage*, a term used in SLA research to represent stages in the development of a learner's second-language grammar, was first used to refer to a pidgin or creole variety that emerged as an "in-between" language for communication among different language groups (Holm 1988: 30–31). *See* **interlanguage (IL), language evolution, nativization, pidgin, pidginization, stabilization, mixed language**.

## Creolization

The social and linguistic processes by which a creole language comes into being. Precisely what this entails is still debated.

Earlier definitions often included the process by which pidgin varieties acquire native speakers (*nativization*), become conventionalized and stabilized, and eventually become the principle language of a creole community (cf. Holm 1988: 6–7). Among the many traditional examples of English-based creoles are the Caribbean creoles found in, for example, Jamaica, Barbados, and Trinidad, and the better-known Pacific Ocean varieties such as Hawai'ian (English), Tok Pisin (Papua New Guinea), and Bislama (New Hebrides). The process of expansion describes how the language acquires more speakers and is used in a greater number of contexts. It also acquires additional words and structures through creative processes available to speakers.

More recent views, however, no longer stress the necessity of a pidgin in creole genesis, and instead focus on the social and historical background of the individual settlements. First of all, there are no attested pidgin varieties in many known situations in where creole languages emerged, for example, in the Caribbean communities (Bakker 1995: 38). And, creole varieties have been attested where children were not yet present (Arends 1995: 21; Singler 1993: 236–238). Therefore, many creoles have emerged among adult speakers where only learners' varieties were present, not a fully developed pidgin language. *See* **contact languages, creole, interlanguage (IL), language evolution, mixed language**.

## Criterion-based testing

Testing (assessment instruments) designed to measure a person's individual language skills according to a set of language features or structures.

It measures what a child can or cannot do in a language, perhaps linked to grade- or age-appropriate criteria (e.g., according to objective measures of sentence length and complexity). Despite its stated goals to measure individual skills for accurate placement, such a test can be used to compare groups of students, for instance, monolinguals versus bilinguals. National norms are so important in this type of testing that they infer their way into many local school districts, especially in light of the critical nature of national testing and links to the effectiveness of particular schools, programs, and individual teachers. *See* **assessment, census surveys, formative testing, norm referenced testing**.

## Critical literacy

A type of literacy—the ability to recognize the *underlying* social and political assumptions of particular authors. Clearly, this type of literacy skill goes beyond basic, functional literacy and requires mastery of cultural literacy and more.

It includes the ability to "read between the lines" to the motivations of a particular author and to spot persuasion and manipulation, being able to recognize expressions of Anglo-American cultural values, and having the ability to analyze texts critically *and* expound on the types of meanings expressed. This implies having sufficient knowledge of the historical, cultural, and social backdrop of the writer and what he or she has written. Any educator familiar with the challenges faced by rural folks, the working-class, women, indigenous peoples, and linguistic minorities knows what a daunting task this can be. Anyone who claims to teach critical literacy skills must be familiar with the kinds of knowledge that critical reading entails, qualitatively as well as quantitatively. It goes much further than merely teaching a child how to read and write and to achieve functional literacy—the endpoint of many English-only programs is just that, functional literacy. See **biliteracy, cultural literacy, literacy, preliteracy training**.

## Critical (or sensitive) period
Refers to a period in the life cycle when there is greater sensitivity to certain kinds of stimuli, an inborn or *innate* advantage. There is popular support for the idea that children have a special talent or propensity for language that older learners do not have. Among researchers in SLA, however, this has been a constant source of controversy, particularly in view of recent positions of the domain-specific or domain-general views of language. See **Critical Period Hypothesis, domain**.

## Critical Period Hypothesis (CPH)
The hypothesis stating that there is a special or sensitive period in development in which a child has a particularly heightened ability to acquire language.

Developed by the biologist Eric Lenneberg, the hypothesis seemed to fit with most people's intuitions and the idea that children seem to have a unique ability to just grab languages out of the air (with no teachers, no textbooks, and no testing). However, critics have questioned what empirical data says to test the hypothesis. The questions: (a) Do children have an inborn advantage; if so, what are its causes? (b) What are the relevant age limits (the beginning and end of this special period)? and (c) What aspects of language development does it apply to (various levels of grammar) (Hoff 2009)?

Lenneberg based his hypothesis on the imprinting of goslings shortly after hatching. There is a sensitive period in which they follow the first moving object (usually the mother) they see. If this period elapses, then imprinting does not occur. According to the hypothesis, the beginning of the sensitive period, a special open window for language acquisition, is age two, the emergence of the *two-word stage* and, therefore, syntax. (This showed a clear bias toward a syntactic view of language and its acquisition. Consequently, his theory was linked to Chomsky's early work, e.g., the Language Acquisition Device or LAD.) This special period was believed to end at puberty (say, 9–13), with a link to brain *lateralization*, when certain abilities became "located" in either the left hemisphere or the right hemisphere of the brain.

Recent work, however, suggests that children show language ability at a much younger age (so they must be acquiring it). For instance, cooing noises and other pre-linguistic sounds emerge at around four months of age; and the beginnings of the acquisition of target-language phonology is evidenced by six months. In addition, lateralization of language functions may appear even at birth, that is, certain abilities are already located in specific areas of the brain at birth. While children do seem to show special language abilities, it may be best to speak of different critical periods for separate areas of grammar, for example, phonology (i.e., pronunciation, or accent); grammar (morphology and syntax); vocabulary; and discourse/pragmatics. There are also a large number of other factors besides biological ones to consider (e.g., individual characteristics, birth order, socioeconomics, and culture). See **domain, innate, Language Acquisition Device (LAD)**.

## Cross-cultural communication

The sharing of information across cultural groups.

It often includes conflicting norms of interaction and interpretation and the lack of understanding that can arise from cultural mismatches (e.g., differences in being talkative, attitudes toward highly personal information, maintaining physical distance, touching and pointing behaviors, gesturing, making eye contact, and a host of other possible factors). Participants in a communicative event may even speak the same language, and for cultural reasons, use that language in clearly distinct ways, at times leading to misunderstandings and conflict (cf. Seelye 1994: 1–10). As a consequence, patterns of usage may be traced back (or linked) to cultural differences and membership in a particular ethnic groups, that can foster stereotypes of one kind or another that can be very difficult to break. See **contact, culture, cultural pluralism, norms of interaction, norms of interpretation**.

## CT (Roentgen-ray computed tomography)

A process by which a computer-generated image of particular areas of the brain is generated.

The Greek morpheme *tomo* means "slice." Before modern technology began allowing biologists, physicians (surgeons), and neurologists to examine the human brain and other vital organs virtually via machines, the typical methodology involved taking physical slices of affected tissue during a biopsy or autopsy to examine damage and to arrive at causes of injury. The development of current technology allows for the noninvasive examination of living tissue (in living patients) by a number of neuroimaging techniques, which allows for the examination of tissue slices—the insides of various organs. By assembling images from various angles, computerized machines can construct three-dimensional images of the organ being examined.

In CT scans, for example, a beam of X-rays is sent through the brain. As this beam passes through, it is affected by the type of tissue through which it passes. The images portrayed by the x-rays are, therefore, a result of the density of the tissue encountered along the way. Dense tissue like bone essentially blocks the X-rays, and soft tissue such as brain matter filters them to a lesser extent. X-ray detectors positioned around the outside of the scanner collect readings from many angles, and a computerized algorithm assembles an image of a "slice" of brain. See **event-related potentials (ERPs), fMRI, MRI, tomography**.

## Cultural literacy

A type of literacy that includes more complex analytical skills than the surface skills required merely to function reactively in society. It involves knowledge of the culturally based behaviors and literacy practices of a culture.

All culturally based behaviors are learned behaviors. They are usually learned in such culturally defined institutions as schools and the media. They involve the values, assumptions, and the kinds of cultural knowledge that are reflected in school curricula. Educators have long known the necessity of a common body of knowledge (e.g., "what it means to be an American" in the US) for meaningful communication to occur among the various sectors of society and to be able to interpret the messages that appear in various media. For example, all citizens in the United States are expected to be familiar with generally accepted beliefs of the roles and responsibilities that they have within a democracy. Living up to those expectations entails understanding one's legal rights and responsibilities (and their limitations), participating in the political process, and supporting various other institutions such as education, health care, and social welfare.

This surely goes beyond merely being able to function, read the mail, and contribute a portion of one's income to the public coffers. At first glance, this may appear to be a quantitative measure—know more stuff and you'll know how to use it, but that may underestimate the complexity of the associations that need to be made in order to arrive at subtle inferences. Nevertheless, one would be hard pressed to find a precise listing of the things an "informed" citizen must know. Every segment of society can conceivably draw up its own list of the books an educated citizen or resident must read. Ask a scientist, philosopher, English teacher, political scientist, music or art instructor, or coach of any sport to list the 100 written works that all productive members of society should be familiar with, and you can imagine how different those lists might be. However, this is the exact job that educators take on in deciding basic school curricula (Field in press: 1011). *See* **biliteracy, critical literacy, literacy**.

### Cultural pluralism
Having many cultures and subcultures co-existing within a society.

As an ideal, cultural pluralism seems transparently good because it broadens the experience of the average citizen within society at large, and it puts every culture on equal footing (as in the famous quotation from the Declaration of Independence of the US, "...all men are created equal"). However, it seems that even the most liberal and benevolent of societies can conceal deep-rooted resentments and animosities among ethnic groups, between a long-standing majority and various minorities, and among minority groups as well. In fact, in some cities and states in the United States, there is no longer a simple majority ethnic group, and pluralism is a reality. In such places, Anglo Saxons may be the largest among several groups, but they are no longer the numerical majority. This may help to explain the reactionary attitude of governmental institutions and the stress on Americanism and English-only programs of education (to create a kind of cultural and linguistic homogeneity). *See* **culture, cross-cultural communication**.

### Culturally transmitted (cultural transmission)
Refers to the ways a specific language is passed from one generation of speakers to the next within a human culture. It is used in opposition to the term *biologically transmitted*, which applies to the *faculty of language* that is genetically, or biologically based.

Specific languages such as English, Spanish, and Arabic are passed from parents and other caregivers to children within a community of speakers—in a sense, inherited. It is cultural in that it involves something that differs from the essential human capacity for language. It includes all the cultural facets of language usage (the where, when, and with whom) and issues of communicative competence. As a linguistic behavior, language encompasses the ability to produce and understand well-formed utterances in the language plus customary behavioral norms of usage in the many contexts of speech, including literacy. *See* **biologically transmitted, communicative competence**.

## Culture

The ideas, customary actions, arts, and beliefs of a group of people that are passed on (or communicated) from one generation to the next. Also, an identifiable social group that is held together by a culturally transmitted set of religious beliefs, values, and standards of behavior (including dress, food, customs, taboos, and superstitions).

The role of a child's culture in both NLA and SLA is a topic of great discussion, particularly in the context of *linguistic relativity*: To what extent does culture shape a child's view of the world? How does culture shape language? And, therefore, how does a specific language influence the child's perception of the world? The question naturally follows that a bilingual has two languages and may participate in separate cultures represented by those languages. So, how or to what extent, does a native language/culture affect the acquisition and usage of a second/subsequent language? Opinions certainly vary as to the extent of the influence of culture upon language and thought. *See* **discourse knowledge, linguistic determinism, linguistic relativity, Sapir–Whorf Hypothesis**.

## Cummins, James (Jim)

A well-known figure in SLA research and literacy development of ELL/EAL students. He is a professor at the Ontario Institute for Studies in Education, University of Toronto.

In the early 1980s, he coined the terms *BICS* (basic interpersonal communication skills) and *CALP* (cognitive/academic language proficiency) that were nearly ubiquitous in early biliteracy research. Though he is highly respected in educational circles, his early work received criticism from some linguists for simplifying the debate about the language abilities of language minorities in the multilingual classroom, and, perhaps, lending credibility to already existing stereotypes (see, e.g., Romaine 1995: 281). For instance, if a teacher expects bilinguals of a certain ethnic and linguistic minority to do poorly in the classroom (based on her individual biases), then a particular opinion of language usage by those bilinguals, when they fall into the patterns he or she anticipates, may actually strengthen his or her biases, justifying the stereotype. He or she may assume that members of this group lack the cognitive skills to succeed in academic subjects. It's a Catch-22: he or she expects certain behaviors, and when he or she notices them, they reinforce his or her preconceived notions of the abilities of group members.

The issue appears to be mistaking the acquisition of formal, academic registers of English with a child's cognitive abilities. The accumulation of academic knowledge and knowledge of the word achieved through schooling and cognition as the capacity to "know" are two separate issues. *See* **BICS, CALP, registers of speech**.

### Dead languages
Languages that are no longer used or transmitted as native languages from one generation to the next. *See* **language death**.

### Decode
The term is used by specialists in educational linguistics to mean roughly to analyze and comprehend a code, particularly with respect to aspects of literacy (e.g., *decoding* print). That is, to decode a written text is to convert the written word into spoken language.

One question that naturally follows is whether simply decoding print, or pronouncing the words on a printed page, indicates substantial comprehension of the text. This is a key issue in studies of literacy and biliteracy. It is evident that many children merely repeat orally what they see written with little ability to understand the many levels of meaning that can be communicated through the written word. This appears to be one possible result of bottom-up approaches that focus on form. Comprehending a text involves being able to "read between the lines," and to discern when a writer might be manipulating the reader (spotting logical fallacies) or simply being untruthful (recognizing propaganda). It involves both knowledge of the world and analytical skills that go well beyond merely repeating words based on memorization of how letters and letter combinations are pronounced. *See* **bottom-up, code, literacy, top-down**.

### Deficit model
The model of language variation that links nonstandard varieties of English to social or cultural deprivation. "A deficit model treats speech differences in terms of a norm and deviation from that norm, the norm being middle-class white behavior" (Wolfram and Fasold 1974: 10). Socially stigmatized varieties are, therefore, typically associated with uneducated and poverty-stricken groups or classes. Such an outdated view, though disproved by considerable scientific evidence, still seems to pop up, most likely influenced by harmful ethnic stereotypes.

Probably the clearest example is the history of African American Vernacular English—abbreviated AAVE (called variously Black English, Ebonics, etc.). Popular opinion long held that it was substandard, that it was an inferior variety of English that indicated the cultural depravity of African American people. This was seen as a mental deficit that was partly a consequence of the cultural and linguistic isolation of African Americans from the more "educated" speech of their European counterparts, and partly a consequence of genetics (obviously, a belief tinged with racism). In the early 20th century, linguists began to look at variation in speech without judging either the people or the language varieties they spoke, that is, without putting them on a social hierarchy of high-low, superior-inferior.

Out of that research came the recognition that a variety that deviated from accepted norms represented by a standard language was merely not standard, or nonstandard. This led to a difference model of language as a behavior. As greater attention was paid to social dialectology in the 1960s (coinciding roughly with the Civil Rights Movement in the US), AAVE became the focus of many groundbreaking studies that revealed its systematicity (as are all languages) and its validity as the language variety learned natively by a good portion of the American population. Thus, as a result of scientific study, a consensus of sorts has formed that AAVE merely differs from Standard American English—it is therefore *nonstandard*, neither good nor bad, higher nor lower, superior nor inferior. After all, "different" does not necessarily mean better or worse. See **difference model, nonstandard, social dialect, standard, substandard.**

## Descartes, René

A French philosopher, mathematician, and scientist during the 17th century. A rationalist, he is regarded as one of the founders of modern philosophy. His theological views (the so-called "ghost in the machine") were evident in his view of human nature and the existence of innate thought, or mind, as independent of the body (a biological machine).

Noam Chomsky (1966) has claimed that Cartesian thought revolutionized philosophy. He traces his theories to ideas that run from Descartes to von Humboldt. Two basic principles are that the general properties of language are universal and that they reflect fundamental characteristics of the human mind (language universals). He also observed that language is creative and independent of the mechanical forces evident in the environment, and it is there by design, and therefore, innate. As a consequence, his views are distinct from those of the behaviorist school and its proponents, namely B. F. Skinner. Recent public discussions have focused on the Darwinian principles (selectional restraints) that have guided the evolution of language, extending the discussion from the design of language to its ultimate origins (e.g., Hauser, Chomsky, and Fitch 2002; Fitch, Hauser, and Chomsky 2005; Jackendoff and Pinker 2005; Pinker and Jackendoff 2005).

## Descriptive grammar

Provides a description of the speech of members of a community (capturing patterns, word choice, and grammatical characteristics), what they actually do with their language in various social settings. It is essentially an approach to language description and teaching.

In this view, there is no prescribed correct or incorrect way to say something because that implies a value judgment (and someone making the judgment). Consequently, a descriptive grammar merely *describes* what people actually do when they use a language and makes no judgments about correct/incorrect, good/bad, proper/improper, or high/low grammar. So, there are no bad grammars (they are all equal, just as all cultures are equally valid). Some varieties of English may differ from Standard American English (SAE), but that does not mean that they are inferior to it or inherently bad. Different is different, not necessarily better or worse. The term is contrasted with prescriptive grammar, an approach to language teaching typically associated with education, which sets out to define correct or proper usage. See **pedagogical (teaching) grammar, nonstandard, prescriptive grammar, standard.**

### Developmental approach

Approaches to research that emphasize the course of language development and that offer explanations for that course of development. For example, children acquiring English apparently learn particular structures in a sequential order (e.g., the processes of negation and question formation). Many explanations focus on the complexity of the processes, assuming that simple is learned before complex, or according to their learnability. See **approach, developmental models, Language-Making Capacity, learnability theory.**

### Developmental English

A course designed to strengthen the academic skills of students who do not exhibit the writing skills necessary to deal with the demands of high school, college, or university courses. They are remedial in nature, though the term *remediation* (implying a remedy for ills) is no longer in fashion. The rationale for the term appears to be that a student may lack specific skills to participate successfully in class with his/her peers; they are yet to develop or emerge in the student's performance. Thus, a developmental course acts to promote and encourage the emergence of particular academic skills (generally, literacy skills in the standard language). See **biliteracy, English for academic purposes, literacy.**

### Developmental models/perspective

Models of language acquisition that emphasize biological maturation. For example, children appear to acquire language in identifiable steps, all predictable based on age and development. Their individual grammars, too, develop gradually from early babbling to the development of various types of sentences.

Developmental models, therefore, allow for certain innate abilities (that gradually unfold) without having to commit to a specific underlying Universal Grammar (UG) that linguistically guides the progressive steps of child language acquisition. Developmental approaches generally view the acquisition of language as a manifestation domain-general models, that it is one of many cognitive abilities that are acquired/learned through the interaction of the organism (the child) and the environment (the social milieu into which the child is born and raised). See **domain, Piagetian/Neo-Piagetian, Universal Grammar (UG)**.

### Developmental sequences

How syntactic operations are acquired systematically, for example, in the development of question formation and negative sentences (Hoff 2009: 238–239).

Children gradually move from childlike utterances to more adultlike structures. For some specialists, the term *sequence* has a specific usage that differs slightly from the term *order*. For example, in the order of acquisition of phonemes, reference is made to the specific order in which they appear in a child's speech. A developmental sequence specifically involves the ordering of processes. It is like the ordering of steps in a recipe or the steps in the process of learning to drive an automobile or other complex activity.

Concerning the reordering of words, the development of negative sentences (negation) follows predictable developmental sequences, just as the development of questions (both yes-no and *wh*-questions). In negation, children first simply say the word *no*, or place it immediately before another word, for example, "No like that." "No!" "No night night." By about the age of three, children appear to learn contractions with a negative element, for example, "Can't get it." "Don't do that." It isn't until much later that children really master the adverb *not* with an auxiliary. In questions, the same types of gradual steps take place. At first, the word order of a question is basically the same as a declarative sentence, with rising intonation added to indicate a question. In yes-no questions, an auxiliary may appear in sentence initial position; *do* remains uninflected for third-person singular. "Do it go inside?" Wh-questions are also usually asked with the *wh*-word in sentence initial position, but the remaining word order remains the same as in declarative statements. Later, subject-auxiliary inversion will occur as the child's grammar becomes more adultlike. Therefore, one is likely to hear, "What you name is?" before something like, "What is your name?" *See* **emergence of speech sounds, morpheme studies**.

## Dialect

A distinct variety (or version) of a language. There are two general dialect types: regional dialects, varieties that can be linked to speakers from various parts or regions of a country, and social dialects, varieties that can be associated with particular social groups. Some dialects, particularly those based on social or ethnic groups, may be considered nonstandard if they exhibit features that do not conform to the characteristics of the national standard. Nevertheless, everyone speaks a dialect depending on the national, regional, and social circumstances of birth (Wolfram and Fasold 1974: 26–35). In the United States and Canada, the study of regional varieties has been mostly one of population movement and contact among older established British dialects and various European languages (Fennell 2001: 209–210). And, in the United Kingdom, dialect studies have focused a great deal on settlement patterns of various groups (e.g., Angles, Saxons, and Danes) and in the emergence of a common language in England. In all cases, contact of English with indigenous/original languages of colonized peoples has shaped national varieties of English to various extents. *See* **dialect awareness, dialect continuum, language, regional dialect, social dialect**.

## Dialect awareness

The awareness of speech variation in the classroom; associated with a movement in the United States.

Students are made aware of the different ways English has changed over the years (e.g., the difference between Elizabethan English and current usage in Great Britain and the US), and how it varies from place to place (modern-day London vs. Los Angeles). The focus, however, is how informal usage outside of the classroom may clash with the formal, academic types of language students need for academic success.

While it is not strictly an urban problem, many school districts have a very diverse student population. There may be speakers of particular stigmatized regional and/or social dialects that are characterized by special vocabulary and grammatical characteristics. For example, nearly all nonstandard dialects feature so-called double negatives (in languages like Spanish and French that share this characteristic, it is typically called *negative concord*). There is also the non-standard usage of the word "ain't". Obviously, prescriptivists and other language purists shudder when student papers manifest such nonstandard traits, which are typically associated with undereducated people from the lower socioeconomic strata (which shows a bias based on social class). The goal is not necessarily to teach nonstandard dialects, or to replace instruction in standard forms of the language. The purpose is to increase the awareness of students and teachers of the differences, and to help both understand that nonstandard dialects are systems unto themselves. They function to meet all the communicative and expressive needs of their respective communities. Nevertheless, the variety that is honored in society, the only variety that is recognized in official, institutional settings (e.g., the government, schools, and the media), is the standard, whether it be Standard British, Standard American English, or other recognized national standard. *See* **bidialectal, dialect, nonstandard, standard, stigmatized**.

### Dialect continuum

A gradual shading of language forms from one regional dialect of a language to another. That is, closely related varieties (according to a family tree model) show significant similarities in various levels of grammar, from lexicon (similar vocabularies) to phonology (similar pronunciation characteristics), and on to other morphological (the ways words are constructed) and syntactic (word ordering) traits. Those differences may seem minimal in borderlands areas and places where regional varieties intersect.

In Western Europe, dialects of Latin stretched throughout Southern Europe once forming a continuum of dialects of the language across former colonial possessions (Chambers and Trudgill 1980: 6–8). These varieties evolved over time into separate national and regional languages with their own histories, traditions, and literatures. It has been said that, if a traveler were to walk from village to village west to east conversing with people as he or she went along, starting, say, in Portugal and hiking through Spain, France, Italy, and so on, the differences are so gradual that our traveler would be able to understand with little difficulty the dialect of the next village. Similar continua apparently exist with Slavic, Germanic, and other families of languages, as well. *See* **dialect, language, regional dialect, social dialect**.

### Dichotic listening tasks

Tasks given to study functions of the different brain hemispheres.

In discussions of where language might be located in the human brain, much attention has been paid to hemispheric functions, that is, human abilities as they appear to be distributed biologically throughout the various regions of the brain. Evidently, what the right ear hears is processed on the left side of the brain (so-called *contralateral* connections); these contralateral connections from the ears to the brain appear to be stronger than those that occur on the same side (or *ipsilateral* connections). In an oft-cited study by Doreen Kimura (1967), subjects were presented with two stimuli simultaneously, one to the left ear and one to the right. Depending on which event the subjects perceived, researchers were able to determine which side of the brain processed the signal, inferring where that particular brain function is located. This type of work has been important in studies of brain lateralization (the assignment of specific functions to either hemisphere), particularly with reference to language and other cognitive functioning. *See* **contralateral, corpus callosum, functional architecture, ipsilateral, split-brain patients**.

## Difference model

The model of language variation that states that differences among regional and social dialects are the result of natural processes of language change—nothing more, nothing less. These changes do not imply a lack of social or cultural opportunity as once envisioned in so-called deficit models. In other words, acquiring the language of one's culture or subculture is the result of the unconscious processes of language acquisition. Whether one learns dialect A, B, C, or Z makes no difference; they are all speech varieties that fill the communicative and expressive needs of a community.

Even though it has been common to assume a hierarchical ranking of cultures, languages, and communities (similar to the concept of a food chain, with the strongest and best at the top), there is no scientific basis to do so. Such subjective measures as intelligence and beauty are patently tinged by one's own cultural biases. The ranking of language varieties on a scale of good to bad is similarly biased and subjectively swayed by cultural, racial, and ethnic stereotypes. Because a person does not like the sound of a particular language or dialect does not "prove" that the "offending" dialect is deficient in any way. *See* **deficit model**.

## Diglossia

The compartmentalization of language varieties according to the situation of use.

Diglossia occurs when members of a bidialectal or bilingual community assign individual varieties to specific domains of usage. For example, many bi- and multilinguals speak a minority or *recessive* language (or dialect) in the home, and another majority or *dominant* language in the workplace, at school, and other official settings. In his seminal work, Fergusson (1959) coined the terms H (or high) and L (or low) varieties to illustrate how languages in bilingual situations show clear separation according to their functions in society. He characterizes diglossic situations as relatively stable, where one variety is used under certain circumstances (e.g., in institutional settings), and under entirely different circumstances. Originally referring simply to formal, written forms (e.g., from an extensive traditional literature) opposed to informal, spoken vernaculars, his terminology has been extended to bilingual situations, as well (e.g., Fishman 1989 and elsewhere), situations in which one language is seen as the H variety (e.g., a majority or prestige variety), and the other as the L variety (e.g., minority or stigmatized varieties).

Typically, bilinguals assign each language to a particular situation, much as registers of speech are assigned according to the *setting* and *participants*. As a consequence, some bilinguals select one language over another based on such factors as the people present, topic being discussed, location of the speech event, and its goals and purposes. This can ultimately lead to a difference in the exposure that the bilingual has to a broad range of registers in each language. They may only be familiar with a limited set of registers in each of their languages, say, only informal registers of a minority language and formal registers of the majority language, leading to an apparent disparity between their abilities in each language. (See discussion in Wardhaugh 2006: 87–93, for further details.) *See* **code-switching, dialect, register, shift, variation**.

## Discontinuous

The theory that the development of a child's grammatical system is not gradual and continuous, but, in essence, discontinuous. It suggests that a child's internal grammar changes fundamentally from a word or semantic-based system to an adultlike, abstract grammatical system (Hoff 2009: 265–266). That is, a child's system develops from one based on meanings of words (e.g., a color goes with an object—qualities and entities that the child senses) to an abstract grammatical system with syntactic categories such as subject and predicate.

In this view, biological maturation allows the child's grammar to develop as the child physically matures. The analogy is that of the effects of puberty; physical changes are programmed into the child's DNA, but they don't emerge until later in life. Similarly, as the child's brain develops, brain density and the number of possible connections increase as a result of the interaction of biological factors and experience. Innate syntactic categories emerge later on in acquisition; they do not have to be present at birth. However, there is no obvious and abrupt change in the child's speech, only the gradual growth of vocabulary and the knowledge of grammar (Clark 2003: 410). *See* **continuity-discontinuity, the tadpole-frog problem**.

## Discourse knowledge

Knowing how to structure larger units of speech, particularly in conversations with others and while speaking in longer narratives. That is, children learn to order information according to the cultural norms set by the community. They learn how language works in their community, for example, precisely how to take turns when speaking, when it might be appropriate to interrupt someone, and who gets to pick the topic of conversation.

This is part of the socialization process of language acquisition and the acquisition of communicative competence. It goes well beyond (in some views deeper than) linguistic knowledge, which is merely being able to generate a coherent, grammatically correct sentence in a language. It also touches on sociolinguistic knowledge—which deals with issues of respect (e.g., according to social rank, age, and gender). For example, when families migrate to the United Kingdom or the

United States, children may bring their knowledge of how speakers structure stories or cultural legends in their original/heritage language. (This also applies to minority language and cultural groups within a nation as a whole.) Discourse patterns can differ greatly from one culture to the next. See **communicative competence, pragmatic knowledge, sociolinguistic knowledge.**

## Dishabituation

When a child's interest is *renewed* or heightened by a new stimulus. See **habituation, high-amplitude sucking (HAS) technique.**

## Domain

A particular area or sphere of influence or activity, for example, the domain of science. The term is used somewhat ambiguously to refer to domains or areas of the mind/brain and therefore, its functional architecture. It is also used to refer to particular areas of speech, the where and how language is used in various private and public domains.

Views of the human mind/brain include how it is evidently organized. Cognitive scientists (and other specialist of the brain) have found that there are domains of human knowledge, that our faculties (capacities) appear to be organized in particular parts of the brain. One of the main controversies is that of the language faculty, whether or not it involves a specific, specialized region (or domain) of the brain, or whether the entire brain is involved. A *domain-general* view says that all human abilities are within one general area of influence; language learning is like any other kind of learning. A *domain-specific* view, in contrast, states that language is unique, and its link to the mind/brain gives it special status with respect to learning. Domain-general views are characteristically linked to behaviorist or connectionist approaches to language learning, and domain-specific views are favored by cognitivists, nativists, and generativists (cf. Karmiloff-Smith 1992: 33–40). See **cognition, domains of usage, functional architecture, functional asymmetry.**

## Domains of language usage

A domain is a particular realm or field of activity. With respect to language usage, domains are particular social realms in which a language is used. For example, a domain may be the home or at school, at work or at play, in a particular profession or sport. Domains, in this sense, may correlate to some extent with *genres*, the situation of speech, and *registers*, corresponding language forms appropriate to those situations. See **domain, register.**

## Dominance/balance measures

Psychological testing designed to measure the relative strength of each of a multilingual's language varieties. Tests typically measure reaction time in word association tasks in both languages (assuming that the quicker responses go to the stronger language), quantity of responses to word association tasks, and the time it takes the bilingual to process written texts. A balanced bilingual performs equally in both languages; a disparity would indicate (psychological) dominance in one or the other. However, such tests are criticized because they often only measure a very small subset of skills in a language, neglecting such issues as communicative competence. See **assessment, balanced bilingual, bilingual, communicative competence, coordinate, compound, subordinate**.

## Dominant

Most powerful or influential.

There are two principal uses of this particular term. (1) A language can be *socially* or culturally dominant and, therefore, most useful in a greater number of social contexts or domains. For example, it may be associated with a numerical majority, particular prestige group, or politically (therefore, culturally) powerful group. Therefore, this language may be more useful or required in a greater number of domains of speech. In the United Kingdom and the United States, English is the language of political and socioeconomic power. It is a majority language, and the language of government, commerce, and education. It is, therefore, the socially dominant language of each nation. (2) The term can also refer to a *psychologically* dominant language in the linguistic repertoire of a speaker, the language he/she feels more comfortable using in terms of knowledge (e.g., vocabulary), proficiency (fluency), and confidence (ease of expression). In the vast majority of cases, a bilingual will favor one language over the other. It may be the speaker's native language, or primary in the sense that it is the most frequently used language in the bilingual's linguistic repertoire. See **asymmetry, bilingual, dominance/balance measures, hegemony, shift, spread**.

## Dominant language switch hypothesis

The hypothesis that young children tend to learn a second language more fully than older learners and become dominant in that second language.

It appears that young children are immersed in quality input in their new language (through their educational and social environments), and, consequently, switch to the second language as their dominant language. It is not merely a matter of mastering the second language and becoming a balanced bilingual; it is becoming dominant in that language. The language becomes dominant in two ways: it is their most used, and becomes also their psychologically stronger language. Therefore, it is not age, *per se*, that determines the difference; it is the ability of younger learners to adapt in new circumstances. This does not appear to be the case with older children and adults, who typically rely more completely on their native language (Hoff 2009: 67). See **age, Critical Period Hypothesis**.

## Donor

In processes of borrowing, the language that "donates" or gives vocabulary items and structures to a recipient language. For example, the word *sushi* has now been borrowed into English. English is the host (the language in which the word now resides), and Japanese is the donor. In pidgin or creole genesis, there is typically one language that provides the vocabulary items, the superstrate or lexifier (lexical donor) language, and another that forms the grammatical matrix or substratum. See **creole, pidgin, substrate, superstrate**.

## Drift

The gradual change of a single language over time, in general terms, from simple to complex or from complex to simple. It is usually applied to languages that drift from one type, for example, from synthetic (highly inflected) to isolating-analytical (relatively few inflections), as in the case of many indigenous languages of North America that have become morphologically more simple as a result of attrition and contact with European languages.

The importance of this is that heritage languages in contact with English typically drift in the direction of English because of its influence on all spheres of life—the effects of language contact, attrition, shift, and various bilingual language phenomena. Bilingualism has its effects over time as two languages characteristically influence each other in the individual bilingual's head, which subsequently spreads throughout a speech community. For instance, English affects Spanish in Southern California in nearly all areas of grammar, in pronunciation, word order, and even morphology, making it more isolating-analytical. The number of English loanwords in local varieties of LA Spanish, for example, can even make it unintelligible (as "pure" Spanish) to native speakers of Spanish from Spain or Latin America (see Silva-Corvalán 1994: 5–6). *See* **contact languages, language typology, typological classification**.

## Dual immersion

An approach to bilingual education that immerses a child in the target language and culture to facilitate acquisition of a majority language, while also maintaining a native (heritage) language. The goal is bilingualism and biliteracy.

Dual immersion usually stands in contrast to *structured immersion*, in which a majority or dominant language is both the topic and medium of instruction, and *submersion* approaches, so-called "sink-or-swim" methods in which language minority children are essentially dropped into a pool of native speakers of the majority language and left to fend for themselves. Although such programs as structured immersion are often construed as forms of bilingual education, they do not include any type of formal instruction in the child's native language. Thus, they are better classed as monolingual education because they use only the majority language as the language of instruction, similar to submersion approaches (Field in press; Baker 2006: 245–250).

Dual immersion programs have received a great deal of attention for their obvious success in various parts of the world (Hakuta 1986: 93–4, 228; Crawford 1995: 138–142; Baker 2006: 244–250). The term, itself, is intended to mean that the child is immersed in two languages and cultures. *See* **heritage language bilingual education, structured immersion, submersion, two-way/dual language programs**.

### Early exit program
A transitional bilingual program in which children have a limited amount of instruction in a new language (perhaps, only two years or less of practice) before they are mainstreamed. See **mainstream/mainstreaming, transitional**.

### Early-system morpheme
See **system morpheme**.

### Echolalia *or* echolalic speech
The meaningless repetition of words or phrases that have been spoken within a person's hearing. This may occur with children during language acquisition, but it may also be a symptom of autism. See **aphasia, innate**.

### Elaborated code
Believed to be context-free, complex speech patterns used in educated situations; a term typically used in opposition to *restricted code*. An elaborated code does not depend on extralinguistic contexts such as gesturing and shared beliefs.

These distinctions were developed in the 1960s and 1970s by the late Basil Bernstein, a British sociologist whose work focused on the connections between language and processes of socialization, particularly the effects of culture and social class on language according to an apparently strong version of the Sapir–Whorf Hypothesis (linguistic relativity). Both terms are typically associated with cultural stereotypes and concepts of social class. Public perceptions of language variation differ from those of linguists and other language specialists. While linguists point to the "equality" of language varieties, there is still a lingering view that some varieties are inherently better than others, and that those who speak superior varieties are consequently privileged and cognitively (intellectually) advantaged. The distinction between elaborated and restricted codes is another manifestation of this. The terms have been met with great skepticism by their critics, though they have also been received by some educators as insightful descriptions of the differences in language usage found in many classrooms around the globe. However, among the criticisms is that Bernstein was less than clear on what exactly constitutes a *code*. His distinctions, too, of (lower) working class and middle class lack definition. He made the very controversial claim that working-class children not only have little experience with the so-called elaborated code, but they might be harmed by exposure to it because it communicates cultural values that go against the child's lower-class upbringing.

Most linguists would probably find his distinctions subjective and biased. For example, he asserted that elaborated code (or, earlier *formal* code) employs *accurate* grammatical order and syntax, complex sentences, propositions to show logical relationships, and a wide range of adjectives and adverbs. Citing the behavior of middle-class mothers, he noted that they explained things *better* and more fully to their children than working-class mothers. Restricted code, characteristic of the speech of members of lower social classes, employs short, simple sentences, sentence fragments, poor syntactic form, and much repetition; and it is less *logical*, however that can be determined (cf. Wardhaugh 2006: 327–332). Using terms such as *accurate, better, more* or *less logical* obviously betrays a cultural bias and a misconception of the nature of language. Many of his descriptions fly in the face of those by sociolinguists who write of the *logic* of nonstandard varieties, for example, in the work of William Labov (Labov 1972. While it may be possible to link socioeconomic class with lack of success in school, it is not possible to link a particular language variety with inherent intellectual capacities, despite one's prejudices. Nevertheless, some of his distinctions resurface from time to time in education, with refined meanings. It can be anticipated that such terms will refer to the perceived deficits of SL learners. *See* **BICS, CALP, code, deficit model, dialect, difference model, language ideology, linguistic relativity, register, restricted code**, **Sapir–Whorf Hypothesis, standard**.

## Embedded language (EL)

According to the Matrix Language Hypothesis of code-switching (Myers-Scotton 1993a: 6–7), stretches of speech from one language that is inserted into another or second language; the language system into which these elements are inserted is the so-called matrix or base language. *See* **Matrix Language (ML), Matrix Language Hypothesis (MLH)**.

## Emergence of speech sounds

The gradual and systematic appearance of speech sounds (phones and phonemes) in a child's speech.

The emergence of language-specific speech sounds seems to follow a general order (they appear in the child's utterances in a reasonably predictable pattern), though certain characteristics of the target language may influence this order; there may also be individual variation from child to child. For instance, the phoneme /v/ appears relatively late in the native acquisition of English, while in Swedish, it is acquired much earlier. This type of discrepancy suggests that the difficulty of producing a sound does not explain completely why some sounds are learned earlier than others. As with other language phenomena, frequency may be a factor, but not necessarily in the frequency that a child hears a particular sound, but in how frequently it is used; that is, the usefulness of the sound in the production of words (Hoff 2009: 168–169). It does not appear that there is one, fixed, absolutely invariable order, but children learning the same language will progress with remarkable consistency.

All children go through similar steps, though some will start earlier or go faster, while others will start later or proceed more slowly. First, cooing begins around the eighth week, and the emergence of articulatory skills begins at around three or four months of age. Vocal play begins around week 16. In addition, early babbling seems to be independent of the particular language to which the children are exposed, but after about six months, children's babbling gradually becomes more like the sound pattern of the language they're acquiring (so-called *babbling drift*). Reduplicated babbling (*da-da*, *ta-ta*) begins around week 36. Nonreduplicated babbling (ta-da) emerges approximately at week 48. At this stage, children's speech will show noticeable intonation contours (or prosody), producing the musical (prosodic) patterns of her/his target language without actual words. First word appears shortly before the first birthday (around 52 weeks of age)—but, remember, some children start earlier, while others start later. As a consequence of this regularity among children from various language backgrounds, many researchers infer that children, indeed, have the same special innate ability for language. The problem lies in defining exactly what that ability means. See **babbling, cooing, developmental sequences, morpheme studies**.

### Emergentism
A theoretical view that new knowledge emerges from the interaction of innate, biologically based learning mechanisms and information that comes from the environment. It differs from constructivism in its claim that what emerges from innate structures operating on environmental input can be more than what is provided by either the innate structure or the environmental input. Connectionist models, broadly conceived, often favor such views; they have put a renewed emphasis on the nature of innate learning mechanisms and processes. See **constructivism, structuralism**.

### Emerging bilingual
A bilingual speaker whose second/subsequent language is developing or emerging. An insipient bilingual is one who is truly only beginning to develop proficiency in a second/subsequent language (hence, becoming bilingual). The term *emerging* is similar, but implies skills beyond the beginning stages, and yet not advanced enough to be called *proficient*. See **bilingual, insipient bilingual**.

### Empiricism
A broad tradition within Western philosophy which asserts that all (reliable) knowledge is derived directly from experience in one way or another, that is, by observation or via sensory data. One thing that empiricists generally agree on is that there are no innate, universal ideas (e.g., of God, justice, or morality). As a consequence, empiricist views of human language and the language faculty tend to be domain general (there is no special domain or part of the brain dedicated to the acquisition and processing of language). All of our human capacities emerge as an accumulation of experience and the gradual biological development of the individual, although this begs the question of the nature of intelligence, consciousness, and the emotions. Empiricist views of the human mind tend to be either that it does not exist (there is only the physical brain) or that brain and mind are one and the same (see, e.g., Dennett 1991).

Empiricist views of human language, for example, the behaviorist views of B. F. Skinner, were at one time dominant in the West. While Cartesian concepts of language and thought still appear to dominate in generative approaches to language and cognition (see Pinker 1994: 15–24), empiricist ideas appear to have prevailed in other branches of linguistics (e.g., applied areas of language learning and teaching). In addition, many recent views of the mind/brain attempt to construct models of the brain and the faculty of language that are in line with current research in the neurological architecture of the brain (interconnected neurons). Such models tend to be reductionist in that they reduce thought and language to neurological impulses and chemical responses in the brain. *See* **approach, behaviorism, domain, Locke, method, Piaget, Rationalism, Skinner.**

## Encode
Refers to the mental processes of representing thought symbolically in language (particularly phonologically in speech, which includes visually in sign languages), or to the processes of changing the way information is represented from one format to another (as in genetic encoding). *See also*, **code and decode.**

## Endangered language
A language variety that may cease to be spoken because there are not enough speakers to keep it going.

Crystal (2000) makes several distinctions of languages according to their ability to survive (viability), including *viable* (no threat to their long-term survival because there are a sufficient number of speakers); *viable but small* (more than 1,000 speakers in isolated communities with a strong social identity, whose existence is assured for the foreseeable future; *endangered* (continued survival is a possibility, but need to expand in terms of the number of young, native acquirers); *nearly extinct* (or *moribund*, spoken by only a few elderly people with no hope of long-term sustainability); *extinct* (the last speaker is thought to have died) (20–21).

There may also be a number of languages that are potentially endangered, those that are minority languages in direct competition with strong, majority languages. The so-called Superlanguages (e.g., English, Spanish, Russian, and Mandarin) can exert a lot of socioeconomic pressure on speakers of minority languages, to the point that speakers within those communities no longer see the importance of maintaining a heritage language. Shift can be accelerated in such situations. As a consequence, to encourage attempts at revitalization, many linguistics organizations (e.g., the Linguistics Society of America) encourage language revival efforts and the preservation (recordings of last speakers) of materials from endangered and near extinct languages. When a language becomes extinct, all humankind loses a unique manifestation of the human language faculty and an instance of the amazing diversity of human language. *See* **attrition, language death.**

## English as a foreign language (EFL)
English taught in non-English-speaking countries (e.g., in Mexico, Korea, Germany, or France). It is contrasted with ESL (English as a second/subsequent language), which is taught in so-called English-speaking countries where English is an official language and acquired natively (e.g., the UK, US, Canada, Australia ...).

The usual drawback to foreign-language instruction in general is the scarcity of native speakers to model pronunciation accurately, particularly the kinds of compressed speech that occur in naturalistic setting among native speakers.

In addition, the fact that national varieties can differ in pronunciation and spelling can be a source of difficulty for students. For EFL programs, a decision must be made *which* English to teach, American, European (British), or Australian, for example. For this reason, more than one national variety may be offered in places like Singapore and Japan. Most European countries offer British English perhaps with a bias toward European forms. However, American English is obviously spoken by more people. In respect to prejudices, thinking of American English as inferior shows an ignorance of the nature of language. There is no English-language food chain or hierarchy with British English at the top, and so-called "colonial varieties" at the bottom. *See* **compressed speech, dominant, English as a second/subsequent language (ESL), hegemony**.

### English as a second/subsequent language (ESL)

English taught inside a country in which English is the predominant or official language (and spoken natively)—in other words, an English-speaking country.

The term *English as a second language* has traditionally been used to denote English instruction given to a child who speaks a language other than English in the home as he or she enters school, or to an adult as he or she migrates to an English-speaking country. However, the term *second* is an ordinal number. The simple fact that English may be the third or fourth language for the child or adult has led to the substitution of the word "subsequent" (which preserves the ESL acronym); this alternative is preferred by many language specialists. However, the phrase *English as a second language* has persisted probably because of its relative transparency, and because it has been traditional.

Nevertheless, ESL has typically been used to refer to the students, as well. In this latter sense, it has become a label that becomes a permanent part of a child's academic records. Consequently, some districts/programs have switched to the term *TESOL* (Teaching English to speakers of other languages) because it seems to reflect more accurately an underlying linguistic reality (Gunderson 2009: 1). A language learner should be recognized for what he or she is, not for any perceived limitations. For example, a child may speak any number of languages before entering school. Thus TESOL recognizes that the child may speak more than one language other than English. Among several alternative terms, English as an Additional Language (EAL) is sometimes used. Also, in many school districts, the acronym ESL has given way to ELD (English language development) when referring to programs, and to ELL (English language learner) when referring to students. *See* **bilingualism, developmental English, ELL, LEP, multilingualism**.

### English for academic purposes (EAP)

English language instruction specifically designed for students (e.g., university students).

Typically, universities offer various levels of English courses through particular programs (often called institutes) for students who have matriculated from foreign countries where English is not an official language. These courses offer instruction in various facets of the knowledge of English, for example, pronunciation, reading (often coupled with writing), and writing course papers (how to order information according to accepted norms). They are tailored for the academic needs of foreign students. In the countries where English is the predominant language, developmental courses (often remedial in nature) may also be offered for individual citizens who are not native speakers of standard varieties of English or who may be speakers of nonstandard dialects whose writing skills in the standard are still emerging. See **biliteracy, developmental English, literacy.**

## English for specific purposes (ESP)

English instruction (either ESL or EFL) for specific occupations, for example, English for hotel workers, airline pilots, or for workers in industry (e.g., in assembly plants).

Many colleges and trade schools that specialize in training adults for the workforce, for example, offer this type of instruction as a service to businesses that employ relatively large numbers of foreign workers. Accordingly, workers who have limited English skills are taught terminology specific to the business, for example, vocabulary used in instruction and safety manuals (e.g., to know how to avoid unsafe practices, and how to fill out insurance forms). When the development of literacy skills is needed, such courses also provide basic instruction in reading and writing. Companies arrange contracts and pay for these services, which can provide a school with funds derived from outside sources (similar to a grant). See **English language learner (ELL), teaching English as a second/subsequent language (TESL)**.

## English language development (ELD)

Generally, a program or course that is designed to teach Standard English to speakers of other languages or speakers of nonstandard dialects of English. As an acronym, for example, it has come to replace ESL (English as a second/subsequent language), mainly as a result of the realization that speakers of nonstandard dialects can benefit from specific instruction in Standard English. See **bilingual, developmental English, English as a second/subsequent Language (ESL), English language learner (ELL), testing**.

## English language learner (ELL)

A term used to refer to a person who is learning (Standard) English nonnatively. It is one of a plethora of words used to describe and categorize English learners. There is some controversy about which acronym-label is the best and most accurate in representing the true linguistic nature of the learner.

To some, the issue of terminology is more than a matter of political correctness, though it is often portrayed as such. It is more a matter of accuracy and resolving the prejudices that are associated with labeling students according to perceived deficiencies. For instance, the term *ELL* has come to replace the highly stigmatized *LEP* (Limited English proficiency) and its rather offensive nickname *leper* that has been carelessly tossed about in "lunchroom conversation" (Wiley 2005: 123–125). The term *limited English* focuses primarily on what a child does *not* know, not on what he/she actually knows. As a consequence of the political importance of Standard English, incipient bilinguals do not get credit or any kind of recognition for knowing their own native language(s). And, by referring to

English as a subsequent or additional language (e.g., EAL), it is hoped that the former prejudices would dissipate. Whether a change of name can alter perceptions and biases is, of course, debatable. The labels ESL and ELL themselves, though not overtly linked to race, can act similarly to classifications based on race (Wiley 2005: 120–121; Field in press). See **assessment, bilingual, deficit model, English as a second/subsequent language (ESL)**.

## Equipotentiality

Having an equal potential in many different respects. In studies of language acquisition, it is generally accepted that all children possess the natural ability to acquire any language natively—they have the equal potential to learn any language. To the child acquiring his or her native language, all languages are equally challenging (difficult or easy). Adult learners of a subsequent language may find some languages more difficult than others, which may affect rate of acquisition/learning and degree of success (Felix 1995: 139–140).

In another usage of the term, the equipotentiality hypothesis states that both brain hemispheres have equal potential for acquiring language, and that left hemisphere (where the language center of the majority of humans is usually located) specialization develops later. The opposite view that the brain is specialized from birth, the *invariance hypothesis*, states that hemispheric specialization is there from birth. Subsequent research supports the idea that the left hemisphere is specialized for auditory processing from the earliest age testable. However, changes over time take place, and the degree of asymmetry changes over the course of development (Hoff 2009: 57). See **corpus callosum, Critical Period Hypothesis (CPH), dichotic listening tasks, hemispheric specialization**.

## Error

Persistent mistakes that reveal underlying patterns, in any area of grammar. They can be phonological in nature (i.e., pronunciation errors), morphological (either omitting obligatory suffixes or applying them incorrectly), syntactic (variation in word order), or pragmatic (patterns of discourse).

While all speakers, native and nonnative, make so-called "performance errors" (e.g., slips of the tongue), language learners may make specific mistakes that appear to correspond to characteristics of their first language. That is, particular errors made by English language learners from the same language background may appear to be regular and systematic (they all make the same mistake), particularly those that are a result of transfer from a previously learned language.

For instance, Spanish speakers may omit personal pronouns in subject position when using English. (Spanish does not require such pronouns because every finite or tensed verb must have an inflectional ending indicating tense, person, and singular-plural often making the use of a subject pronoun redundant.) For example, the Spanish verb translated as "I sing" is *canto*. The root *cant-* represents "sing," and the *-o* ending indicates first person, singular, present tense. English is required (for lack of such inflectional endings) to express the pronoun "I" overtly, while Spanish will only use personal, subject pronouns to avoid ambiguity (distinguishing, e.g., *él* "he" from *ella* "ella" which both require the same inflectional ending) or for emphasis. Therefore, beginning learners of English who speak Spanish as a native language may unconsciously omit such personal pronouns in speech. Errors such as these create recognizable patterns in bilingual speech, sometimes referred to informally as "accents." *See* **contrastive analysis, error analysis, interlanguage (IL), learners' variety, performance analysis, transfer**.

## Error analysis (EA)

Involves observing errors made by second language users to establish patterns. EA is the logical outgrowth of contrastive analysis (CA). It claims no ability to predict specific errors or where language learning might be easy (Cook 1993: 19–24).

In the developing field of SLA, error analysis in the later 1960s was seen as providing indications of underlying processes of language acquisition. In the early stages of CA, behaviorist concepts of habit formation in language understandably saw patterned errors as evidence of a conflict between L1 and L2 habits. However, in view of the tremendous influence of Chomsky and generative approaches to grammatical analysis, researchers began looking past mere product (what was produced in the performance of language) to what might be going on in the child's brain and how a child's theories of the nature of the TL may evolve. The Chomskyan view that language is a rule-governed behavior was thought to explain developmental sequences in the acquisition of particular structures (e.g., subject-verb agreement in English), especially when systematic errors in children's speech (output) could not be traced back to L1 influence.

In spite of its promise, EA was subjected to similar criticism as CA. For the most part, its weakness lay in the attention to errors. A number of researchers have pointed out that errors are only a relatively small part of the language acquisition process. Importantly, speakers of particular languages may not show errors when producing certain structures (e.g., relative clauses in learners' varieties of English by native speakers of Japanese) because they simply avoid them. Moreover, when examining data, it is simply not possible to conclude whether the absence of certain structures is a result of avoidance or merely the low frequency of those structures (Larsen-Freeman and Long 1991: 61–62). As a consequence, error analysis eventually fell out of favor with researchers and gave way to a different kind of analysis, performance analysis (PA), with increased focus on how language learners go about processes of acquisition. However, it was a necessary step in the field of SLA (cf. Cook 1993: 19–24). As with CA, it has not been completely abandoned by researchers; its continued usefulness has mostly been subsumed by performance analysis. *See* **contrastive analysis (CA), error, performance analysis (PA)**.

## Event-related potentials (ERPs)

Measurable electrophysiological activity in the brain.

When neural circuits "fire" or transmit information, there are changes in the electrical potential (relative voltage) of the neurons in that particular circuit that can be detected on the scalp. By attaching tiny electrodes to the scalp of the test subject, these chemical-electric impulses can be measured and monitored. This is one way to measure damaged tissue that may have resulted from injury, for example, brain trauma after an automobile accident, fall, fight, or other type of lesion resulting from disease or stroke. When abnormal levels of activity are present, this may suggest damage.

ERPs are also used to study the intact brain in operation. The location of ERPs linked to different mental activities is seen as an indication of the area of the brain responsible for such activities. As a method of monitoring events, it has the advantage of being noninvasive (e.g., nothing is injected into the test subject). When this method is used with young children and infants, all they need to do is wear a cap or net holding the electrodes. A disadvantage associated with this technology is that it is one dimensional. Unlike more sophisticated, multidimensional methods, it can only record what can be detected on the surface of the scalp (Hoff 2009: 47–48). *See* **CT (Roentgen-ray computed tomography), fMRI, MRI**.

### Eye movement(s)

The movement of the eyes when doing specific tasks.

Tracking eye movement is a technique for observing what a reader does when encountering an ambiguous sentence. Experimenters observe where the eyes go (e.g., how far back in the sentence) to identify the point at which the sentence becomes ambiguous, and, therefore, clear up (disambiguate) the difficulty. This technique is also used for bilingual subjects to observe how they parse sentences in their respective languages. Observing the choices a reader makes when encountering a syntactic ambiguity in an L2 can illustrate the strategies available to him/her based on L1 and proficiency levels in the L2 (Francis 2005: 270–271). *See* **head-turn technique, high-amplitude sucking (HAS) technique processing**.

### Faculty of language (language faculty)
The mental ability to know a language. It includes the genetically transmitted mental capacity to acquire and use human language, including all biological and anatomical facets of speech, from neurological structures involved in the perception and performance of language to the physical mechanisms of speech (ears, eyes, and touch for input and perception, and the vocal tract—lungs, tongue, lips, and other places of articulation necessary for output and performance, including the hands). *See* **cognition**.

### Family tree model
In the genetic classification of languages, a simple model patterned after a genealogy of human families, with parents and offspring. However, in the genealogical classification of languages, there is only one parent (ancestor or progenitor), the mother. The offspring are classified as daughters; offspring of the same mother are sister languages.

Perhaps one of the most well-known language families in Western culture is the Romance languages. Latin (the language of the Roman Empire) was spoken throughout much of Western Europe, with varieties on the Iberian Peninsula and along the northern areas of the Mediterranean Sea. Consequently, over the centuries, varieties of Latin spoken in Portugal, Spain, France, Italy, Switzerland, and Romania evolved into autonomous language systems with their own speech communities, national boundaries, and literatures.

The concept of language families, however, captures the important linguistic idea that related languages often share many characteristics and features, which typically makes the acquisition or learning of sister varieties (e.g., Spanish by speakers of Portuguese) relatively easy when compared to the learning of totally unrelated. *See* **typological classification**.

### First language
A somewhat outdated term for a person's native language; the one learned first in the home, and often referred to as the *mother tongue*.

The term has generally been replaced by native language (NL) because "first" implies a chronological order, first, then second, third.... However, it is common knowledge that many children around the world know more than one "first" language, so it would be nearsighted to use the ordinal number (hence, the development of the term *Bilingual First Language Acquisition* (BFLA). Likewise, the term *second language* has been replaced by such terms as *subsequent language, additional language,* or *language learned nonnatively*. For the purpose of a language census, mother/maternal tongue may be used to refer to the language of the mother, while paternal tongue refers to the language of the father. *See* **Bilingual First Language Acquisition (BFLA), L1, native-language acquisition (NLA), second/subsequent language acquisition (SLA)**.

### Fluent English proficiency (FEP)

The term refers to those who have reached near native-speaker status in English or who have transitioned into mainstream classes (along with native speakers of English). It does not apply to native speakers, only to those that were previously classified as ESL, LEP, or ELL.

There are two basic problems with the classification. One is that FEPs, even though they are placed with native speakers (or NSs), are still not native speakers. They still may lag significantly behind their native-speaking peers in areas of academic language and measures of literacy. The second is simply the reliability of testing and assessment. See achievement, assessment, English language learner (ELL).

### Fluent/fluency

Indicates the ability to speak freely, in a flowing manner.

The term itself is often debated by specialists. Most definitions include being able to speak readily (without hesitations and stops), over a wide range of topics (implying the knowledge of different registers of speech), and eloquently. Speaking readily does not, however, necessarily indicate overall proficiency or competence (one can speak quickly only on a narrow range of topics). And, person can speak quite rapidly in a language and yet make many grammatical mistakes, perhaps interfering with comprehensibility. A proficient speaker generally knows also how to speak accurately according to native-speaker norms. *See* **accuracy, proficiency, competence**.

### fMRI (functional magnetic resonance imaging)

The use of computerized MRI scans that correlate blood flow with specific functions of the brain. An fMRI, therefore, associates blood flow in the brain with specific activities, albeit indirectly. When a person is given a particular task, blood flow increases in the area of the brain in charge of such tasks.

The benefits of this particular methodology are that it is noninvasive (no injections of dyes or chemicals), and there is no exposure to harmful ionizing radiation (X-rays) that occurs with CT scans. These types of studies are generally used by cognitive scientists to understand and locate brain functioning. Despite their obvious successes (e.g., in locating damaged tissue), many neuroimaging studies have not shed much light on many of the controversies (and internal debates) facing the behavioral sciences. They have, at best, confirmed what has been established by other clinical methods. But, tasks involving language, for instance, translation studies and the like, lack enough specificity to solve theoretical debates of neural pathways and whether or not both/all languages in a multilingual's repertoire share a common circuitry (Bialystok 2005: 426; Paradis 2005: 412–413).

See **activation, brain-imaging techniques, CT (Roentgen-ray computed tomography), MRI (magnetic resonance imaging), neuroimaging**.

## Form

The form of the word is what it looks or sounds like, its specific phonological shape, how it's spelled, or how it's signed. When discussing the types of knowledge that one must have in knowing a *word*, knowing its form may include all the forms in which the word may appear (*go, goes, went, going, gone; attack, attacks, attacking, attacked*), all of its grammatical functions (e.g., noun, verb, or adjective), all of its customary meanings, and other facets of meaning associated with a person's knowledge of the world. See **bilingual lexicon, lemma, lexicon**.

## Formal

The type of speech considered appropriate for particular *formal* situations according to custom or rule. For example, a formal event (dinner or ball) may be characterized by particular forms of dress and behavior; typically, one expects to follow a number of rules that determine when and how one speaks. The term is used in opposition to *informal*.

In the past, the term formal may have been associated with the number and intensity of rules: the more formal speech is, the more rules that one must observe. It is now generally accepted, however, that informal speech also follows a set of rules that can be just as complicated as those for formal usage—they are just different registers of speech that are marked by such contrasts as information and involvement, formality and informality. Registers are also contrasted by specific linguistic features. For example, in formal academic registers, students are typically advised by their teachers and professors to avoid sentences ending in prepositions and to avoid the use of colloquialisms such as contractions, slang, and so-called "dirty words." However, informal registers are marked by such usages. And, it is by degrees: for example, the more informal a conversation is, the more frequent the occurrence of contractions.

Formality can also be influenced by language *mode*, that is whether the medium of interaction is spoken (signed) or written. The end result is that registers of speech constitute a continuum of sorts, with features that cluster along a line that stretches from one extreme to the other. For example, spoken language *tends* to be less formal, and written language is generally more formal. But, notice that written forms such as romantic fiction will also include representations of spoken dialogues; however, the reverse is also true that literate, formal forms may have an influence on speech in formal contexts. In general, written modes are associated with formal-informational registers, and spoken language is associated with informal-involved registers; but, this is not an ironclad rule. We can write using informal registers ("Know what I mean?") and speak using relatively formal registers. Again, topic and physical location, purpose, and participants typically influence language forms in dynamic ways. See **genres, informal, informational, modes, registers, standard**.

## Formal grammar

Approaches to grammar that feature formal expression, a set of rules for the formation of phrases and sentences, typically using some sort of abstract (mathematical) symbolism. In generative approaches, syntactic rules generate the full range of allowable sentences in a language. See **descriptive grammar, generative linguistics, structural linguistics**.

### Formative (testing)
A type of testing that is designed to identify areas in which a student needs to either improve or continue to develop in some skills area. When the results of a test point to areas in which a child needs work, the teacher can intervene and offer immediate focused help. (In linguistics, the term *formative* may also refer to *morpheme*, either a derivational morpheme, e.g., one used to create or derive a new word form, or an inflectional morpheme, used to express abstract, grammatical distinctions such as tense.)

When administered at the beginning of the school year (or when a student transfers to a new district), formative testing can help educators spot problem areas (e.g., vocabulary building, reading comprehension, etc.); when given at the end of the school year, these tests can be used to measure individual (and group) progress. However, there may be a temptation for some school administrators to uses the scores as data for comparison, or to motivate underachieving groups. In the educational sense, formative is often contrasted with normative, or norm-referenced testing, which is used to compare individuals or groups of students. See **No Child Left Behind, norm-referenced testing, summative testing**.

### Fossilization
The gradual slowing or stopping of language acquisition.

Language development may slow down to a halt at a particular level of proficiency, often at the point where effective communication (communicative effectiveness) has been reached. In other words, when a speaker gets to the point where he/she can perform all the necessary functions of language in a second/subsequent language, motivation to progress may cease. The speaker's progress may fossilize, that is, slow down or stop completely (Selinker 1972). See **fluent/fluency, proficiency, motivation, transfer**.

### Fossilized variation
A term used by SLA specialists to describe the effects of fossilization.

It represents a kind of learners' language (or IL), with fairly predictable and systematic errors in pronunciation (an "accent") and grammar (either using incorrect forms or *avoiding* a preferred form). "Variation" implies that sometimes the mistakes occur, and sometimes they don't. That is, mistakes may occur in greater frequency under certain conditions (e.g., in formal, written situations). There will be both grammatical and ungrammatical utterances together, with variation, that can become fossilized (do not continue to develop). In contrast, native language acquirers progress in predictable orders with little variation and keep going until the language is fully mastered according to community norms.

The terms "mistake" and "error" have also been controversial in studies of language acquisition because they turn the focus away from what the learner has accomplished, the level of proficiency that he or she has attained. This has been particularly the case in the development of contrastive analysis, error analysis, and their successor, performance analysis, which focuses clearly on progressive stages in the development of a language. *See* **error, error analysis (EA), fossilization, interlanguage**.

## Function word/item

Words that have specific functions (or duties) in a sentence or clause.

Unlike content words, they are not names of things, actions, attributes, or anything similar. They are said to express *relational* meanings (indicating the meaningful relationships among words), and they typically do not stand alone. They must go with content items, with the exception of pronouns, which stand in place of entire noun phrases. For example, prepositions and conjunctions of various kinds function to link ideas by joining individual words and various word groups together.

In the sentence, "The book is on the table," the underlined portion indicates a physical or spatial relationship between the *book* and the *table*. The preposition *on*, therefore, expresses a relational meaning. In this particular case, the word *on* would be meaningless if it stood alone: "The book is on…." In addition, function words are notoriously difficult to translate from one language to another. A function word that exists in language A may not exist in language B, or there may be so many choices that a long explanation is required with respect to usage (e.g., the word "the," the definite article in German, has numerous equivalents that depend on gender of the noun, singular or plural, and distinctions of case). *See* **content word/item, system morpheme**.

## Function

The particular job a word is to serve in a sentence. In some approaches, function includes the kinds of abstract meanings that a word can communicate (e.g., the meanings expressed by auxiliary verbs).

In certain approaches to language learning, it has been traditional to think that form follows function, that a word form is learned when there is a clear need to use it. However, sophisticated learners can learn a form without fully knowing its function, that is, the contexts in which that form must be used (as a result of word choice) and those in which it customarily appears (as a result of frequency). This is evident in student writing when words are used incorrectly or out of context, or when a particular construction is used without the student truly knowing what it means (Bardovi-Harlig 1995). In addition, native language development proceeds quickly and effortlessly in ways that are not dependent on a need for the child to express himself or herself. Children are active participants in the learning process, and their grammars expand as they are exposed to various registers of speech. The expansion of a child's grammar, therefore, is natural and a response to input, not necessarily driven by a need to communicate.

In sociolinguistic studies of language usage, the term *function* is also used to refer to the various things that speech accomplishes. For example, we make requests, ask questions, give commands, and so on. Each act of speech (or speech act) links forms and expressions with their functions (duties, jobs) in speech. *See* **registers, input, Input Hypothesis, speech act**.

## Functional approach

The belief (or approach to language evolution) that the function of speech drives the evolution of language from simple to complex. It is extended to include descriptions of language acquisition in children.

For example, the processes of acquisition in children begin with the uttering of individual speech sounds and gradually progress through stages, from first words through the development of multiword utterances, and onto more complex sentences. They go from simple sentences, in general, and begin linking clauses with various conjunctions (coordination, then subordination). A functional approach suggests that the child needs to develop increasingly complex utterances, that the child's communicative needs drive the progression from single-word utterances to longer, complicated sentences (from a child grammar to an increasingly adult-like grammar). But the simple fact is that language acquisition will progress in steps despite the child's environmental needs. Functional approaches ultimately fail to account for the systematic acquisition of language by all children regardless of their linguistic, socioeconomic, and psychological circumstances in the vast majority of cases.

## Functional architecture

How the brain appears to be organized according to its functions.

Much of what we know about brain architecture is inferred from studies of various aphasias, via actual observations using brain scans of various kinds (e.g., CT and fMRI), and other techniques that assume an asymmetry in brain functions. The brain, as a physical organ of the body, appears to be an undifferentiated mass, but it functions to control such involuntary responses as reflexes, breathing, sleeping and waking, plus all the other sense-functions as seeing, hearing, smelling, tasting, and touching. It stores memories of our experiences and thoughts—the brain is the place where we *think* and carry on conversations with ourselves and with others. In Chomskyan terms, it is the "language organ." Obviously, without the brain, we would not be able to survive. See **aphasia, dichotic listening tasks, fMRI, neurolinguistics.**

## Functional asymmetry

A characteristic of the human brain in that each hemisphere serves different sets of functions. Therefore, the hemispheres are not evenly balanced with respect to brain functions. See **equipotentiality, hemispheric specialization.**

## Functional bilingual

A bi- or multilingual person who is relatively proficient in each (all) of her language varieties, and can function in society in either language variety.

The term usually refers to a bilingual who speaks one language natively (with a high degree of proficiency) and the other in a more limited way, for example, a native speaker of Spanish who speaks a learner's variety of English, or the reverse, a native speaker of English who knows Spanish well enough to function within the Spanish-speaking community.

Minimal standards are generally used to discuss functional bilingualism. For example, an immigrant may know enough English to read bills sent by mail, write checks (and balance a checkbook, which also implies numeracy and simple arithmetic skills), and respond to notes sent home by teachers regarding children. This person may be able to read headlines in a daily newspaper, deal with getting directions from strangers, and buy items at a market or from various kinds of shops, well enough to successfully negotiate daily transactions, but not necessarily enough to engage in social interactions that require sophisticated language skills. See **biliteracy, fluency, functional literacy, literacy, proficiency**.

## Functional literacy

Identifies the kinds of skills an individual needs just to function satisfactorily within a society.

It includes the ability to *decode* print—that is, to convert the printed word into understandable expressions and structures or their spoken equivalent. For example, all citizens in developed countries are expected to be able to read road signs and warning labels (e.g., poison, represented the skull and crossbones), street names, and job applications. They need to be able to read the bills (coupons, advertisements, and offers) and school notices that they receive in the mail and perhaps gain important political information about their communities from local newspapers. They will need to pass tests for a driver's license. It also implies a degree of *numeracy*, basic arithmetic skills required to balance a checkbook. These abilities form the core of *basic* literacy skills that are deemed important for basic survival. Not coincidentally, this type of literacy is often the goal of educators for many of their students, in particular immigrants and ELLs in short-term, English-only programs (and adult education ESL classes). See **biliteracy, critical literacy, cultural literacy, decode**.

## Functionalism

A general approach to the study of language that is based on the belief that the function of speech drives the evolution of language from simple to complex.

That is, language evolution is parallel with the evolution of species in that the first or original language(s) of human beings were simple, and that over time they became more complex as the range of uses gradually expanded. The more a person needs to use a language (the more functions it needs to fulfill), the more complex the language will become. This is one of the bases for theories of creolization that pidgin languages expand linguistically as their functions also increase. In the case of creole genesis (according to the Bioprogram Hypothesis), children took the degenerate input of their pidgin-speaking parents, nativized it (they became native speakers), and, therefore, created complex creole structures. See **creolization, functional approaches, functions of speech**.

## Functions of speech

The things one accomplishes with speech (in addition to the mere exchange of information); what language is used for.

These functions include apologies, requests, demands, commands, instructions, complaints, and compliments. One may make a request or purchase, greet a friend or acquaintance, deliver a sermon or joke, tell a story, or do a classroom assignment. The expressive functions of language include communicating emotions and sharing ideas and insights, all the normal things that human beings discuss with each other. In functional approaches to language development and evolution, the needs of humans to use speech (e.g., to achieve increasing degrees of specificity) grew, and, as a consequence, the number of functions grew. Hence, language itself expanded to become more complex. Nevertheless, functional explanations fail to account for the fact that children automatically acquire all the "functions" and grammatical devices of their native languages irrespective of their communicative needs. *See* **functional approach, speech act**.

## Gender

As a grammatical term, it refers to the category that divides classes of nouns, for example, into masculine, feminine, or neuter.

As with many grammatical categories, gender distinctions may seem arbitrary. For example, the word "moon" in English is translated into German as *der Mond*, a masculine noun, and in Spanish as *la luna*, a feminine noun. Conversely, the English word "sun" is *die Sonne*, feminine, in German, and *el sol*, masculine, in Spanish. "Man" is masculine in German (*der Mann*) and "boy" is likewise masculine (der Junge), while "woman" (*die Frau*) is grammatically feminine but "girl" (*Das Mädchen*) is neuter. However, frequently, masculine nouns denote biological males, and feminine nouns denote biological females (see Corbett 1991).

The term *gender* has also been brought into the sociolinguistics study of human sexuality to refer to psychological characteristics and sexual identity. An entire subarea of sociolinguistics, therefore, is linked to gender studies, gender/sex roles, and the apparent differences in the speech of males and females, or gendered speech (see Tannen 1994; Lakoff 1975). Emerging gender studies also include gay, lesbian, bisexual, and transgender issues, which include rhetorical patterns and characteristic speech patterns. See **grammatical, identity**.

## Generative approaches/linguistics

Approaches to the science of language historically based on Chomskyan notions of generative grammar. In the history of linguistics, it is especially noteworthy because of its impact on views of cognition and language acquisition, particularly the issue of *innateness*.

Many criticisms of Chomsky's theories pertain to the notion of Universal Grammar (or UG), a theory of knowledge that purports to explain how children acquire their native language(s) so quickly, efficiently, and in a predictable order, without the aid of overt instruction. One of its main concerns is the internal structure of the human mind, that is, that all humans are born with the knowledge of language as a common inheritance, or biological endowment. It is hardwired into their brains and independent of other aspects of cognition. In this view, NLA is merely learning which particular aspects of this underlying, Universal Grammar apply to the specific language being acquired.

However, if all people share the same knowledge or underlying principles of language, then, it stands to reason that all languages, as specific instantiations of this UG, should be more alike. Why, then, are human languages so incredibly diverse? And, if NLA is uniform across languages, then the acquisition of a new or second language should be much like the first. This is clearly not the case. There is a consensus among experts that SLA differs in a number of fundamental respects from NLA. In particular, the role of a native language (how it influences SLA) needs to be accounted for. Despite their initial impact, generative approaches have not been able to provide a complete enough picture of SLA to satisfy all of its critics.

Other criticisms are the role of data in support of a theory and the esoteric nature of generative theories, in general. For example, other approaches to language universals and acquisition prefer a data-first orientation. They seek to use the widest possible range of languages as sources of data and to focus on specific aspects of syntactic processes (Bowerman 1985: 1258–1259; Slobin 1985: 1158–1159; Comrie 1989: 1–5). Regarding generative theory, volumes have been written on the various versions (e.g., Cook 1988; Radford 1988); they presuppose familiarity with its development since the mid-1950s. Generative linguistics has gone through many revisions during that time, for example, Transformational Grammar, Principles and Parameters, X-Bar Theory, Government and Binding, the Minimalist Program, and Optimality Theory. As a consequence, the term *generative linguistics* has expanded to refer to several interlocking (perhaps overlapping) theories and subtheories.

Nevertheless, because of its near ubiquitous role in language studies in the 1960s, 1970s, and later, generative linguistics (or grammar) is part of discussions of bilingual acquisition (see, e.g., Larsen-Freeman and Long 1991: 114–116; Hoff 2009: 25–27). See **generative grammar, Cartesian linguistics, cognitive revolution, Universal Grammar (UG)**.

## Generative grammar
A set of rules or procedures that determine what is or is not a sentence (or well-formed utterance) in a language. As formulated by Chomsky in his earliest work, it is a set of rules that operates on a finite set of elements to generate all the possible sentences of a language. See **Chomsky, generative approaches/linguistics**.

## Genre
A kind of literary or artistic expression (e.g., poetry, prose, epic narrative, or novel) and extended to refer to the characteristics of communicative activities (acts of speech) distinguished by the situations of speech; the external situational factors that determine registers of speech (Biber 1988: 70–71).

"By *genres* are meant categories such as poem, myth, tale, proverb, riddle, curse, prayer, oration, lecture, commercial, form letter, editorial, etc." (Hymes 1974: 61). Typically, the precise variety of speech (including word choice and grammatical characteristics) is referred to as a *register*. See **register, situation of speech, speech act**.

## Grammatical
Having to do with the grammar (rules) of a language, distinct from actual meaning. When a sentence is grammatical, it is constructed within the limits of native-speaker norms and the native speaker's knowledge of the grammar of her/his language. The opposite term, *ungrammatical,* is applied to sentences that clearly do not conform to the internalized grammar of a language (Lyons 1968: 133). The oft-cited example, "Colorless green ideas sleep furiously," written by Noam Chomsky, is used to illustrate that a sentence can be formed according to the grammatical rules of English and yet yield a meaning that is nonsense; grammaticality

and meaning, therefore, can be teased apart—part of the generativist claim of the autonomy of syntax and the argument for innateness.

The term *grammatical* is often contrasted with "acceptable." A sentence may be relatively well-formed (but may contain mistakes) and, therefore, comprehensible, but may not conform to the formalized grammatical rules of a sentence. It may be acceptable in the sense that it can indeed, be understood. This may be the case when performance errors (online slips ups) are made for various reasons, in the speech of a child acquiring the language (which may be grammatical in the child's grammar), or in the speech of an SL learner who is yet to master the grammar of a target language. In the case of the SL learner, the process of *transfer* may influence sentence structure (syntax) in the target. *See* **generative approach, grammar, innate, rule, rule-governed, transfer**.

### Grammatical morphemes

Words and word endings (i.e., affixes) that mark grammatical relations, such as articles, propositions, auxiliary verbs, and noun and verb endings. These distinctions were used in the well-known morpheme study of Roger Brown (1973). *See* **function word/item, morpheme studies**.

### Guest (language)

In some approaches to code-switching, a guest language is the one from which elements (typically words or structures) are taken and embedded into a host language, that is, the morpho-syntactic matrix into which it is inserted.

In contrast, in linguistic borrowing, all loanwords (or other borrowed material) from a lexical donor are generally considered belonging to the host language when they have been fully adapted (integrated) into the borrowing language phonologically and morphologically. They are pronounced as if they were native words, and receive prefixes and suffixes as if they were native words. In discussions of the differences between code-switching and borrowing, there is some debate about one-time or *nonce* borrowings, whether they are incidences of online code-switching or the beginning stages of borrowing, as a new loanword gradually becomes absorbed into the recipient (host or matrix) language (Field 2002: 8–11). *See* **borrowing, code-switching, host language, intrasentential, Matrix Language Frame (MLF) model**.

## Habituation

The *loss* of interest in a stimulus that is repeatedly presented to a child and that gradually becomes habitual or boring. Thus, when a child is first presented with a sound or figure that he or she perceives to be novel (demonstrating his or her ability to discriminate one sound or figure from another), the child's interest is piqued. In the high-amplitude sucking (HAS) technique, the intensity of sucking goes up, at first (*dishabituation*). But, when he or she gets used to it and it becomes boring and, in a sense, habitual (*habituation*), the strength and intensity of his or her sucking gradually decreases.

Previous work in the development of older children (e.g., by Piaget) was restricted to data observed from their manual search abilities, what they could physically and unambiguously demonstrate. In recent studies of the perception of infants and neonates, it was noted that they can, indeed, register responses (reactions) to various stimuli by two additional means: sucking and looking (the head-turn technique). This has opened new avenues for peering into the mind of the infant, helping researchers discover the types of knowledge that human beings are apparently born with regarding language, geometric shapes, number, and human intentions (Karmiloff-Smith 1992: 12–15). *See* **dishabituation, head-turn technique, high-amplitude sucking (HAS) technique**.

## Head-turn technique

A widely used procedure for investigating what young infants seem to be sensitive to; an alternative to the HAS technique.

In one application, the child is presented with two displays simultaneously, and researchers note which one the infant prefers to attend to (listen to or look at). It is also used according to the habituation/dishabituation paradigm to test an infant's ability to discriminate between sounds (e.g., between the syllables *ba* and *ga*). One particular syllable is presented to the child repeatedly until he or she loses interest. When the syllable he or she hears changes, he or she registers a response. For example, in one study, a toy monkey banging cymbals together would appear when a new sound was presented; the child learned to expect the monkey to appear when he or she heard a new syllable. Eventually, as soon as he or she heard a novel syllable, he or she would look toward the place where the monkey would appear in anticipation of his appearance, showing his or her ability to discriminate among numerous sound combinations (Hoff 2009: 150–151). *See* **dishabituation, high-amplitude sucking (HAS) technique, habituation**.

## Hegemony

Leadership or dominance, especially of one nation or social group over another. This can result in the hegemony of one language or dialect over another. That is, a particular language (e.g., Standard British English) may be associated with a particular majority, prestigious, or dominant group and, therefore, become the preferred language of a society. This typically manifests itself in the relative status of one language variety in education (the medium of education), the media (radio, television, and the Internet), government (in official documents and diplomacy), and business/commerce (banking and international finance). *See* **standard, standardization, dominant**.

## Hemispheric specialization

The idea that human brain consists of two sides, or hemispheres, each with its own sets of functions or abilities. In studies of language and the mind/brain, this refers mainly to left-hemisphere specialization (Hoff 2009: 56–59).

Apparently, the vast majority of people have their language centers (portions of the brain specialized for language abilities) on the left side, although specific abilities (e.g., prosody) appear to be spread throughout the entire brain (on either side). There are two opposing views on how this specialization is reached: the equipotentiality hypothesis, and the invariance hypothesis. The former argues that both sides of the brain have equal potential for language learning, while the latter argues that specialization is there from birth (but changes with maturation). *See* **Broca's area, contralateral connections, corpus callosum, Critical Period Hypothesis, dichotic listening tasks, functional asymmetry, Wernicke's area**.

## Heritage language

The original language of a community. The term is typically used in the United States to refer to both the languages of immigrant communities and those of indigenous, Native Americans. Though it might be assumed that a degree of proficiency is implied, the emphasis is on the community. For example, Vietnamese is the heritage language associated with Vietnamese American citizens, whether they speak the language or not. And, of course, Irish Gaelic is the heritage language of people of Irish descent.

There are criticisms of the term *heritage*. In the United Kingdom and Australia, for example, the term sometimes gives way to *community language* (referring to English as an *additional* language, not second language). For one, the term "heritage" looks to the child's past (and perhaps present minority status) rather than to his or her future.

As part of recent discussions, it has been found that institutional language maintenance may have a linguistic cost. For example, when a language is maintained by a community and it is its principle language, social and cultural identity may also be maintained. When a heritage language begins to die, or becomes moribund, however, many structural features may be lost because of restricted usage. Little by little, this language is used in fewer situations. For example, it may be relegated only to home usage, then used only in symbolic fashion through various kinds of insertional code-switching (during particular religious or cultural events). In such cases, language death may be inadvertently hastened as a result (Baker 2006). *See* **code-switching, language attrition, language death**.

### Heritage language bilingual education

A type of educational practice in which children's home language is used as the medium of instruction, for example, in specific programs used for indigenous languages such as Navajo, Ojibwa, Cherokee, Dakota, Inuit (Eskimo), native Hawai'ian, and also for Spanish in areas where it is a common home language—where it may be the majority language in the community. To add an element of ambiguity, the term *heritage language* in the United States is also extended to include a broad range of immigrant language (e.g., Russian, Spanish, and Vietnamese) (Wiley 2007: 75).

Concerning indigenous languages, the goal of heritage language schools, in general, is to preserve the ancestral language and culture; therefore, bilingualism and biliteracy are the intended byproducts. However, there is some question of the effectiveness of institutional language maintenance. Where endangered languages are concerned, there can be a good deal of ambivalence within the community about the future of their language. Well-meaning educators (and linguists) may be convinced that they represent the best interests of the community, but the social, political, and economic pressure to shift to English may be so strong that languages are lost despite their best efforts. This has happened with hundreds of indigenous languages in North America that have "died" as a result of disuse; it occurs worldwide as a common theme of studies of language attrition (cf. Edwards 1994: 104–118; see also Dorian 1989). If learning English means that a community has a better chance to survive, gain access to educational programs, and advance in society, it may be a tough sell to motivate them to preserve a language that is no longer perceived as useful (cf. Crystal 2000: 76–88).

Regarding immigrant languages, heritage language schools have sprung up in grassroots fashion, founded by language minority groups who are keenly aware of the cost of language attrition and loss of cultural values that assimilation presents. Many of these schools are private, so presumably, parents and other community members who support the schools are from upper sociostrata. The students come from language-minority homes, and the parents choose to place their children there. On average, instruction is half in the minority language and half in the majority language, although the minority language may be used exclusively in the early grades. Eventually, the children are able to transfer skills and knowledge to the majority language. *See* **bilingual education, endangered language, heritage language, language death**.

### High-amplitude sucking (HAS) technique

A widely used procedure for investigating the things to which young infants are sensitive; it is also an alternative to the head-turn technique.

In recent approaches to child development, researchers have noted that children can communicate (register a response or reaction) via sucking and looking, two things besides crying that they seem to do well. The latter, looking, is used in the head-turn technique in which the infant turns his or her head in order to attend to something, and the former involves non-nutritive sucking on a device (similar to a pacifier) that is attached to a machine that calculates the rate and intensity of sucking. After habituation and a child's sucking rate decreases (e.g., as he or she loses interest in a sound presented repetitively), the child's rate of sucking picks up again when he or she is presented with a new sound (stimulus). The increase indicates that the child has perceived a change, a new sound or distinguishing characteristic. This technique has been used to measure infants' capacity to discriminate among various different phonemes and, more explicitly, to discriminate among particular features of phonemes (e.g., onset time of voicing) relevant to categorical perception (Hoff 2009: 149–150). While early research in language acquisition seemed to suggest that the beginnings of this type of perception were relatively late, recent work has shown that very young infants are sensitive to the pronunciation patterns of different languages, and by four months of age, they can perceive phonological cues to clause boundaries in their native language (Karmiloff-Smith 1992: 37). *See* **dishabituation, habituation, head-turn technique**.

## High-Low language status

Refers to the relative status of languages, particularly in multilingual settings. In situations of diglossia, one variety typically assumes a preferred social status (the language of power, or High variety), while the other one is socially viewed as lower, less important, or subservient in some way (the Low variety).

There is an asymmetry in language status because there is an imbalance in the social relations among ethnic and language groups—a phenomenon known as social stratification. This asymmetry extends to the language varieties spoken by various groups (cf. Labov 1972: 44; Wolfram and Fasold 1974: 15–17). The culturally dominant or majority language, therefore, may be referred to as the High (or H) variety while a minority language or dialect may be referred to as the Low (or L) variety (Fishman 1970 Wardhaugh 2006: 87–93). For example, in the United States Standard English is considered the H variety and all others pale in comparison with respect to prestige. English is the language of power because of its preeminent role in education, government, the economy, and the media. All other languages and nonstandard dialects are considered L varieties, for example, Spanish, Russian, and Arabic, despite their H status in nations where they are official languages, and such nonstandard dialects as African American English and Chicano English because of their associations with minority ethnic groups. *See* **dominant, hegemony, recessive, social stratification**.

## Holophrastic speech

The one-word stage in child speech. In essence, one word serves as an entire phrase, and intonation basically determines its meaning. For example, the word "mama" may mean that the baby is uncomfortable; it may be a request for more of something, or an expression of happiness. The words "me" may mean such things as, "I want some," and "mine" may communicate "That object belongs to me!" *See* **two-word stage, telegraphic speech**.

## Host (language)

The recipient language in processes of borrowing. For instance, as English borrows words from other languages, English becomes the host language of the new words.

Loanwords are typically adapted phonologically to the sounds of English. A word such as *chutzpah* from Modern Israeli Hebrew may be pronounced "English;" that is, the initial sound, a velar fricative (the so-called "guttural" sound that resembles clearing one's throat) is usually replaced with the /h/ sound of a word like "happy." (Of course, in British dialects, initial /h/ is often not pronounced at all—it is silent, e.g., in the typical pronunciation of *Hampshire*.) Vowel quality may be similarly influenced. In the United States, the Spanish word *tortilla* [tor-ti-ya] is often anglicized; the glide (phonetically represented by /y/) is often omitted, yielding a pronunciation something like [tor-ti-a], a slight difference, but quite noticeable to speakers of Spanish. A more striking example would be the pronunciation of the double-l (ll)—a glide in Spanish, as an /l/, as in [tor-ti-la], which would represent a strong English accent. Nevertheless, English becomes the host of the word, which has entered the American English lexicon with the Mexican Spanish definition of "flat, round, bread-like substance used in the preparation of Mexican food dishes." See **borrowing, donor, guest language, recipient**.

## Hypothesis

A basic concept or assumption that attempts to explain the patterning of linguistic data; perhaps a weak form of *theory*. In language acquisition, the term applies to the ways a child analyzes information of the language he or she is acquiring natively; he or she constructs hypotheses about the nature of that language, its apparent rules or regularities. (A language with no regularities would be unlearnable, so the child must operate from a basic set of assumptions in the construction of particular theories.) As the child observes patterns, he or she may test his or her hypothesis in performance by applying perceived regularities. See **Language Acquisition Device (LAD), hypothesis testing, theory theory**.

## Hypothesis testing

A process by which a child forms and then evaluates his or her hypotheses about the nature of the grammar he or she is learning. She or he relies on some sort of feedback (either positive or negative evidence) or interaction with native (proficient) speakers to correct his or her initial hypotheses as she or he moves from a simple, child grammar to full proficiency.

For example, children construct a preliminary hypothesis about how to make a past tense verb based on the evidence they receive. The first step appears to be a rule or regularity that occurs with regular verbs: put an *–ed* ending on the verbal root. Thus, *look* becomes *look+ed*, *learn* becomes *learn-ed*. (The adultlike pronunciation of such suffixes may take more time, as hypotheses of pronunciation of this particular affix in various linguistic environments also emerge.) The child then tests his or her hypothesis by applying the rule to verbs like *see*, *sing*, and *run*, producing *see+ed* ("seed"), *sing+ed* ("singed"), and *run+ed* ("runned"), respectively. When he or she does not hear the same forms in the speech of (adult) caregivers, he or she eventually adjusts his or her hypothesis to the input he or she receives.

In generative approaches, it is believed that a child's hypotheses are constrained (limited or restricted) by an innate, UG that is part of his or her biological endowment (or LAD). This greatly aids his or her in first constructing a possible theory of the grammar of his or her target language, and the possible adjustments that he or she must make to reach adult or adultlike grammars (Elliot 1981: 8–11; Cook 1993: 16–17). This is important when considering how children go from no knowledge of the target of acquisition to the ability to generate adultlike sentences. *See* **acquisition, Language Acquisition Device (LAD), Language-Making Capacity (LMC)**.

## Ideal speaker

The native speaker as the judge of grammatical utterances in a language. This speaker knows what constitutes a well-formed utterance in that language, having acquired the rules of that language via unconscious processes of acquisition. She or he may not be able to articulate this knowledge consciously (as a formally trained linguist), but intuitively, she or he is the ideal judge.

This term is linked to generative approaches to language and the work of Noam Chomsky and his colleagues. It also leads to questions about what constitutes a language, how a speech community is formed, and what the term *native speaker* means precisely. Some linguists assume that a "language" is nothing more than an aggregate (conglomeration) of idiolects, or individual versions of a language as defined by a community. For example, English is spoken worldwide, but every speaker's version of English (the individual *lect* or *idiolect*) has its own specific characteristics in performance and vocabulary. The "English" of the average speaker in London, for example, can vary considerably from other speakers in the same city, more so from speakers in the north or west of England. It will vary to a much greater extent when contrasted with the average speaker of American English in Los Angeles or New York.

The effects of contact with speakers of other languages depend on a host of social variables. For instance, individual speakers of English are in intimate contact with French in parts of Canada or Spanish in the Southwest United States. Words of foreign origin may occur on a moment-by-moment basis in the speech of English speakers for cultural items (foods, cultural events, etc.) Thus, a portion of the vocabulary of a native speaker of English from El Paso, Texas, may consist of Spanish words fully adopted into his/her mental lexicon—whether or not the person actually speaks Spanish at all. Therefore, even in the same locale, the mental vocabulary of one speaker of English may differ from another in character both quantitatively (depending on level of education and knowledge of literate registers) and qualitatively as a result of cultural contact with speakers of other languages. Issues such as these may bring into question just what a native speaker needs to know to qualify as the ideal speaker. *See* **community, community bilingualism, dialect, idiolect, speech community, standard**.

## Identity

How one views oneself; a person's concepts of his/her individuality or group reference/affiliation.

The word *identity* implies a degree of sameness (e.g., in the adjective *identical*), so terms like "social identity" imply the perceived sameness of an individual with others in a social group. It includes a sense of belonging to social, cultural, or ethnic groups (as in social identity, cultural identity, and ethnic identity). Most current conceptions of personal (individual) identity assume that it is dynamic, and that it can change from situation to situation. Thus, it is not necessarily tethered to static demographic categories such as race, age, gender, and socioeconomic status and their associated stereotypes.

Social and cultural identity figure prominently in studies of language acquisition because they play roles in attitude and the different types of motivation necessary to learn a new language and either maintaining a heritage language or shifting to a socially dominant, majority language. *See* **Acculturation Model, attitude, endangered language, gender, heritage language, individual bilingualism, integrative motivation, language loyalty, popular culture**.

## Idiolect

An individual's lect (*idio-* "one's own, personal" + *-lect*). In that every person has her own influences and sources (models) of language acquisition, each of us acquires an individual language variety. The extent to which idiolects overlap and intersect within the larger community of speakers is the extent to which idiolects are mutually intelligible. This also helps to account for some individual variation.

For example, in Los Angeles, California, it is very common that an individual's parents have originated from another state in the United States or an entirely different country. In the study of bilingual families, all possibilities occur (Romaine 1995: 183–189): parents may come from the same town in Latin America; one may have been born in an Asian nation and the other in Mexico; or both parents may be native speakers of Spanish (Vietnamese, Russian...) but born in the United States. Thus, an individual child may be raised with multiple linguistic and cultural influences, all shaping her individual identity and language usage. One result is that regionalisms (words associated with a specific part of the country) may exist side-by-side as synonyms of sorts. For example, the words *sofa, divan, davenport, couch*, and even *chesterfield* (a Canadian word) may refer to the same item of furniture prominent in homes, and be part of an individual's linguistic competence. *See* **dialect, lect, standard**.

## Immersion

A general term that refers to a teaching environment in which a target language is both the topic of instruction and medium of instruction.

However, immersion seems to be a feature of widely differing types of programs. For example, so-called dual immersion programs feature being immersed in both the majority and minority language, so there are two target languages. It is considered a strong form of bilingual education because proficiency and literacy (biliteracy) in both languages are the goals; such programs foster additive bilingualism. In structured immersion classes, immersion is in the majority language; the minority language is used only in the beginning, if at all. In contrast to dual-immersion programs, it is considered a weak form of bilingual education—it is most likely an ESL program with a misleading name. Such programs are typically subtractive. Submersion programs are known as "sink or swim" approaches. There is no pretense of bilingual education, so, therefore, they are monolingual for all intents and purposes. See **additive bilingualism, dual immersion, structured immersion, submersion, subtractive bilingualism**.

### In-between group

A minority group that is caught in the middle between two cultural or linguistic groups. For example, many second-generation immigrants find themselves not identifying fully with (a) their new adopted culture and language or (b) with their parents' homeland (the old country), culture, and language.

As old cultural associations gradually fade, this in-between group may identify socially with others like them, as they adapt to a new language and culture. In some cases, members of the older generation see their influence waning, and distance themselves from the younger generation who struggle with a new social identity as an ethnic and/or language minority. If minority status also implies some kind of social rejection by the new host culture, an in-between group (neither A nor B) can emerge as a distinct community with its own social identity, and its own norms of speech and behavior. This has been the case in some sectors of the Chicano-Latino population in the United States, for example, those who are neither Mexicans nor Americans (i.e., White Anglo Saxon Americans). This has occurred worldwide as a consequence of colonization, as the result of the importation of guest workers, for example, Turks, in Germany, and as a consequence of the globalization of densely populated urban environments. In many areas, members of in-between groups have carved out separate social status and identity. In-between individuals can be contrasted with those who consider themselves *both*, that is, bicultural and bilingual, able to live and move freely in either/both cultures and languages. See **three-generation rule**.

### Incipient bilingual

One who is beginning to be bilingual, that is, a monolingual person who is learning a second or additional language. See **emerging bilingual**.

### Incipient bilingualism

Bilingualism at its beginning stages, as members of a language-minority community begin to shift toward a majority language in daily usage. As a result of contact, individuals within an immigrant community, for example, will acquire/learn the socially dominant language of their surroundings. They may do this for utilitarian reasons (for employment) or for the purpose of integrating into the majority language culture. As the number of bilinguals increase, bilingualism itself will spread. See **bilingual, bilingualism, shift, spread**.

### Individual bilingualism

An individual's proficiency in both/all of his or her languages, typically with degrees of proficiency in each language.

The term is often used in contrast to *community bilingualism*, mainly because one cannot equate behaviors of a community with those of an individual. The influences are neither necessarily identical nor to the same degree. Community-wide attitudes toward individual bilingual language phenomena may influence individual behaviors, but it takes groups of individuals to shape the behavior of communities. Various language mixing behaviors can convey messages of social identity, status, and in-group membership; the community interprets what is acceptable according to community norms. For instance, in a particular community, code-switching can become the "unmarked choice," meaning that it is the preferred way of speaking in specific situations (Myers-Scotton 2006: 158–170). *See* **bilingual language phenomena, borrowing, code-switching, diglossia**.

## Infant-directed speech

Speech directed by adults and other caregivers to infants and young children. It can also be referred to as baby talk (an ambiguous term that also may refer to the ways that baby's "talk") and child-directed speech. *See* **child-directed speech, motherese**.

## Informal

Refers to the everyday; casual, supposedly lacking in formal rules. With respect to language, it is the type of speech considered appropriate for everyday, casual situations. Although informal speech is often contrasted with *formal* speech, there may be as many conventions observed in informal interactions as in formal interactions. It is not merely the absence of rules. *Informal registers* of speech may be influenced a great deal by pop culture, and may be just as complicated to acquire as *formal registers*. Informal speech may also be influenced by *nonstandard dialects* and the use of slang and other vernacular forms, for example, words like *ain't* and so-called *double negatives* (e.g. "I didn't do nothing"). *See* **formal, genres, registers**.

## Informational

Pertains to the amount of information a particular speech event conveys. For example, a formal lecture at a university is expected to present a lot of information (e.g., specialized vocabulary and new concepts that require definition and explanation), while a casual conversation among peers is usually marked by informality. It may contain relatively little actual new information (but show a greater degree of conversational interaction and social involvement). Registers of speech, therefore, will contain relative amounts of information. At one end of a continuum of registers of speech are those high in informational content (and low in personal involvement), and at the other end, are those low in content (but high in involvement) (Biber 1988: 43).

It is often remarked that monolinguals assign different varieties of speech to various speech events much as bilinguals assign different languages to different events (Finegan 2008: 318–319). With respect to bilinguals and bilingual performance, informal registers of one language may cluster at one end of a continuum of usage and formal registers of the other may cluster at the other end. A relatively strict "division of labor" such as this may mean that a bilingual is exposed only to particular registers of each of his or her languages in specific social contexts. For example, most formal–informational interactions may occur in the majority or dominant language, while informal–involved interactions in the minority language, leading to a skewed range of proficiencies. As one can imagine, educators who are sensitive to such distinctions will try to facilitate the learning of a wide range of registers in both languages so that bilingual speakers will be able to take advantage of their bilingual capabilities. See **bilingualism, formal, genres, involvement, proficiency, registers**.

## Innate

Refers to abilities or capacities that are in-born or present at birth (programmed into human DNA and, therefore, a biological endowment). This topic is important to discussions of SLA, particularly in view of the belief that children acquire their native languages (NLA) effortlessly and efficiently while adults appear to struggle so much with language learning later in life. Debates generally center on whether children have a real biological or developmental advantage, and if so, what the relevant age limits might be and what specific types of language abilities appear to be involved.

Unless somehow impaired, all humans will walk at a certain point in their development, even though we are not born ready to walk right away. Likewise, all humans are born with the ability to talk, sign, or *do* language, at least in the sense that we are born with the ability to acquire human language. There are possible exceptions, for instance those born with specific language impairments or disabilities. While most language acquisition specialists acknowledge that at least some facets of language acquisition are apparently innate, there is little agreement on what precise abilities or capacities that entails. Issues of innateness are hotly debated in both NLA and SLA research. See **behaviorism, Cartesian linguistics, Chomsky, generative approaches, Language-Making Capacity (LMC), Universal Grammar (UG)**.

## Input

In theory, everything a learner hears from a target language can be considered input whether or not it is immediately recognized and understood. Some forms may be heard a number of times before full productive knowledge is reached.

In discussions of the Input Hypothesis, this observation has motivated the coining of a separate term, *intake*, to refer to that particular type of input that the learner can use to promote the development of his/her second language (in the development of her interlanguage) (Larsen-Freeman and Long 1991: 140, 144). In other words, it is language information that the learner can use as a basis to comprehend (hence, acquire) additional linguistic data of the target language. See **comprehensible input, Input Hypothesis, intake**.

## Input Hypothesis

A hypothesis proposed by Stephen Krashen (1985).

According to the hypothesis, we acquire language by understanding messages, that is, through *comprehensible input*. According to the hypothesis, the input required for acquisition (not just basic comprehension) must be just beyond what has already been acquired, or one small step past what has been acquired. In this way, learners can progress from their current state of learning, or $i$, to the next state, or $i + 1$. If it is too far past the acquirer's ability, it will not be understood. If the acquirer has already learned and assimilated the word, phrase, or construction, there's no challenge—acquisition is moot (Larsen-Freeman and Long 1991: 224, 240–249). See **acquisition, Acquisition-Learning Hypothesis,**

Affective Filter Hypothesis, comprehensible input, Krashen, Monitor Theory, native-language acquisition (NLA), Natural Order Hypothesis, and second language acquisition (SLA).

## Instrumental motivation

Refers to a type of motivation that individuals may have to learn an additional or foreign language. Instrumental motivation is the kind that comes from needing a degree of proficiency in an additional language for utilitarian purposes.

For example, English is the language of business in the United States, Canada, the United Kingdom, Australia, and so on. In order to get or keep a job, one must be at least proficient enough to function on the job. One must be able to fill out job applications, tax forms, and so on, and to understand instructions and, perhaps, respond to customer/client concerns. For access to information and technology available only in English, a certain amount of proficiency is necessary. The same applies to the motivation to learn German in Germany, Dutch in the Netherlands, and French in France. Conservative elements in those countries expect in-migrants and residents to achieve at least some measure of competence in the national languages. *See* **functional bilingual, functional literacy, motivation, integrative motivation**.

## Intake

Refers to the kind of input that can be used to promote growth of an individual's interlanguage, perhaps just slightly beyond the learner's current abilities. It also implies the information/data of language that a child acquirer actually retains (Sharwood Smith 1994: 8–9). *See* **comprehensible input, input, Input Hypothesis**.

## Integrative motivation

In the acquisition of a second language, the type of motivation that is believed to be required to reach native-like or near native-like ability. By definition, it is a complex of attitudinal and motivational variables that reflect a genuine interest in learning a new language to come closer to the community (Gardner 2001: 1–19). It does not necessarily mean withdrawing from one's original community, but a degree of identification with the new community is implied. It leads to more thorough acquisition of a target language beyond a functional or instrumental level. *See* **instrumental motivation, motivation**.

## Interaction/interactive

Mutual exchanges of information; reciprocal actions. Every speech act is an exchange of information among participants. Hence, interactive approaches to second-language teaching (English or other languages) involve the interaction of students with other students; they are also referred to as "student-centered" approaches. They are contrasted with "teacher-centered" approaches and the "full-frontal" teaching methodology disdained by some proponents of newer cooperative-learning techniques of traditional pedagogical approaches that feature teacher lectures and students' passive participation.

An interactive approach to language learning is based on the assumption that true acquisition is accomplished by the effective interaction between a learner and a proficient speaker of the target of acquisition (e.g., caregivers in child language acquisition). An active exchange of information occurs as participants negotiate meaning (accommodate one another to make sure messages are being communicated and understood) in various ways, for instance, through language (e.g., a particular choice of words) along with contextual clues such as gestures and facial expressions. Meaningful interactions make it possible for learners to analyze input and acquire new forms and expressions. The important distinction between approaches that emphasize interaction and those that don't is the need for the active role of the learner, inferred from NLA and the view of the child as an active participant in the acquisition process, rather than passive observer. *See* **comprehensible input, interactionism, speech, speech act**.

## Interactionism

The theory that maturity (e.g., with respect to language acquisition) is reached through personal interaction with others.

In current views of the nature–nurture debate, it is an alternative to both behaviorism and nativism. While it allows for some innate learning capacities of the child, it places greater emphasis on the child's experience and learning environment. It appears to offer a kind of middle ground between two extremes, where the child is seen as possessing some inborn capacities for acquiring language (quickly, effortlessly, and without a teacher). In addition, social interactionism is a related view that stresses the importance of social interaction of the child (hence, student) with caregivers. Constructivism, the view of child development associated with Piaget and his followers, is interactionist in principle. *See* **behaviorism, constructivism, empiricism, nature vs. nurture, nativism**.

## Interference

Refers to the influence of a native language (or mother tongue) on the performance of another, usually second language. The term was used in early studies of language contact, but has fallen into disfavor because it implies random, uncontrollable effects. The term *transfer*, which can include systematic effects, has come to replace it. Many researchers prefer nuanced terms such as (native language) *influence* that appear to be more neutral (not associated with a particular school of thought or theory).

## Interlanguage (IL)

Abbreviated IL, refers to the stages that a second language goes through on the way to proficiency in a target language. These stages at which learners' grammars of a target language develop range from $L2_0$ to $L2_n$. Beginners start at zero ($L2_0$) or no knowledge of the target, and reach a final stage that varies considerably from one learner to the next ($L2_n$), $n$ representing a variable, or however far that particular learner will advance in SLA towards native-like proficiency (Larsen-Freeman and Long 1991: 60–61; Cook 1993: 17–20; Myers-Scotton 2006: 358).

The term was originally coined by Reinecke (1937) to refer to rudimentary "go-betweens," or intermediary languages used for business and inter-group communication, that is, pidgins and creoles where each group maintains its own native language and develops an auxiliary language for the purposes of trade (Holm 1988: 30). The term was expanded to include stages in the process of SLA most notably by Selinker (1972). Its current usage maintains a sense of betweenness; however, this betweenness is between the polls of zero and relative proficiency in one language (someone's native language). See **creoles, fossilization, learner's variety, pidgins**.

## Intersentential code-switching

A switch from one language in a bilingual's repertoire to another that occurs between sentences or utterances.

For instance, a bilingual may switch from one language to another in response to a change in the situation of speech, for example, when there is a new participant to the conversation or when the topic changes. This typically occurs when a bi- or multilingual store clerk is approached by a customer who apparently speaks one or another language in the bilingual's linguistic repertoire. The clerk may switch to the language he/she thinks the customer most likely speaks, depending on the appearance of the new participant (style of dress or other cultural characteristics) or from overheard speech (the customer was speaking the other language with a companion). See **code-switching, intrasentential**.

## Intrasentential code-switching

A switch or alternation from one language to another midsentence, that is, within sentence boundaries. Intrasentential code-switching is generally conversational, when both languages are switched "on." It is not necessarily in response to a change in the speech situation, as in the case of intersentential code-switching. Because of the speed and ease of the utterance, the two languages are spoken simultaneously.

In many bilingual communities in the United States, United Kingdom, and elsewhere, code-switching and borrowing may be tolerated and accepted by the bilingual community at large. This tacit approval may even encourage such behaviors in individuals. In other similar communities (or sectors of the same community), such behaviors may be looked down upon and actively discouraged. Language purists (those conservative elements within a community that wish to maintain sharp distinctions of usage) typically view conversational code-switching as corruptions of both languages (Field in press). They may view such mixing as corruptions, so to speak, as neither A nor B, or as an indication that neither language is being spoken "correctly" or properly according to community standards and norms. This is one reason why particular kinds of language mixing receive names that are somewhat pejorative (e.g., *franglais*, the mixing of French and English in Quebec, *Spanglish*, *Konglish*, and *Taglish*, and perhaps *Banglish*, for Spanish-English, Korean-English, Tagalog-English, and Bangla-English mixing, respectively). See **bilingual language phenomena, borrowing, code-switching, diglossia, intersentential**.

## Involvement

A discernible quality of speech that pertains specifically to the degrees of personal involvement of speakers in informal interactions/conversations. It is typically contrasted with *information* (informational quality) in description of registers of speech.

Involvement describes the degrees of familiarity among participants in a speech event. The more involved the conversation is, the closer the personal and emotional ties among participants. Speech forms typically associated with involvement are the frequent use of first- and second-person pronouns (relative to the use of third-person pronouns), the "I-you" emphasis in conversational interchanges, and other speech characteristics linked to informal registers of speech (e.g., sentence-ending prepositions, contractions, colloquialisms, and so on). Involved, informal registers are contrasted with those that are relatively more informational and formal. However, the differences between two polls are a matter of degrees. *See* **formal, informal, informational, registers, situation of speech, speech event.**

## Ipsilateral

Refers to the connections between the body and the brain that occur on the same side (e.g., left side of brain, with left side of the body). It is used in contrast to *contralateral* connections. *See* **contralateral, corpus callosum, hemispheric specialization.**

## Islands

Words, phrases, or clauses from one language embedded or inserted into another typical of conversational code-switching; sentence constituents in bilingual speech.

The presence of embedded-language islands is a prominent topic in recent studies of code-switching. According to Myers-Scotton (1993a and elsewhere), there are two kinds, matrix language (ML) islands and embedded-language (EL) islands (Myers-Scotton 1993a: 136–148). ML islands are stretches of speech that clearly belong to the host language (the presumed morpho-syntactic base or matrix of the code-switched utterance). EL islands are those that are embedded or inserted into the ML during fluent, insertional, intersentential code-switching (see Muysken 2000: 17–18; Myers-Scotton 2006: 241, 252–253).

Many specialists in contact linguistics agree that all bilingual phenomena (including the emergence of new languages in situations of long-term, intimate contact such as pidgins, creoles, and other bilingual mixtures) show the systematic effects of contact-induced change (e.g., Field 2002: 1–4). Many, if not all, language-mixing behaviors appear to be characterized by some sort of language matrix, whether it is a native language in SLA, the host language in borrowing, or the substrate variety in the emergence of pidgin and creole varieties. *See* **bilingual phenomena, borrowing, code-switching, contact linguistics, creolistics, interlanguage (IL), Matrix Language Frame model, transfer.**

## Joint attention/gaze

When a child and parent look intently at the same object at the same time while engaging in conversation.

It may have been thought at one time that the child would fix his or her gaze on whatever the mother or other caregiver was talking about, trying to learn as much about that object or activity as possible (e.g., naming objects). However, it is not an easy task to attract and keep a young child's attention on a single object for more than a moment. To keep a child engaged in conversation, it is best when the conversation keys on what the child is attending to or watching (Clark 2003: 32). As many parents realize, wherever the child's eyes go, so goes the child. If he or she sees an interesting object, he or she will most likely point to it or try to touch it. It is easy to see how objects are named in such a scenario. The object draws the child's attention (mother looks at the object, as well, to estimate danger, etc.), and the child wants to name it—information supplied by the mother. *See* **naming insight, segmentation, speech stream, word order**.

## Knowledge (of language)

What a speaker knows about a language variety; the internalized knowledge of a language that has been acquired.

There are apparently two basic types of knowledge regarding language; tacit and explicit (focal). Tacit knowledge is the type that a speaker may not be able to express or articulate to another person. It is typically based on the unconscious acquisition of the rules and patterns of one's native language, and involves perhaps instinctive linguistic knowledge of how to make a well-formed utterance in a language (associated with the notion of "native speaker intuition"), and how native speakers often base their opinions of grammatical correctness on feel, rather than conscious, objective analysis (cf. Haegeman 1994: 6).

Explicit, or focal, knowledge, in contrast, can be expressed, much like a teacher's ability to point out particular rules of a standard variety, and how one *should* form a sentence according to the stated rules of a language contained in grammar books. It involves conscious analysis and awareness, often according to a standard variety or specific community norms. See **acquisition, discourse knowledge, learning, linguistic competence, pragmatic knowledge, sociolinguistic knowledge, rule**.

## Krashen, Stephen

Influential researcher in the fields of language acquisition/learning and teaching in the United States. His approach and various theories are often associated with the influence of *Noam Chomsky* on the cognitive sciences and concepts of *innateness* and the abilities of children to learn their languages naturally. His distinction between *acquisition* (how children seem just to "get" their native languages) and *learning* captured a key insight into the differences between the unconscious learning of a native language by children (acquisition) and the typically conscious learning of a second language by adults (learning).

There are a number of important hypotheses of SLA attributed to Krashen that have had a great impact on language teaching. However, almost from the beginning, these hypotheses have generated considerable controversy among specialists; some are very critical of so-called strong versions. For example, in discussion of his Acquisition-Learning Hypothesis, researchers like to point out that it is not always clear what is "learned" versus what is "acquired", whether or not conscious knowledge can become unconscious skill (e.g., through constant practice), and to what extent a second language can be "acquired." It is very likely that Krashen's viewpoints appeal mostly to the intuitions of teachers. There is no question that he has left his mark throughout the literature on language acquisition and teaching methodologies. At the very least, as with all hypotheses and theories, they have been excellent starting points, serving to identify particular areas in need of continuing research. *See* **Acquisition-Learning Hypothesis, Affective Filter Hypothesis, Input Hypothesis, Monitor Theory, Natural Order Hypothesis, whole language**.

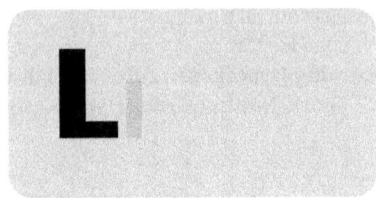

## L1, L2
Abbreviations for language number one (L1), and language number two (L2), respectively. These are typically technical terms used for convenience despite the connection to the outdated terms *first* or *second language*. See **native-language acquisition, second/subsequent language acquisition**.

## Language
While it is certainly easy enough to give an example of *a* language, language as a human ability requires a more subtle definition.

Language can be viewed in at least two fundamental ways, as (1) a mental process occurring in the brain, and (2) as a system of communication that functions in society. It involves neurological processes that are biologically linked to human cognition and the ability to communicate with other members of our species through a system of spoken or visual, albeit arbitrary signs. It is also creative; a finite set of elements (e.g., words and rules) can produce an infinite set of utterances. We speak new sentences every day, and comprehend those we've never heard before. Only human language can differentiate between strings of words syntactically, for example, in the well-known expressions of "Dog bites man" versus "Man bites dog" (Pinker 1994: 84); animal communication systems are greatly limited in this respect. And, we can refer to past events or ones that may occur (a quality known as *displacement*). Language also involves the social processes that link people together, allowing us to communicate our thoughts internally (as we carry on inner conversations with ourselves while thinking) and externally to others via social networks. It is hard to imagine thinking without language.

In general, languages as communicative systems have the following characteristics: They are linguistic systems, either oral (spoken) or visual (signed); they have a speech community (an identifiable group known as speakers who share some sort of history); they possess a shared literature or oral tradition (e.g., a writing system, books, legends, etc.); and possibly, some sort of political or natural boundary (mountain range, river, lake, or ocean). A language is typically defined and named by its speakers, and, in essence, belongs to a culture. And, when a person "knows" a language, he/she knows its individual sounds, how those sounds combine into words and other word groupings (how to create a well-formed sentence), and all its other grammatical and pragmatic characteristics (how it works). See **dialect, processing, sign**.

## Language Acquisition Device (LAD)
In early versions of Chomskyan linguistics (Generative Grammar), the Language Acquisition Device (or LAD) was seen as a metaphorical black box. It represented

what was unknown about the human mind/brain and the language faculty. Impenetrable by actual scientific observation, it was nevertheless a potential source of information. It represented what can be inferred from the problem of the knowledge of language: young children appear to know a great deal about how language works, but they have very little evidence upon which to build hypotheses. As a scientific theory, the idea of an LAD helped motivate a paradigm shift in the cognitive sciences, a different way of viewing (a) the task of language acquisition and (b) the nature of language (Cook 1993: 13–17).

The shift was away from a view of language as human behavior, a view that was promoted by behaviorist schools of thought and reinforced structuralist views of language that dominated language teaching in the United States and elsewhere. In contrast to the behaviorist view, language acquisition was seen as a mental process that takes place over time in the mind/brain of the child (hence, a mentalist view of language) and not merely a behavior learned through repetition and mimicking the actions of adults. The problem was twofold: in perception, the child must mentally come up with some kind of structural description to identify subjects (nouns) and predicates (verbs). In performance, he or she must also construct a grammar that would generate appropriate responses.

The LAD was seen as guiding the processes and enabling the child to evaluate and eliminate grammatical sequences that were not possible based on his or her input. It restricted the possibilities as the child fashioned his or her own grammar from the ground up. In turn, the child's developing grammar was not seen as an inferior or defective version of an adult grammar; it was seen as an autonomous and expanding recreation of the target language. In recent versions of Chomskyan linguistics, the LAD has been abandoned in favor of concepts of UG; the search for a particular region of the brain responsible for acquisition has yet to produce satisfactory results. *See* **generative approach, innate, structuralist, Universal Grammar**.

## Language attrition

The gradual loss (or disappearance) of a language as members of its speech community die out or move away and are not replaced by new, native speakers.

The term is also expanded to refer to linguistic processes in the gradual loss of forms and structures of the language itself (as a system) due to language contact and processes of *shift* (Crystal 2000: 21–23). In addition, this latter sense of the term can apply to the gradual loss of proficiency of children in their L1 as they shift to a new, dominant language (and, consequently, neglect the use of the L1— i.e., native or former primary language). It also can occur in the speech of adults as the domains of usage shrink in their heritage language, or in the gradual loss of a second language learned in school that is seldom or never used in actual conversation (see Lambert and Freed 1982).

The end result of attrition is usually referred to as death, but many researchers do not like its association with a disease metaphor, which likens the loss of a language to a terminal illness. Languages do not die; they are not living organisms that live, become ill, and die. Their speakers, however, do eventually die. So-called living languages are those that have a regular supply of new speakers because children are continually born into the community who then become native speakers.

In the process of shift, the number of new native speakers may slow to a trickle and stop. *See* **attrition, endangered languages, language death, shift**.

## Language background scales

The measurement of a person's usage of a language variety in different contexts, that is, according to different relationships and situations of speech.

It is also a kind of self-assessment that shows the same limitations as all self-assessment measures. Because language choice/usage can be almost entirely unconscious, such self-reports rely on impressionistic estimates that can exaggerate or underestimate the usage of one language or another. Such scales and related language use surveys are limited in the kinds of situations that they can list; many opportunities for language choice are simply not listed because simple inventories cannot be exhaustive. In addition, whether a particular bilingual is aware or not, a minority language may not be used at all on an everyday basis despite subjective judgments that it is used frequently (Baker 2006: 32–34). *See* **assessment, census surveys, self-assessment**.

## Language change

The gradual evolution of a specific language variety. It is often imperceptible to contemporary speakers, but it proceeds nonetheless. One obvious example is the development of all forms of English revealed in a diachronic study of the language, for example, in the transition from Old English (Anglo-Saxon) to Middle English, to Modern English, and on to Present-Day English. *See* **contrastive analysis, language evolution**.

## Language choice

The more-or-less conscious choice of one language variety over another based on situational factors. For example, in diglossic situations, individuals and groups typically assign specific language varieties (languages, dialects, registers) to specific domains of usage. As in many other areas of life, choices have consequences.

For example, a child may know that a particular language needs to be used at school as a result of its status; if she or he does not possess enough proficiency in the language, she or he may avoid using it. Thus, she or he may be viewed by the teacher or other educators as quiet, nonverbal, or even reticent when in fact, she or he is just unfamiliar with the situation of speech and lacks the level of proficiency that is expected of her or him (in that situation).

Other possible consequences are both language maintenance and language shift. On the one hand, when a community of speakers wishes to preserve a heritage language, choice can lead to planning by political groups thereby ensuring that the heritage language is used and taught in a wide range of situations (genres). Reading materials can be provided, motivating the practices of literacy. On the other hand, when a community in effect abandons a heritage language in favor of a politically and economically dominant language, such planning may not develop within the community of speakers (perhaps, only by well-meaning linguists). *See* **diglossia, heritage language, language maintenance, language planning, productive knowledge, shift**.

## Language contact

When speakers of two (or more) languages share the same physical and cultural space, for example, in a community or social grouping. In other words, languages are said to be in contact when the same group of speakers share two languages (one speaker, two languages).

For example, English and Punjabi are in contact in parts of the United Kingdom, as well as in India and Pakistan. In the United States, Spanish and English are in direct contact, and in Quebec, Canada, French and English are in close intimate contact. That is, entire communities of people are exposed to two (or more) languages on a daily basis, and individual members of the community may speak both or either language that is used in the bilingual community. In some environments where one particular language has almost total dominance in domains of public usage, contact may be restricted to inside the homes of individual bilinguals. The apparent affects of language contact, therefore, depends on relative size of the bilingual (minority-language) community. See **bilingual community, contact**.

## Language contact phenomena

Also referred to as *bilingual language phenomena*. Particular phenomena such as borrowing, code-switching, and diglossia that occur as a normal consequence of language contact and societal bilingualism. See **bilingual language phenomena**.

## Language death

The gradual extinction of a language variety. Obviously, languages are not living organisms that can live or die apart from their speakers. Hence, a so-called dead language is simply one that no longer has any native speakers—its *speakers* have died. The normal cultural transmission of a language from one generation to the next, parent to child, has ceased.

As in the case of Ancient Hebrew, Latin, and Sanskrit, language systems can live on in very specific areas of life, particularly for religious or other cultural reasons. However, because they are no longer passed from one generation of native speakers to the next, they cease to "live" because they stop growing and changing; every living language is in a constant state of change, even though the changes may be imperceptible to its speakers. All languages evolve over time as a result of external and internal processes of adaptive change. See **endangered language, language attrition, language change, language maintenance**.

## Language evolution

The gradual processes of language birth, change, and, perhaps death. It is linked to processes of language acquisition/learning as language emerges or develops in recognizable stages (see, e.g., DeGraff 1999). See **contrastive analysis, developmental models/perspective, language change, language death, pidginization, Pidginization Hypothesis**.

## Language ideology

A theory or construct of the moral and social nature of language, commonly that languages possess intrinsic moral, social, and political value. Thus, a particular ideology may lead to assumptions about the relative merit of a specific language variety and engender a clear bias in favor of one particular variety.

Though the term "ideology" is ostensibly neutral in meaning (e.g., an informed ideology takes facts into consideration), in sociolinguistic studies of language and cultural hegemony, it is often associated with suppositions of "proper" usage (e.g., according to a prestige or standard variety) and the lack thereof. Some stigmatized varieties are even thought to have characteristics of "bad" grammar or even no grammar at all. Along with concepts of good or bad grammar, there is the belief that language homogeneity (e.g., one national or standard language) is more beneficial to a society than language diversity (in which many varieties may compete and multilingualism flourishes). Wolfram and Schilling-Estes (1998) define "ideology" as "ingrained, unquestioned beliefs about the way the world is, the way it should be, and the way it has to be with respect to language" (9). *See* **dialect, nonstandard, Standard English**.

### Language loyalty

Most often refers to the sense of loyalty that people feel toward an ancestral or heritage language. (It is implicit that part of that loyalty is deeply felt cultural ties to an original homeland and to a traditional way of life that are often threatened by the language and culture of a majority language and culture.) The depth of loyalty may determine whether or not this traditional language variety is maintained or gradually abandoned. *See* **attrition, language attrition, language maintenance, shift**.

### Language maintenance

The planned preservation of a language variety within a bilingual nation or community.

In contrast, *language loss* (leading perhaps to language death) occurs when a bilingual community shifts toward one or the other of its languages, typically to the dominant social variety. In that case, maintenance may stop, leading to the gradual decay and loss of the language, in terms of both the number of speakers and the knowledge of all aspects of grammar and lexicon. Maintenance also implies the normal transmission of a language from one generation of speakers to the next; in that case, language change is generally slow. But, in situations of advancing shift, contact-induced changes may accelerate (Thomason and Kaufman 1988 9–10; Myers-Scotton 2006: 68).

An example of language maintenance is the French of Québec, Canada, in spite of considerable pressure from English on all sides. Politically, French has been declared the majority language and the dominant language of Francophone Canada even though it belongs to a numerical minority nationally. Elsewhere, of course, English is the majority language. To afford equal status to two putative majority languages, Canada considers itself to be a bilingual nation. In Anglophone areas, proficiency in French is encouraged, as is English in Francophone sections. Both languages are consequently maintained in specific areas where they might be spoken by a numerical minority with the stated intent that neither language will be pushed out by the other. *See* **attrition, endangered languages, language death, shift**.

## Language minority/linguistic minority (LM)

A community of people who speak a numerical minority language. The term stands in contrast with *language majority*. For example, in the United States, the vast majority of people speak English, the politically and socially dominant language of the nation. Spanish speakers are a numerical minority, so they comprise a language minority in the United States at present. This is in spite of the fact that Spanish is the majority language in many nations where Spanish is the politically and socially dominant language (e.g., Spain and Mexico). See **asymmetry, dominant, recessive, shift**.

## Language mixing

A term that is used to describe various behaviors, for example, the *transfer* of aspects of a native language (or substrate) into a second/subsequent language, the *borrowing* of forms and structures from one language into another, and various kinds of *code-switching*. Some theories of *creole* and *pidgin* genesis assert that they are the results of language mixing and the interaction of substrate (recipient and matrix) and superstrate (lexical donor) languages.

The term might also be appropriate for the behaviors of bilingual children, who seem to mix their languages from time to time in systematic ways. This has given rise to many discussions of how children mentally organize their languages, whether they have one unitary system (which includes words and processes from both/all of their languages) or two, autonomous systems, one for each language. See **contact languages, mixed languages, one system (or two), Separate Development Hypothesis**.

## Language modes

Psychological states in the online processing of bilingual speech that are activated (or "on") when a bilingual uses those languages.

According to the work of François Grosjean, a bilingual has a monolingual mode for each language that is activated (and which acts to block the other) when the bilingual is in the presence and interacting with speakers of one or the other language, and a bilingual mode in which both (or all) languages are activated in the presence of other bilinguals (Grosjean 1995: 259; 1997: 225–226; 2006: 40–43). When a language mode is activated, all words and structures in that language are accessible for immediate retrieval, and in the bilingual mode, all languages are more or less equally activated. When a bilingual is in the bilingual mode, she may engage in various code-switching behaviors, particularly when interacting with other bilinguals who may mix languages in various ways because both languages are at the ready and readily accessible. See **mode, language processing**.

## Language processing

How the brain deciphers and responds to linguistic data, and initiates output in the form of speech, sign (gestures), and writing.

Briefly, processing entails how the mind/brain interprets input data of an acoustic or visual signal, retrieves meanings of individual words according to tacit phonological knowledge, and interprets whole utterances according to syntactic and semantic information. In turn, the mind/brain (theoretically, that facet of the mind/brain known as the language processor) must assemble messages from the conceptual level (the idea stage) to the final output of an actual response, or, in the case of initiating utterances, how the brain creates a message and produces it.

In some models of language processing, performance involves the dynamic interplay of several types of memory, for example, an explicit competence (the knowledge that one can articulate to oneself or to others) and an implicit competence that can only be inferred from actual output (from performance data). The implicit competence that underlies the physical manifestations of speech (i.e., that neurologically control the various articulators in the vocal tract) is known as *procedural memory*, which allows a child to acquire unconsciously the ability to speak a language freely and automatically (the characteristic of automaticity). This stands in contrast to *declarative* memory, the ability to recall consciously experienced events or facts. Declarative memory is usually linked with language learning, explicitly taught points of grammar and vocabulary.

Controversies arise in discussions of bilingual language processing when linking procedural (implicit) memory with NLA and declarative (explicit) memory with SLA. The main points of contention are age (whether the ability to acquire procedural knowledge cuts off at any particular age) and whether explicit memory can become implicit, procedural memory eventually leading to automaticity in a second (or additional) language (cf. Paradis 2004: 7–12). *See* **activation, bilingual interactive activation (BIA), bilingual interactive model of lexical access (BIMOLA), connectionism, modular, parallel distributed processing (PDP).**

## Language skills

Four general areas or skills that include two passive abilities (listening and reading) and two productive/performance abilities (speaking and writing). The term *skill* is used to represent the kind of knowledge that is acquired unconsciously through observation and active participation, for example, skill on a musical instrument or in a particular sport. It is contrasted with the types of knowledge that are learned through conscious study and memorization, for example, content areas of academic knowledge (biology, chemistry, and linguistics) (Baker 2006: 7). With respect to bilinguals (and biliteracy), language skills can vary according to language.

Bilingual language skills are those that an individual has acquired natively, for example, with respect to literacy and mathematics. An important issue is whether or not a bilingual can utilize skills acquired in a first or native language to the learning task in the second language, in particular, the set of literacy skills. For years, researchers have reassured educators that such things as L1 reading skills (in an alphabetic system like Spanish, French, English, and so on) can, indeed, be transferred to the SL learning situation in positive ways, thereby reducing the time required for acquisition/learning. This, in turn, implies that learners without "nativized" (L1) literacy may be at some disadvantage. Lack of literacy skills in an alphabetic system like English may have an effect on those who have mastered other types of writing systems (e.g., Chinese) in their acquisition of English literacy, but those students will most certainly retain academic knowledge, study skills, and their values of literacy. For example, literate language learners can still apply literacy strategies (e.g., using context to figure out meanings or skipping unfamiliar words until the meaning is known) to the context of a new language (Hakuta 1986:

93–95; Baker 2006: 330–331). *See* **acquisition, biliteracy, literacy, skills areas, transfer.**

## Language socialization
How the child learns to communicate in appropriate ways within his or her cultural or social group. Research aims to describe children's language usage, how language develops as a means of social interaction, and the factors that affect its development. In general, research in language as a social behavior includes studies of cultural and gender differences in speech, and studies of specific culturally bound usage in such areas as narration (story telling, conveying information), conflict resolution (dealing with personal conflicts), telling jokes, and other types of discourse (Hoff 2009: 14). *See* **discourse knowledge, pragmatic knowledge, sociolinguistic knowledge.**

## Language typology
The systematic classification of languages according to phonological, morphological, and syntactic traits. As an outgrowth of historical linguistics and genealogical classification of languages (language families), its ultimate goal is to establish structural characteristics common to all languages, that is, universals of language. *See* **genealogical/genetic classification, typology, typological classification, universal.**

## Language universals
Features of language that are thought to be common to all languages, although some current approaches in language typology seem to challenge these assumptions.

There are two fundamentally different and contrasting ways of determining such universals, the generative approach and a typological approach. The former, associated with Chomsky and his colleagues, presumes that certain characteristics of language are innate to humans, and therefore universal (based on a philosophical universalism). Thus, generative approaches are theory-driven; that is, they rely on theoretical presuppositions and rational explanations of selected data to support those presuppositions. The latter approach proceeds in basically the opposite direction, from wide-ranging data to the formation of theories (Comrie 1989: 1–5, 15–16). *See* **formal grammar, generative grammar, structuralism, universals.**

## Language use surveys
Surveys that are intended to determine usage (language choice) patterns. They are typically designed for language-minority groups, for example, to measure how frequently a minority language is used in or outside the home in contrast with usage of a majority (prestige, or national standard) language.

A thorough census survey may contain information about geographical areas (number and density of speakers), migration history, language usage by generation (grandparents, parents, children), socioeconomic data, and other cultural characteristics (e.g., attitude and motivation). While such information can be useful for planning educational services according to the needs of the community—to increase exposure to the dominant language and access to literacy materials, libraries, and specific courses—it may also contribute to stereotyping of individuals according to place of residence (particular neighborhoods), ethnic minority, or socioeconomic level. Locale, socioeconomic level, and ethnic status may correlate with academic performance (achievement), but they do not exist in a cause-and-effect relationship. Wealth does not cause success, any more than relative poverty or minority status portends failure. See **achievement, deficit model, diglossia, language choice, restricted code, self-assessment, tracks (streams)**.

### Language variety
A general term used to refer to a language, dialect, or register of speech. It is, in a sense, theoretically and politically neutral. For instance, it is not always possible to separate such terms as dialect and language. Some politically distinct languages can be so similar that they appear to be dialects of each other, for example, Serbian and Croatian which were once considered one language (by linguists). See **dialect, language, register**.

### Language-Making Capacity (LMC)
The ability of children to acquire their native languages through a set of general learning strategies. The concept of an LMC stands in contrast to an LAD, the early Chomskyan notion of a special structure in the brain of the child that only needs to be activated by exposure to language input to kick in.

The difference between the two, LAD and LMC, is more than a semantic one: they involve nearly opposite approaches to language acquisition. Generative approaches generally start out with assumptions of the innate knowledge of language (UG). Developmental approaches such as those of D. Slobin and colleagues appeal to a general learning capacity that all children evidently possess. While they are willing to concede that some aspects of this capacity are indeed innate, they prefer to describe it as a capacity that involves common learning strategies or principles (not access to an already existing universally available grammar). Developmental approaches start out with actual language acquisition data—from a broad range of languages, and formulate hypothesis based on the data (Slobin 1985: 1158–1159). See **acquisition, Language Acquisition Device (LAD), Universal Grammar (UG)**.

### Late-exit program
Transitional programs that provide substantial instruction and practice for child learners (perhaps throughout the primary grades) until they are transitioned into mainstream classes. See **early exit, mainstream/mainstreaming, transitional**.

### Late-system morpheme
See **system morpheme**.

### Lateralization
A point in human development when it is believed that certain abilities, for example, cognitive functions of language, become located or centralized primarily in either the left hemisphere or the right hemisphere of the brain.

Recent work, however, shows that lateralization of language functions may appear even at birth, that is, certain abilities are already located in specific areas of the brain at birth, and that many types of cognitive abilities are spread across both hemispheres. See **corpus callosum, Critical Period Hypothesis (CPH)**.

## Lau v Nichols

An important court case that looked to clarify issues of language rights for language minorities. It is often cited as a landmark case in bilingual education.

*Lau v Nichols* was a lawsuit that began in 1970 in San Francisco, California, in the wake of the Civil Rights Act of 1964 (Baker 2006: 192). It involved a group of Chinese children with limited skills in English whose parents claimed that their children were being denied the help they needed to succeed in school. The case appealed to Title VI of the Civil Rights Act of 1964, which had banned discrimination on the basis of national origin.

The US Supreme court accepted the case after other courts had rejected it. They ruled in 1974 that the San Francisco Unified School District had violated the children's civil rights by not offering educational services in Chinese. It was not enough to provide the same textbooks and instructional materials used for proficient English speakers to students who did not understand English. The Lau decision, typically cited as legal precedent for all language-discrimination cases, recognized the close ties between language and national origin, and that discrimination based on language was essentially discrimination based on national origin. It tested the limits of the Bilingual Education Act (1967), which established funding for bilingual programs, by challenging the practice of merely providing English instruction to children who did not speak English. Programs were subsequently established to provide help for students as they gradually progressed from bilingual-education classrooms to so-called mainstream classes. See **bilingual education, mainstream/mainstreaming**.

## Learnability

Refers to the specific characteristics of human language that make it possible for children to acquire it merely through exposure.

It seems to match up with a child's innate language learning capacity, making it possible for any child to acquire a language given the opportunity and exposure. Controversy centers on the apparent circularity: a language is learnable because children acquire it; and children can acquire any human language, therefore they are learnable. The logical problem of learnability, then, is to find out exactly what makes specific constructions learnable, and how that might influence language instruction (teachability and learnability) (Larsen-Freeman and Long 1991: 270–287). It is also likely that questions of learnability have arisen as a result of claims of innate categories (e.g., those of Chomsky such as Noun-subject and Verb-predicate) that especially enable children to acquire any human language merely by being exposed to input from that language. See **Language Acquisition Device (LAD), Language-Making Capacity (LMC)**.

## Learnability theory

A theory (or collection of theories) to what makes language acquisition possible given the nature of the input a child receives.

The problem appears to be how the child proceeds from no knowledge of the target language to native-speaker status, constructing intermediate grammars along the way (mental computations that generate utterances) based on the language that the child actually encounters—the input. The concept of learnability is relevant also for SLA (is learning a second language the same as learning the first?) and bilingual acquisition (learning two "native" languages simultaneously from the beginning) (Pinker 1996: xv–xvi; Yip and Matthews 2007: 30–31). See **learnability**.

### Learner's variety
An alternative term for interlanguage (IL), chiefly referring to whatever stage a particular learner may have reached. See **interlanguage**.

### Learning
Typically used to denote the conscious learning of a language by adults, especially in classroom situations. See **acquisition, Acquisition-Learning Hypothesis**.

### Learning strategies
One of several factors in language acquisition, in particular, the behaviors linked to learning as a process. They include an individual's learning behaviors, for example, to such individual (or cultural) traits as being prepared, planning ahead, taking notes, paying attention, asking for clarification, repeating examples, and being able to visualize (image) concepts. Such learning strategies are particularly helpful in analyzing classroom behaviors relative to SLA. See **age, aptitude, cognitive style, motivation**.

### Lect (-lect)
A social or regional variety of a language; also, used as a suffix in compounds, for example, *idiolect*, and *sociolect*. See **idiolect, sociolect**.

### Lemma
The mental representation of a word (root morpheme).

In many psycholinguistic theories of the mental lexicon, a "word" is represented in the brain according to a collection of properties: its form (or label) and all other information about its various forms, for example, syntactic information about where it may occur in an utterance, morphological information about all forms in which the particular word might appear (e.g., *go, went, gone*), and semantic information about the word's meaning, including connotations that depend on a speaker's knowledge of the world (c.f., Levelt 1989: 6). There is considerable discussion of the bilingual lexicon and how words from a bilingual's respective languages might be "tagged" with information that identifies language of origin, helping the bilingual to maintain two, independent mental stores of lexical items, one for each language (De Bot and Schreuder 1993: 193–195; Myers-Scotton 2006: 298–299). See **lexeme, lexical item, lexicon, one system (or two), Separate Development Hypothesis, word**.

### Lesion method
A method of investigating the brain by locating damaged areas (lesions) and matching them with specific impairments. This was most likely one of the only

ways that earlier scientists had in investigating the function of particular areas, for example, Broca's Area and Wernicke's Area, both found to play significant roles in language processing.

Lesions can occur as a result of injury, for example, those incurred in traffic or other types of accidents or during times of armed conflict. They may also occur from internal injuries due to stroke or disease. The lesion method, therefore, involves identifying damaged brain tissue and correlating it with an impaired function (e.g., an aphasia). See **aphasia, corpus callosum, functional architecture**.

## Lexeme

The underlying mental representation of a word or word root. In psycholinguistic studies of mental word storage, it is sometimes used interchangeably with (or instead of) *lemma* (for theoretical reasons).

In addition, the lexeme (as a lexical item) is what appears in printed dictionaries as a basic form from which other forms are derived or associated. In other words, the form of the printed word that a person would look up in the dictionary (e.g., when one sees the form *brought*, one must look for the base form *bring* in order to find its meaning). As a term, lexeme may refer to the mental representation of a word, hence its association with lemma. However, the usage of the term *lemma* is typically restricted to the mental representation and not an actual realization of a spoken, written, or signed word. See **lemma, lexical item, word**.

## Lexical access

The mental recognition and retrieval of lexical items from one's mental lexicon. It involves being able to locate the particular form appropriate for a specific intended meaning in production (an abstract concept finds a label), and the reverse, being able to locate a meaning when a particular form is heard or seen (a word form finds its meaning). See **access, word recognition**.

## Lexical category

Refers to word class or part of speech, for example, classes of nouns, verbs, adjectives, pronouns, determiners, and so on. Lexical categories are traditionally assigned into two broad groups, content words and function words, based on their shared characteristics. See **content word/item, function word/item**.

## Lexical item

A word or word root. It is among numerous terms intended to reduce ambiguity; it is often used interchangeably with *lexeme*. The term *lexical item* typically refers to an entry or unit in a speaker's vocabulary (mental lexicon). The term *word* can obviously refer to the written word, but also to meaningful units of speech that are not necessarily in a dictionary, for example, phonological words such as *gimme*, *cudja*, and *gonna* that are the products of compressed speech. See **compressed speech, lexeme, lemma, mental lexicon, phonological word, word**.

## Lexicon

Synonymous with dictionary, but used by linguists and other language specialists to refer to our "mental" lexicon, our total knowledge of the words we know in a language.

The lexicon is a mental store of a speaker's vocabulary items (words and morphemes) in a language. According to many approaches on what it means to "know" a word, the mental lexicon includes (a) all the forms a particular word may take (e.g., *go/goes-went-gone-going*), (b) it's grammatical function (e.g., *verb*), (c) it's core meaning, and (d) all the possible meanings it can have according to the speaker's knowledge of the world (idioms, specialized usages in a wide variety of discourse contexts). For instance, the word *red* expresses a particular color, but it can be made into a verb (*redden*) and can be used to apply to political views and even military entities (the *Red Army*). See **access, competence, lexical access, mental lexicon**.

## Limited English proficiency (LEP)
Language learners who are limited with respect to their proficiency levels in English.

The term has fallen into disfavor in recent years because of its negative connotations and is usually no longer used in official documents (though some school districts and programs still may use it). The term *ELL* (English language learner) has replaced it and its particularly offensive nickname *leper* frequently overheard in "lunchroom conversation" (Wiley 2005: 123–125). The term *limited English*, also focuses only on what a child does *not* know, not on what he or she does know. The more cynical among us doubts, however, if a change of name can alter perceptions; prejudices toward "foreigners" and their languages can be stubborn. The label itself, like all labels that carry pejorative senses, though not overtly linked to race, can act similarly to classifications based on race (Wiley 2005: 120–121). See **English language learner (ELL), English language development (ELD), fluent English proficiency (FEP)**.

## Linguistic competence
Refers to the ability to produce well-formed sentences in a language according to native-speaker norms.

The term includes also the degrees to which a learner/speaker has mastered the *grammar* of a language, including aspects of phonetics, phonology, morphology, and syntax. However, true mastery of a language includes a number of other competencies (types of knowledge) regarding usage, not just grammatical correctness, and awareness of a vast array of cultural and social issues in which all speech is situated. See **discourse knowledge, pragmatic knowledge, sociolinguistic knowledge**.

## Linguistic determinism
The view that language determines, and, therefore, limits human thought and knowledge, going beyond the notion of linguistic relativity that language merely influences thought. According to this view, in that language and knowledge are culturally transmitted, the thought processes of one generation are transmitted to the next.

The idea that our native languages influence or determine thought has been extensively discussed, back to the early 19th century and the German philosopher and linguist, Wilhelm von Humboldt (1767–1835) (Gumperz and Levinson 1996:

2–12). Humboldt suggested that we think and express our thoughts as members of a community and that language structure (its inner form) systematically represents those thoughts accordingly. Humboldt was also influenced by work done on the indigenous language varieties of the Americas that illustrated the remarkable diversity of human language. With a profound respect for this diversity, the concept of *linguistic relativity* emerged, which follows from the idea that people who speak different languages, therefore, must also think differently: Our thought patterns are not absolutely determined by biology or the objective nature of reality; they are relative to the culture in which we are raised and the language that expresses that culture, its knowledge and belief systems. Edward Sapir and Benjamin Lee Whorf pursued work in linguistic relativity (but they weren't the first), with Whorf's work leaning in the direction of linguistic determinism. See **linguistic relativity, Sapir–Whorf Hypothesis**.

## Linguistic diversity

Within a single society, the usage of many, diverse language varieties. This may include separate languages and/or varieties of the same language (regional and social dialects). Linguistic diversity characterizes large metropolitan areas worldwide, but it is not confined to them. In the United States, for example, many language minorities have traditionally occupied rural areas of the Mid-Atlantic and Midwestern states (e.g., Polish, Czech, and German) and massive agricultural areas of the Southwest (e.g., Spanish speakers in Texas and California). The need for low-cost field laborers and other workers has created many opportunities in the Americas, Europe, Australia, and elsewhere for various minority groups. There is hardly a place on earth where diverse languages don't coexist in some fashion. See **community bilingualism, contact, cultural pluralism**.

## Linguistic relativity

Suggests that we all look at the world (nature) according to the words and structures of our native languages. Therefore, each language contains and communicates a particular worldview.

According to this view, people do not see an objective reality shaped by universal characteristics of thought and language; our views of the world are shaped by the culture and language in which we live. As a concept, linguistic relativity goes back to the early 19th century, and it resurfaced in the early 20th century in the United States, perhaps articulated most clearly by the American anthropological linguist Edward Sapir and his student, Benjamin Whorf. See **linguistic determinism, Sapir–Whorf Hypothesis, universalism**.

## Linguistic repertoire

The language varieties a speaker may possess or know, including dialects and registers of one or more languages. For instance, in the Spanish-English bilingual's repertoire, there may be different regional (national) and social varieties of Spanish and English, including various registers of each. One may include types of literacy, from functional to cultural and critical literacy, the registers associated with each, and the semantic knowledge necessary for various levels of literacy (knowing what words mean and how to use them).

It is important for educators (and bilinguals) to be aware of the differences. For example, if a student is being tested for proficiency in a standard variety and does not score well, this may not be an accurate assessment of his/her overall ability in the language (both standard and nonstandard varieties are dialects). And, fluency in spoken forms may not be any indication of proficiency in written forms. Linguistic repertoires include all varieties, regional, social, and situational; for the bi- or multilingual, those varieties are multiplied by the number of languages that he/she knows. The well-rounded student will be proficient in a variety of registers, both spoken and written forms. See **dialect, genres, literacy, registers, relative proficiencies**.

### Literacy myth

The belief that literacy (especially in a language like English) yields many social benefits, including the emergence of higher-order thinking.

Public perceptions of the value of literacy are generally extremely positive. However, there are numerous persistent myths about the power of literacy and its links to education. According to this mythology, by becoming literate, a person is more likely to be happy and informed, find a job, and earn more money; literacy is thought to lead to rational thinking and even a degree of skepticism (she's or he's less gullible and vulnerable to manipulation). Some of the claims for literacy are quite grand, including "a recognition of the importance of time and space, complex and modern governments (with separation of church and state), political democracy and greater social equity, a lower crime rate, better citizens, economic development, wealth and productivity, political stability, urbanization, and a lower birth rate" (Gee 1996: 26). It is often considered a social panacea and a gateway to various types of knowledge. But, literacy does not equal thinking or knowledge. The development of particular skills may provide a means, but it does not guarantee an end. See **language ideology, literate/literacy, Standard English**.

### Literate/literacy

Colloquially, the ability to read and write in a language. These terms are always relative (fluid and changing) and often dependent on governmental standards of measurement (for estimating the number of citizens who are literate in a nation). A minimal definition in some nations may be the ability to sign one's own name (put an "X" on a printed form). There are a number of types (or degrees), for example:

*Functional literacy* is perhaps the most elementary understanding of being literate in society. It implies the ability to read and write enough to get by, including being able to read surface mail such as bills and notices (decode the printed word) and being able to maintain a bank account (including basic math or numeracy skills). In education, the standards are higher and refer to complex abilities to read English-language literary texts and academic language and to engage a broad range of topics critically in written responses. That is, *cultural* literacy generally encompasses the knowledge of what it means to be a good, productive citizen, knowing and supporting culturally based practices and institutions (e.g., education, social welfare). *Critical literacy* typically entails being able to read "between the lines" to the social and political motivations of the authors of traditional and nontraditional literary texts, for example, the social contexts of authors such as Charles Dickens, John Milton, the American Ernest Hemingway, and to a host of current poets and lyricists that dot the pages of popular magazines.

One conclusion regarding literacy on a mass scale, perhaps, is that it can only be done with the lowest common denominator as a guide and functional literacy as its goal. Further, society's perceptions of literacy since the 20th century have evolved, making expectations once held of society's elite apply universally to all groups—a type of inflation of literacy standards (Wiley 2005: 104–107). Some minorities fall victim to the increasing demands placed on them: they have a "schooling problem" that may be a consequence of the inflated standards of literacy—the gap between increasingly artificial academic environments and the "real" world (Gee 1996: 23). Resnick and Resnick (1988) describe the historical backdrop of how continually rising expectations have shaped views of literacy. In the early 19th century, high levels of literacy were expected only of the upper and middle classes, while minimal, more basic levels were required of the lower classes, the factory workers, mechanics, and general laborers. Recent views of literacy have obviously risen to include all sorts of "new" *literacies*, for example, computer, communications (various media), and techno literacy. See **biliteracy, critical literacy, cultural literacy, functional literacy**.

## Loanword

Synonymous with borrowing; that is, a borrowed word. In other words, a form-meaning set from one language that is used in another. For example, California English has borrowed (rather, its speakers have borrowed) the word *tortilla* to represent the round, flat bread used in the preparation of various Mexican food dishes. It is now an English word (in the dictionary); it is also a loanword from Mexican Spanish. See **borrowing**.

## Locke, John

Philosopher and founder of British Empiricism, the school of thought that attributes all human knowledge to experience. There are various views of empiricism; some versions are Mentalist in that they acknowledge a difference between the brain as a physical organ and the mind as existing independent of the physical world. Such concepts go back to the ancient Greeks (Plato and Aristotle). Other versions lend themselves to behaviorism and views that deny the existence of Mind and Thought as independent of the brain. Such views are regarded as "reductionist" in that they reduce all thought to electro-chemical activity in the brain.

Understanding the underpinnings of various approaches to human knowledge, cognition, and the language faculty is to know the assumptions upon which various approaches and methodologies are based. As a consequence, Locke often appears as having the opposite philosophical view from Descartes, a Rationalist, and, therefore, Noam Chomsky who has based many of his views of cognition and the language faculty on the ideas of Descartes (hence, Cartesian linguistics). Philosophical views lead to specific views of the human mind (psychology). For example, Locke's views of language are seen as forming the philosophical bases for behaviorism and behaviorist ideas of language, for example, by B. F. Skinner and the views of Jean Piaget, though he was not considered to be a behaviorist (Steinberg 1982: 86–88). *See* **approach, Cartesian linguistics, Chomsky, empiricism, Krashen, method**.

**L**

## Mainstream/mainstreaming

Mainstream classes are regular classes in school that are populated mostly by native speakers of the majority language and that do not offer assistance for language-minority students.

In the United States and other former colonial nations, it is implied that the mainstream is also associated with the historically dominant Anglo Saxon language and culture of the founders of the nation. These founders established the political system and have traditionally dominated government, commerce (the distribution of land and wealth), and education. Education, therefore, reflects a bias toward the dominant language and culture (according to a traditional language ideology). The term *mainstreaming* can also refer to the practice of placing language-minority students into majority-language classrooms (the mainstream), whether from the beginning of instruction or gradually through some sort of transitional program. The term is also used for disabled individuals or those with special needs, when placing them in normal school classes (or similar work environment), perhaps with some accommodation. See **bilingual education, language ideology, Standard English**.

## Maintenance

See **language maintenance**.

## Map (mapping)

The process of identifying or understanding new words, associating a particular form to its accepted meaning.

When a child learns a new word for a new object or concept, she or he must make the connection between a form (a set of phonetic elements—the phonological or visual shape of a word) and its meaning and the reverse, project a meaning (e.g., entity, action, quality, or concept) onto its appropriate form(s) or word(s). For example, when a child acquiring English hears the form [dor] representing the word "door," she or he must map that form (a string of individual sounds) onto the object that it signifies. Conversely, when she or he sees an object generally identifiable as a door of some sort, she or he can retrieve the form [dor] from his or her mental lexicon. See **access, mapping problem, perception**.

## Mapping problem

Represents the task that a child has to isolate and identify the correct form or word for an object or other entity from the speech stream (referred to as the *segmentation problem*—identifying which specific stretch of sounds refers to the object) and selecting the exact object (meaning or referent) that the word points or refers to.

Specialists note that the possibilities seem endless. The word "door," for example, could refer to an object's color, its handle, its shape, or the material it is made of. It could also refer to an action that child is to take, like closing or opening it (Hoff 2009: 205). *See* **bootstrapping, mutual exclusivity assumption, whole-object assumption, segmentation problem, taxonomic assumption**.

## Matrix language (ML)

In systematic approaches to code-switching, it is the language variety that forms the basis, or underlying morpho-syntactic system into which embedded-language islands are inserted. In this view, much code-switching appears to be insertional. An alternative view of code-switching is that it is alternational, that there is a true alternation of language varieties with no clear matrix that influences the surface manifestation of fluent, conversational code-switching (see, for example, Muysken 2000: 3). The question whether code-switching *per se* is either insertional or alternational (or both) is still a source of some controversy. *See* **code-switching, intrasentential code-switching, Matrix Language Hypothesis (MLH)**.

## Matrix Language-Frame (MLF) model

A model of code-switching proposed by Myers-Scotton and her colleagues to explain the systematic nature of code-switching.

Such a model proceeds from the assumption that people who engage in code-switching do so with the expectation that they will be understood. So, the ways their languages go together in the apparently unplanned alternation of languages must be systematic or comprehensibility could not possibly occur. In so-called "classic codeswitching," one language forms a morphosyntactic matrix (the ML) into which chunks of the other are placed (the EL).

According to Myers-Scotton (2006), the MLH model is based on three premises. The first is that the ML and EL are not involved in equal parts; the matrix influences the overall grammatical structure of the entire utterance. Second, morpheme types are significant; there is an asymmetry between content morphemes and system morphemes (which closely parallels the traditional distinction between content item and function item). The third is that both languages are psychologically activated or "on," but the matrix appears to be dominant (243). For other views of different types of code-switching, see Muysken (2000). *See* **4-M model, code-switching, content word/item, function word/item, intrasentential code-switching, system morpheme**.

## Matrix Language Hypothesis (MLH)

The hypothesis that one language, the matrix language (or ML), plays a greater role in code-switching than the other. This ML provides the grammatical base, or morphosyntactic frame (including word order and which morphemes are realized), into which elements of an embedded language (EL) are inserted or placed (Myers-Scotton 1993a: 7). *See* **4-M model, code-switching, embedded language (EL), matrix language (ML), Matrix Language-Frame (MLF) model**.

## Mean length of utterance (MLU)

A way to estimate grammatical development. It is typically the average length of a series of utterances based on the number of morphemes they contain.

At first glance, it seems that an indication of gradual growth would be the number of words a child is capable of using. However, the quantity of a child's utterances does not necessarily reveal how he or she is mastering the grammar of his or her language (Elliot 1981: 102). Roger Brown (1973) proposed that the number of morphemes (an average based on 100 utterances) would be a better gauge because it showed the acquisition of inflections and other grammatical characteristics more clearly. Brown arrived at five stages of acquisition that corresponded with MLU: Stage I up to 1.75; II to 2.25; III to 2.75; IV to 3.50; and V to 4.00.

Some criticisms of Brown's metric have centered on the difficulty of determining a child's utterance (when does it begin or end), and which morphemes should be counted. For example, the irregular past was counted as a single morpheme while the regular past (root + -ed) was counted as two; and, Brown failed to distinguish between function words and bound, inflectional affixes. Mastering the usage of a particular function word (e.g., a pronoun) may be considerably different from mastering verbal inflections in a language rich in verbal morphology (e.g., Italian or Russian). *See* **function items/words, morpheme, morpheme studies**.

## Mentalism/mentalist

Simply put, a view that assumes ideas, words, and language exist apart from purely physical or physiological processes, and, therefore, that mental processes cannot be explained only in physical, bio-chemical, or neurological terms (Steinberg 1982: 85; Cook 1993: 15). In its more extreme forms, mentalism asserts that things in the material world exist only subjectively in the conscious mind.

In many modern approaches to psychology and theories of mind, mentalism focuses on thought processes such as consciousness (reason, logic), qualities such as knowledge (wisdom), and mental states such as happiness or anger, especially in regard to an infant's early attention to (and perception of) human faces and language input (Karmiloff-Smith 1992: 118). A mentalist view of language is typically seen in opposition to behaviorist views as it seeks to explain linguistic phenomena and other human activity in terms of mental processes rather than behavior. *See* **behaviorism, Cartesian linguistics, Chomsky**.

## Metalinguistic awareness

Awareness of how language works; the ability to think consciously about and reflect on the nature of language (Hoff 2009: 317). It involves the ability to treat the medium of language as an object of conscious thought, in contrast to merely using language unconsciously to comprehend and generate utterances. In a number of studies, bilingual children appeared to have greater metalinguistic awareness and a more analytical view of language than their monolingual counterparts, suggesting that the ability to control two languages enabled bilingual children to perform better on a number of tasks (e.g., counting the number of words in a sentence) (Baker 2006: 157). *See* **cognitive style, learning strategies**.

## Method

A procedure or set of accepted procedures of teaching, exposition (e.g., in the interpretation of texts), or in conducting research in an academic discipline.

In bilingual studies, methods (or a methodology) refer to traditional ways research is done into language acquisition (qualitative vs. quantitative methodologies), or ways that practitioners go about teaching (according to basic beliefs). *Method*, as a term, is also used as a specific instance of a general approach (although the usage of approach and method may overlap somewhat in the literature), and involves specific practices and tasks known as techniques.

Much as a worldview influences how we see the world around us, acceptance of a general approach determines how we view knowledge. The Scientific Method was based on concepts of a stable universe plus physical, chemical, and biological laws and principles. It led to a system of proofs and techniques (as part of its methodology) that underlie much of modern science. Similarly, different research paradigms start with a fundamental approach to knowledge, and their methodologies, therefore, conform to accepted practices. By analogy, teaching methodologies start with a general philosophy of learning (how human beings learn) and include basic assumptions of the learner and the role of teachers (as conduits of information or facilitators of natural learning processes).

For example, in the first half of the 20th century, behaviorism dominated educational psychology in much of the world, so methods that emphasized language learning as habit formation dominated classroom instruction. One behaviorist approach that is still used was called the Audio-lingual method (ALM). Students memorized scripts and performed drills to establish good habit patterns in the target language. They were discouraged from being creative in spontaneous conversation because it was feared that they would make mistakes, and those mistakes might become habitual. In the 1980s, the *Natural Approach* of Krashen and Terrell (Krashen and Terrell 1983) reflected a change to more cognitive approaches involving teachers acting as "facilitators" of language acquisition, providing students with comprehensible input (with little negative feedback in the form of error correction). This particular methodology features a lot of interaction among students who are given problems to solve (e.g., timed tasks to obtain information from various sources), and active participation in classroom discussions. *See* **approach, Audio-lingual method (ALM), qualitative methods, quantitative methods**.

## Mixed language

One language that shows an equal or near equal distribution of forms and structures from two (or more) autonomous language systems.

Three of the most often-cited mixed languages are Ma'a, spoken in parts of Tanzania; *Michif*, spoken in bordering areas of south-central Canada and north-central United States; and *Media Lengua*, spoken in central Ecuador (Bakker and Mous 1994). Ma'a appears to have a Bantu grammar (or grammatical matrix) (Mous 2003), while Michif has the nominal system (noun phrases) of French intertwined with the verbal system of Cree, an Amerindian language (Bakker 1997). Media Lengua consists primarily of the vocabulary of Spanish embedded into the grammatical system of Quechua, the indigenous language of the Inca

Empire (Muysken 1981, 1997). In the literature on *language evolution*, opinions have ranged from a complete denial that any language could possibly be mixed (with equal parts of two or more languages) to an affirmation that *all* languages are mixed in some way (e.g., English, with its Germanic history and enormous French influence) (Meillet 1928: 90–102; Field 2002: 11–15). *See* **language change, language evolution, language mixing, split languages**.

## Mode (of communication)

Whether a message is signed, spoken, or written.

For teachers, classroom situations often require a written mode, for example, a term paper or a spelling test. Hanging out with your friends talking about music downloads usually requires a spoken (or texted) response. Typically, written responses are more formal, though we can certainly write informal notes to each other, for example, texting, while spoken responses are characteristically more informal. The term is used in a psychological sense, as well, as referring to language modes as mental states in which a language or languages are activated in a bi- or multilingual speaker's mind. *See* **formal, informal, language modes**.

## Modularity

The view that the mind/brain is composed of modules, interlocking compartments, components, or relatively autonomous regions, especially those that assert that language is separate from other cognitive functions. Language itself is also looked at as consisting of smaller, interconnected modules. For example, there is a phonological module responsible for pronunciation, a morphological module for word formation, and a syntactic module governing the relationships among words and their ordering in utterances.

The term is also applied to a particular theory proposed by J. A. Fodor that sees the mind as modular with separate systems (faculties), for example, for vision and language, with their own separate sets of features and cognitive processes (Fodor 1983). *See* **Chomsky, connectionist models, generative approaches**.

## Monitor Theory

A theory by Krashen proposing that SL learners take consciously learned knowledge of the target language of acquisition and use it to monitor their performance in that language.

The theory separates language acquisition into two systems: an acquired system and a learned system. The acquired system (the language knowledge that is acquired, rather than learned) initiates utterances—or acts as the impetus for speech-output. The learned system (the knowledge of language learned in formal settings) acts as an internal, mental editor or monitor. It needs time and conscious knowledge of the target language system to edit the acquired system. The implication is that too much monitoring via conscious knowledge will slow down the more natural, acquisition process(es). *See* **Acquisition-Learning Hypothesis, Affective Filter, critical period, Input Hypothesis, Krashen, Natural Order Hypothesis, second language acquisition**.

### Monolingual/monolingualism
Knowing or using only one language. A monolingual person (or a monolingual) is one who knows to use (read and write) one language. Monolingualism, therefore, is the quality or condition of knowing one language, and is the theory or practice of using one language, for example, of a society (societal monolingualism). It is often used for educational programs that promote the usage of one politically predominant (or majority) language over others (recessive or minority varieties). See **bilingual, bilingual programs, bilingualism, unilingual/unilingualism**.

### Morpheme studies
A series of studies that investigated the order in which grammatical morphemes are acquired by children.

Perhaps the most influential was the groundbreaking work of Roger Brown (1973) and colleagues concerning the order in which grammatical morphemes appear in children's speech. It has provided grist for a lot of subsequent work on NLA and SLA as it begs the question why particular grammatical morphemes or inflections are acquired before others. Other significant studies include the work of de Villiers and de Villiers (1973) which corroborated the work of Brown, and studies by Dulay and Burt (1973, 1974) that were designed to establish a reliable way to measure MLU in language development. Though not without controversy, such studies have been used to gauge progress in learner's speech (Dale 1976: 29–30; Elliot 1981: 103–104).

The study by Brown included the longitudinal (qualitative) study of three children (Adam, Eve, and Sarah) as they acquired English. Brown's list of 14 morphemes included words (function items such as *a*, *the*, and *be*), plus five inflectional suffixes (*-ing* marking progressive aspect, regular noun-plural *–s*, possessive *–'s*, regular past tense *–ed*, and the third-person verbal *–s*). The consistency with which children acquire these morphemes clearly implies an underlying cause. However, there is a great deal of debate on what that underlying cause is.

Brown's study also noted that, while the order among children is remarkably similar, there may be considerable differences in the rate of acquisition: some children go faster, while others go slower. One of the most obvious possibilities was that there is some kind of frequency effect—that is, the more often children hear a word in the speech of their caretakers, the more likely they are to pick it up. Function words such as *a* and *the* are among the most frequent words in the English language, yet Brown's study found out, somewhat surprisingly, that they are acquired relatively late, after nouns and verbs, for instance. So, frequency had no apparent effect. (For discussion, see Hoff 2009: 234–247). See **function word/item, grammatical morphemes**.

### Mother tongue (maternal language)
A child's first language, the one acquired essentially from birth from one's mother or other members of the community. (A paternal language is the one learned from one's father, which may differ from the one of the mother.) It is the child's native language in the vast majority of cases, assuming it is the mother who is the primary caregiver for the child and the one with whom the child has interacted in early childhood (See Corder 1993). See **native language, transfer**.

## Motherese

The style or register of speech used by parents to their babies.

It has a special character, for example, higher pitched and exaggerated intonation contours. Mommies tend to refer to things in the child's immediate environment, use a lot of repetition when they ask questions or give commands (e.g., "Are you hungry, hungry, hungry?" "Don't touch, don't touch, don't touch!"), use special words like *baba*, *'nana*, and *sketti* (for "bottle," "banana", and "spaghetti," respectively), and may use nouns in the place of pronouns, for example, *baby* instead of *you*, *mommy* instead of *me*, and *Fido* or *the doggy* instead of *it*. In some cases, people use a type of motherese to talk to pets (one assumes as a way to show affection). *See* **child-directed speech, infant-directed speech**.

## Motivation

The inner drive or sense of urgency that an individual has in order to acquire/learn a language. It seems to affect mastery a great deal.

There are two general types, *instrumental* and *integrative* motivation. The former, instrumental motivation, refers to the usefulness that the language has for a learner, for example, how important it is for a job, for academic purposes, and so on. Integrative motivation refers primarily to the speaker's desire to become like native speakers of the target language. For instance, to fully integrate oneself into American culture, the mastery of English is necessary; this includes performance as close as possible to native-speaker norms. It is sometimes contrasted with *attitude*, which is a mental disposition toward the language and its speakers. *See* **attitude, integrative motivation, instrumental motivation**.

## MRI (magnetic resonance imaging)

MRI (magnetic resonance imaging) is also known as nuclear magnetic resonance imaging (NMRI). This is a fairly new method of observing brain regions when they are activated during the performance of a particular task.

The subject is placed inside a large, cylinder-shaped magnet. Radio waves 10,000 to 30,000 times stronger than the magnetic field of the earth are then sent through the body. This affects the body's atoms, forcing the nuclei into different positions. As they move back into place they send out radio waves of their own. The scanner picks up these signals and a computer turns them into a picture. These pictures are based on the location and strength of the incoming signals (cf. Thomas 1989: 1226; Hoff 2009: 412). *See* **CT (roentgen-ray computed tomography), fMRI, SPECT/PET scans**.

## Multilingual/multilingualism

An individual who speaks two or more languages (more than one); the usage of two or more languages in a community. As is the case with bilingualism, there may be different degrees of proficiency in each language, questions of self-assessment, and problems of testing. As a term, *multilingualism* is often used interchangeably with *bilingual*. It is also used to refer to societies in which there are multiple languages in use. *See* **bilingualism, relative proficiencies, self-assessment/rating**.

## Mutual exclusivity assumption

The assumption that two words cannot refer to the same entity; it is associated with theories of NLA and the early acquisition of word meanings.

Some researchers believe that children have basic assumptions about how speakers use words that restrict possible word meanings. For example, the mutual exclusivity assumption suggests that, to a child, a new word always refers to a new object (entity or referent). That is, when the child already knows the word *doggy* and hears a novel term *kitty*, she or he will look around to find its referent, a new animal or previously unnamed thing that she or he has not noticed before. The two words *must* be mutually exclusive (she or he already knows what a doggy is). Recent research indicates that young children can also factor in *perspective*, so, for example, *dad*, *father*, *Mr. Jones*, and *honey* may refer to the same person. As a result, some researchers refer to this assumption as the *contrast assumption*, that different terms may contrast with each other and are not necessarily mutually exclusive. So, the same animal may be called *doggy*, *Fido*, *the pet*, and so on (Clark 2003: 98–100). *See* **mapping problem, operating principles, perspective, taxonomic assumption, whole-object assumption**.

## Mutual intelligibility

When speakers of two distinct language varieties understand each other's speech, their varieties are said to be mutually intelligible. In contrast, people who say they speak the same language (perhaps different dialects) may not understand each other at all; their varieties are said to be mutually unintelligible. *See* **dialect, language**.

## Naming insight

A child's realization that things have names.

As children are first acquiring language, they come to discover that everything has a name, a stage in their development typically referred to as the *naming insight*. They get to this stage sometime during their second year, typically between 15 and 18 months of age. This realization may lead to what has been called a "naming explosion," or word spurt, but opinions differ whether all children experience such a sudden growth spurt at a particular point in time or whether vocabulary growth is gradual (Aitcheson 2000: 95). The evidence suggests both: that some children's lexical development is more gradual over time, while others show evidence of a sudden leap forward in vocabulary size (Hoff 2009: 203). *See* **mapping problem, taxonomic assumption, whole-object assumption.**

## Native bilingual

A bilingual person who has acquired two (or multiple) languages as a child, perhaps from birth. In other words, a native bilingual is a person with two (or more) native languages. *See* **Bilingual First Language Acquisition (BFLA).**

## Native language (NL)

A person's first language, typically learned from her parents and/or principal caregivers. It is the language that we acquire unconsciously as children from family and caregivers, within the community where we are raised. This term has generally replaced *first language* which, unfortunately, implies a chronological order. In clear instances of sequential (or consecutive) language acquisition, a native language is acquired first, than an additional (second or subsequent) language. In such cases, it is possible to talk about first and second languages, but actual acquisition scenarios don't always seem to fit into clear categories. And, many of us learn more than one "first" language.

The term is not without controversy, and a number of questions have been raised. For example, what are the relevant age limits? In Bilingual First Language Acquisition (BFLA), when a child is exposed to more than one language from his/her caregivers, which one is first? In the attempt to deal with such questions, numerous terms have been coined to represent contrasting conceptions of NLA. For example, *primary language* is sometimes used to refer to a native language. However, the term also denotes the language a person feels the most comfortable using. It may be his or her *dominant* (strongest) language, the one that is preferred by the individual and/or the community. Therefore, it could be a language that was not necessarily learned natively (as a *mother tongue*), but it functions as one would expect a first language to function. Consistent with this usage of "primary," a secondary language is one that is used less frequently than the primary language; it may be an auxiliary language, or one in which the speaker is less proficient. See **Bilingual First Language Acquisition (BFLA), critical (sensitive) period, second/subsequent language**.

### Native-language acquisition (NLA)

The acquisition of one's first, or native, language. In general, terms like *language acquisition* refer to the natural acquisition (or learning) of one's native language. The distinction is particularly relevant to studies of bilingualism because the various routes to bilingualism shape the outcome, and, ultimately, degrees of proficiency in the bi- or multilingual's linguistic repertoire. The question of how a child acquires his/her first or native language is seen by many as the most important question in science today.

Researchers have been asking for the last several decades such questions as when language acquisition begins, and if/when this ability ceases, if at all. For example, children that begin learning a language after a certain age appear to have some difficulty learning it, and their first language invariably leaves recognizable traces (via processes of transfer). While explanations for causes vary considerably, age does appear to play a role. See **acquisition, Acquisition-Learning Hypothesis, age, Bilingual First Language Acquisition (BFLA), Critical Period Hypothesis, transfer**.

### Native speaker (NS)

For purposes of classification in institutional settings (e.g., on school rolls or census data), one who has learned a language as a native (or first) language.

In the literature on language acquisition, it is not necessarily so clear cut. Researchers are still debating the effects of age, social circumstances, and testing. For example, is native-speaker status quantitative (how much of the language must a child know), or is it qualitative (how well does the child pronounce words when speaking, or how well does she write), which may depend critically on academic opportunity and exposure. See **native language, native-language acquisition, nonnative speaker (NNS)**.

### Native-like control

To have control of a language (almost) equal to that of a native speaker. Learning of a second/subsequent language usually implies that a language learner will never quite have equal abilities like the native speaker. Nevertheless, some learners achieve such excellent control of the language as to "pass" for native speakers. The reasons are elusive, however, and may depend on social circumstances (e.g., socioeconomically advantaged groups) or individual characteristics (e.g., *personality, motivation,* or *aptitude*). See **native speaker**.

### Native-speaker intuition

The intuitive knowledge of grammatical correctness that a native speaker of a language has, mostly in the form of a feeling or impression. It is typically unconscious and, therefore, tacit (unexpressed). The term is most often associated with generative approaches to language acquisition. *See* **acquisition, generative approach, ideal speaker, knowledge (of language), native speaker**.

## Nativism/nativist

The philosophical view that certain abilities are *innate*, or "hard-wired" into the brain. It is also the position of some cognitive scientists that all human beings are born with *innate* cognitive abilities, particularly the ability to know a language—typically associated with the philosopher René Descartes, Cartesian linguistics, and the generative school of linguistics. *See* **Chomsky, Descartes, generative approaches, innate**.

## Natural Approach

Krashen and Terrell's (1983) groundbreaking work. It is an approach to SL teaching based on a model of SLA detailed in Krashen's 1985 work, *The Input Hypothesis*, that included five interrelated hypotheses: the *Acquisition-Learning Hypothesis, Natural Order Hypothesis, Monitor Hypothesis, Input Hypothesis,* and *Affective Filter Hypothesis*. It emphasized naturalistic input without the traditional structure lessons of the Audio-lingual method (e.g., with a good deal of gesturing and simplified language, but no translation, no drill, and no memorization) to maximize unconscious acquisition processes. *See* **Acquisition-Learning Hypothesis, Affective Filter, critical period, Input Hypothesis, Krashen, Monitor Theory**.

## Natural Order Hypothesis

A theory of language acquisition proposed by Krashen that proposed to explain why particular grammatical morphemes were learned in a particular sequence.

According to this hypothesis, children learn easier things (forms and structures) first and progress onto more difficult ones. There is a natural order learners will follow irrespective of the order in which the rules of the target language are taught in ELD classes during SLA. Evidence for a natural order comes from the morpheme studies that indicate a regular order in which English inflectional morphemes are learned in NLA (Brown 1973). The reasoning, however, is circular because it is not clear what makes a pattern or rule *easier*. If easier rules are learned first, then rules that are learned first must be easier. We need a definition for the word "easier." Current research looks at *complexity* to determine what may be relatively easy or difficult. The more complex that a structure is, the more knowledge of grammar that is needed to learn it. So, a simple rule or pattern is learned before a more complex one. *See* **Krashen, morpheme studies, second language acquisition**.

## Natural Partitions hypothesis

The idea that the world objectively includes entities or things that naturally take labels as nouns, offering some explanation why children typically learn classes of nouns before they learn classes of verbs and other so-called parts of speech. There are natural boundaries (partitions) that limit what a label can refer to.

For example, a child sees in her or his environment things like tables, chairs, dogs, and so on that easily fall into types; children can match noun labels with the things she or he sees based on her or his knowledge of the physical world.

Therefore, nouns have real meaning based on objective and observable facts. This makes the learning task easy because reality determines meaning; the child learner only needs to find the correct label for the correct object. In addition, noun meanings are very similar among the world's language; one is very likely to find exact or near exact equivalents among nouns like *book*, *table*, and *chair*. Verbs, on the other hand, involve relationships among people and things (according to the so-called relational relativity hypothesis), for instance, the grammatical and semantic relationships that are expressed in various language-specific ways. For instance, the verb *give* entails someone giving something to someone else; *go* entails someone (or thing) going somewhere. Verbs, therefore, can encode meanings in more diverse ways, for example, verbs of motion in Spanish which do not find exact equivalents in English (Hoff 2009: 189–190). To learn labels for things, the child only needs to match a label to a "meaning" she or he already knows through simple observation, while verb meanings involve more complex relationships that are encoded in the grammar of her target of acquisition. See **linguistic relativity, the Whorf–Sapir Hypothesis**.

### Nature versus nurture

The age-old debate whether humans are born with certain capacities (nature) or if our individual abilities are learned according to conditioned behavior, stimulus and response (nurture). What is at stake is an understanding of the abilities we all bring to the table at birth (abilities to walk, talk, think…) and the effect of the environment into which we are born.

The side which assumes that children have deep innate abilities (knowledge, and even ideas) is generally referred to as *nativism*; it is a descendant of Rationalism (e.g., the philosophy of Descartes, and back to Plato). It asserts that knowledge cannot come from experience alone; there have to be underlying capacities for learning, or the type of knowing that does not come just from memory. There are also differences between the unconscious acquisition of skills (such as the ability to do language) and conscious learning. Acquisition resembles learning to ride a bike, play a sport, or develop talent on a musical instrument. It is not like learning the history of Europe or memorizing the names of plants and animals. Nativists point out that (a) all children acquire language rapidly (faster than they would if they were adults, implying a special kind of ability); (b) they acquire language effortlessly (it is easy for them, not difficult as language learning can be for adults); (c) and they "get" their language(s) without overt instruction or instructor (characteristic of adult learning).

The extreme view that experience shapes the mind from birth is called *empiricism*. (All research done in a laboratory is *empirical* because it is based on observable phenomena, but it does not necessarily follow from empiricism as a philosophy.) As a philosophical view, empiricism is closely associated with the philosopher John Locke; by definition, it opposes the idea of innate knowledge, and the rationalist views of Noam Chomsky and his colleagues that underlie Generative linguistics. The Empiricist side of the debate assumes that children are born with no prewired mental advantages and learn everything, including language, via direct experience. See **behaviorism, Chomsky, Descartes, empiricism, Locke, nativism**.

## Negative evidence

The evidence of language forms and structures that children get through negative feedback, error correction, and attention to form. It is negative in the sense that errors are pointed out in the hope that they will avoid those errors in the future. This is typical of classroom situations in which an instructor marks down performance for the number of errors committed. The phrase is usually used in contrast to positive evidence, that a child learns the grammatical patterns of his or her language from the well-formed sentences uttered by those in her or his environment. Any mistakes she or he may make will vanish as she or he receives more input and corrects her or his theories of language accordingly.

It is often noted in NLA studies that children are not often overtly corrected for mistakes in grammar (e.g., *Me love you*); it is more likely that parents and other caregivers will correct children for saying things that are not true, not for saying things that are incorrect according to adult speech norms. Because all of the utterances that a child hears are potentially positive evidence, there is controversy about the amount and quality of negative evidence that a child receives. Different types of evidence, then, play significant roles in the various views of learnability, particularly when it comes to children generating (or producing) novel utterances. *See* **hypothesis testing, positive evidence**.

## Neural circuit

Interconnected nerve cells. When presented with a stimulus or performing a task, energy passes from one to the other, causing them to fire (become activated) together.

The obvious analogy is with an electronic circuit board, where charges pass from one point to another along materials that conduct electricity. The more circuits involved, the greater possibility of complexity. Another analogy might be so-called closed-circuit television, in which cameras and screens are connected to each other in a circuit-like arrangement, with no outlet to persons or equipment outside of the small and immediate network. Continuing the analogy, neural networks can be massive arrangements of circuits with pathways leading from one area of the brain to another. Connectionist approaches seek to investigate the neural patterning of the mind/brain to create computer models (e.g., artificial intelligence) that can mimic the abilities of the human brain. *See* **activation, CT (Roentgen-ray computed tomography), connectionism, modular, parallel distributed model (PDP)**.

## Neural networks

Inter-connected strands or pathways (along which activation spreads) of neurons that branch out into associated groups (presumably with a specific function). Current modeling of the brain has greatly influenced the ways that psycholinguists view language processing. *See* **connectionism, neural circuit**.

## Neuroimaging

The use of sophisticated machines and computers to create images of the brain and to pinpoint brain activity. Such images are used to form hypotheses about language processing (the wheres and possibly the hows). See **brain-imaging techniques, event-related potentials (ERPs), fMRI, MRI, PET**.

## Neurolinguistics
Specifically studies brain architecture and the various anatomical systems and subsystems (neural pathways) within the physical brain and their connections with speech. The multidisciplinary branch of linguistics (and neurology) that investigates the connections between neurological structures of the brain and the knowledge of language. See **brain-imaging techniques, fMRI, neural networks**.

## No Child Left Behind (NCLB)
Legislation enacted in the United States in 2001 that replaced all previous federal laws concerning bilingual education. It made school districts and states accountable to the federal government for the performance of LEP (ELL) students. They are required to (a) identify languages other than English used by the student population; (b) develop academic assessment (in both skill and content areas); (c) assess proficiency in English annually for all LEP students; (d) include grade 3 through eight LEP students in the assessment of reading and mathematics; and (e) assess reading skills in English for all students who had been in US schools for three years.

Some of these requirements were subsequently relaxed somewhat in 2004, but in essence, LEP students were still to be tested in both English and mathematics, and local educators became responsible for their progress, risking punitive actions (e.g., loss of funding, lower pay) for consistently low test scores. There is no mention in this actual legislation of bilingualism and development (or maintenance) of native language skills, or preservation of heritage languages. Critics point out that compulsory testing, or "high-stakes assessment," will transform the established curriculum, leading to a "teach to the test" mentality in those specific areas that are continually tested, rather than a focus on educating children in a traditionally broad manner in the arts, sciences, and humanities. The ramifications have also led to the massive reorganization of school districts and programs and the creation of charter schools (with special mandates), and the upswing of private and parochial schools where parents have greater control over curricula and school spending. See **assessment, bilingual, bilingualism, testing**.

## Nonnative speaker (NNS)
Typically for classification purposes (e.g., on school rolls or census data), one who has learned a language as a subsequent (or "second") language, for instance, in school, and not natively in the home. See **native speaker, native-language acquisition, second/subsequent language acquisition**.

## Nonreduplicated babbling
Consists of different syllables, in contrast to canonical babbling which contains repetition of the same syllable over and over. See **babbling, babbling shift**.

## Nonstandard

A *variety* of a language that exhibits features differing from the so-called standard. For instance, a nonstandard variety of English will show more frequent occurrence of forms and structures that differ from those associated with *Standard English*.

The usage of nonstandard forms and structures is usually frowned upon by *prescriptivists*, for example, educators whose job includes teaching the standard variety. Some of the most notable nonstandard features shared by most nonstandard varieties of English are the usage of words like *ain't* and the occurrence of *double negatives* (multiple negation). (In languages like French and Spanish, where multiple negation is required, the process that generates double negatives is typically called *negative concord*.)

However, any other version of a language, say English, or dialect thereof, whether linked to a particular region or social group, is not merely something that *diverges* from a putative standard (e.g., in the sense of normal versus abnormal). Any variety of English that can be associated with a particular group, community, region, or nation is, in essence, a dialect. It may be difficult to think of a national standard as a dialect (a dialect of what?), but the truth remains that one national standard differs from the next, most noticeably in vocabulary and pronunciation and how words are spelled. So, vocabulary, accent, and to a lesser extent grammar account for the most obvious differences among dialects and between Standard American and Standard British (cf. Chambers and Trudgill 1980: 3–5). Because a standard is the model against which different dialects are typically compared, it is often excluded in the discussions of dialects, but it is one nonetheless. It just happens to be the one that beat out all of its competitors.

Nonstandard varieties of English are often linked to a local *vernacular*, the language used in the home and within large segments of the population. Nevertheless, it is often associated with a lack of exposure to the standard, according to ethnic or racial stereotypes, and worse, a general lack of education. Sociolinguistic research has shown that nonstandard varieties are systematic and logical, and warrant equal status as dialects in their own right, just as Standard English is a dialect (Wolfram and Fasold 1974: 5–7). An older term, *substandard*, is no longer in use because it implies a subjective hierarchy of language varieties ranging from superior to inferior. See **deficit model, difference model, standard, standardization, vernacular**.

## Norm

What is considered normal or acceptable in a community. Speech norms consist of forms and structures that members of a community use on a daily basis, irrespective of technical status as *standard* or *nonstandard*. They often include a full range of grammatical and discourse characteristics, including the rapidity of speech.

The term is often linked to *vernacular* usage, and with native-speaker norms in relation to a language learner in the development of a second or additional language. The term *norm* specifically refers to what members of a speech community accept as normal or acceptable language behavior. A certain amount of variation is to be accepted, but it is still within limits set by the community. Norms may also become idealized, as the most desirable or best way to say things. Once norms are set, it is possible to speak of codifying various aspects of language and standardization (Wardhaugh 2006: 5–6, 35–36).

The term "norm" is also used to refer to a national mean average on test scores. *See* **nonstandard, standard, standardization, vernacular**.

### Norm-referenced testing
Standardized testing that compares one student with others, allowing a teacher to compare the performance with a national average, or norm, often according to percentile ranking. *See* **census surveys, formative testing, normative testing, self assessment**.

### Normative
With respect to academic testing, practices that establish norms and expectations for average student/learner achievement, for example, those norms that approximate where students should be according to age and grade-level.

In an age when teachers' jobs are often at stake, critics of normative testing (e.g., norm-referenced testing) point out that it puts pressure on teachers and students to improve performance (when students score below norms), and that it unfairly measures academic performance and literacy in bilinguals who may still be developing proficiency in English, the language of education in the United Kingdom, United States, and so on. Results of normative testing may blur the distinction between (a) language acquisition/learning and (b) academic achievement, which is then often equated (perhaps unintentionally) with intelligence. It seems obvious enough (to the critics) that getting at the *causes* of underachievement (low scores) is more important than the testing itself. However, assessment appears to be a necessary evil (so to speak). As a consequence, test design (precisely what is measured) and the interpretation of test scores have taken on added importance, particularly in educational systems that stress mandatory nationwide testing according to national standards (e.g., according to NCLB legislation in the US). *See* **formative testing, No Child Left Behind, norm-referenced testing, placement, summative testing**.

### Norms of interaction
Culturally defined norms of behavior that determine when and how we speak (Hymes 1974: 60). For example, many people whisper at the library, in church, or at a funeral. They yell and scream at a professional or college sporting event. Some may let children speak whenever and however they please, which may not be so in other nations and cultures. There are also customary rules of body movement, touching, and so on that they follow in certain specified situations, for instance, making eye contact may have distinct cultural norms of interaction.

Anglo-Americans, for example, do not usually touch their professors except perhaps to shake hands. In some cultures and subcultures, these norms may be quite different, with lots of touching that may seem more appropriate among close friends. In other cultures, one never directly criticizes a teacher or professor or makes direct eye contact out of respect. This is not so with the average American, who feels quite free to ask questions and express that a professor is not being clear or behaving properly. It is not customary for many American students to show deference to a professor, or to open doors for him/her, while in other cultures, it is quite the contrary—deference is the norm. This does not necessarily imply a lack of respect; respect may just be expressed in different ways. *See* **norms of interpretation**.

## Norms of interpretation

The counterpart to *norms of interaction*, which, in contrast, determine how we interpret the behaviors of others, whether or not they belong to our own community (Hymes 1974: 60–61). These norms define our opinions of when people are being polite, aggressive, rude, quiet, and generally how we behave in personal interactions. A contemporary example would be how we view appropriate cellular/mobile phone behavior. For instance, talking loudly on a personal communication device in a crowded elevator may seem rude, as if one were carving out personal space in a public area.

Our perceptions of the behaviors of members of other cultures often reveal much about our own. For example, if a member of one culture interprets the behavior of another as quiet or polite, then that implies that his/her culture is noisy or rude by comparison. Californians may be viewed by residents of other states as self-absorbed and shallow, perhaps, a result of media portrayals of pampered Hollywood celebrities and self-centered teenagers. Californians, who typically say "Excuse me" when they get within two feet of each other, may think New Yorkers (who don't say such things) are pushy, rude, and aggressive—the stuff of comedy routines. In the United Kingdom, Londoners may have their opinion of the behavior of those from Newcastle upon Tyne, or those from Portsmouth, for example (and vice versa), based on speech or other culturally bound behaviors. *See* **norms of interaction**.

## Obsolescence/obsolete

When a language is no longer useful in a community, it becomes obsolete, like old, outdated pieces of technology. It is typically the result of *language attrition*.

For example, languages within a bilingual community are often compartmentalized according to situations of usage (*diglossia*). Actual usage of the traditional language may be increasingly restricted to fewer and fewer situations. It may be used only in the home or for traditional events, for example, culturally defined religious events. Little by little, particular registers of a community's traditional or heritage language gradually fall into disuse, specifically those used outside of the home and in situations of formal usage. Registers of the dominant language effectively take their place. Bilingual communities, therefore, may find that their old, traditional language is no longer used in a variety of settings—it has become obsolete. *See* **diglossia, language attrition, shift, register, three-generation rule**.

## One system (or two)

This is an ongoing controversy regarding how a bilingual child's languages are represented. One side asserts that the child has one, unitary grammatical system encompassing both or all of his or her languages, and the other side asserts that the child has an independent system for each (two systems).

Recent research suggests that, in many cases, each language in the bilingual's repertoire develops similarly to the ways the languages develop with monolinguals of the respective languages (Yip and Matthews 2007: 33–35). They follow the same developmental steps, and there appears to be little difference in the language acquisition process when both languages are learned simultaneously. Proficiency levels in each language may vary, however. Some bilinguals may resist the acquisition of one language for sociocultural reasons. The heritage language may stop being used because the number of domains in which it is used cease to exist outside the home (language attrition). In that event, the linguistic character of the heritage language may be affected, too, as forms and structures are no longer available in the language because of attrition. Children will not necessarily acquire a language merely because they are around it (Myers-Scotton 2006: 327). *See* **Separate Development Hypothesis**.

## Operating principles (OPs)

Innate principles or strategies for analyzing and organizing language input in some approaches to language acquisition. This contrasts with generative approaches which claim that children have innate grammatical categories of noun and verb.

For example, the work of Daniel I. Slobin and colleagues is based on the extensive cross-linguistic study and detailed accounts of how children in diverse languages acquire their native languages. This approach begins with the empirical data. Slobin *et al.* note that children seem to be especially gifted pattern makers, and that they appear to focus on the patterns of speech to which they are exposed. Slobin (1985) suggests that children pay attention to (a) the order of words; (b) the order of morphemes in words (c) word endings (inflections); (d) consistent relationships between expression (form) and content (meaning); and (e) generalizations (analogies). By systematically analyzing the data, the researchers can reasonably predict where new information will likely appear. The fact that children form generalizations from the data they hear or see helps explain children's overgeneralizations (e.g., *\*go-goed-goed*, *\*sing-singed-singed*). See **developmental models/perspective, Language Acquisition Device (LAD), Language-Making Capacity (LMC), overgeneralization, positive evidence**.

## Order of acquisition

Refers to the order that particular items first appear in a child's speech. Their regular appearance is an indication that particular aspects of speech are being acquired. For example, the order in which inflectional morphemes appear in a child's developing grammar shows the order in which they become part of that grammar. The suffix –s that goes on classes of nouns to indicate plural in English typically appears in children's speech before the suffix –s that goes on verbs in the present tense to indicate subject-verb agreement (the 3p-pres –s), suggesting that there is a reason why children learn one before the other.

In the well-known work of Dulay and Burt (1973, 1974) to measure MLU in developing grammars, the order of acquisition of morphemes was established following specific criteria. The morphemes may first be absent in performance; then they begin to appear, but not necessarily accurately (e.g., as an overgeneralization—one form fits all possibilities). So, every noun plural is formed the same way (*foot-foots*), ignoring strong (or irregular) forms such as *foot-feet*. The final step is to apply the morpheme correctly in all obligatory contexts according to adult, native-speakers norms (Larsen-Freeman and Long 1991: 62–63). See **mean length of utterance (MLU), morpheme studies, Natural Order Hypothesis**.

## Overextension

A type of error in a child's acquisition of lexicon in which a specific word is used to refer a wide range of objects, for example, calling all furry, four-legged animals—including cows and horses—*doggie*. The word's meaning is broadened or extended to cover a greater range of meanings than its equivalent in adult usage. Although it was originally thought that this phenomenon was widespread, research has shown that it is relatively rare, and that it disappears as the child acquires more specialized vocabulary (Hoff 2009: 191–192). The term is used in opposition to *underextension*, in which a word is used for only one specific example, for example, when the word *kitty* refers to only one cat. See **taxonomic assumption, underextension**.

## Overgeneralization

When a particular rule or pattern is applied to any case that is similar, for example, when the regular past-tense suffix *–ed* is applied to all verbs. Based on the speech he or she hears, a child may put an *–ed* on the verbs *sing*, *see*, and *catch* producing *singed*, *seed*, and *catched*, respectively. This is apparently how children (and others) go about hypothesis testing: observe a rule or pattern, apply that pattern, and then wait to learn how that matches with the speech of peers and caregivers (which are not always the same). See **hypothesis testing**.

### Parallel distributed processing (PDP)

One of the earliest connectionist models (a model of the human brain originally derived from a computer analogy). It stresses the parallel and simultaneous (rather than sequential) nature of neural processing during the performance of various mental tasks and activities (Rumelhart and McClelland 1986). Multiple signals spread as various, interlocking networks become activated, taking (i.e., distributing) information to various parts of the brain along observable routes. Such an account may help explain the interesting human ability to do more than one thing at a time, known as multitasking, for example, driving an automobile while simultaneously thinking of something else.

Many recent computer applications seek to explore this type of simultaneous (parallel) processing. For example, early computer programs could do one thing, compute (calculate quantities and numbers). Now, computer users can interact with various applications (apps) simultaneously (via multiple processors) and jump from (with a click of a mouse) one application/network to another without having to close or terminate another program or network. *See* **activation, connectionism, language processing**.

### Parental involvement

How parents actively support their children's education. It involves culturally accepted parent–teacher cooperation (e.g., through consultation/conferences, support of a teacher's goals for the child, and help with the child's homework). Therefore, one of the apparent goals of schools is to educate parents of their responsibilities and the importance of their involvement with their children's academic performance. *See* **mainstream**.

### Parse

To analyze or separate a sentence or other utterance into its constituent parts. In the online task of speech comprehension, the listener or reader must process input, and analyze acceptable (grammatical) word combinations into meaningful chunks. For example, the listener must locate the grammatical subject and ascertain any other external arguments such as direct or indirect objects and the relationships among them (albeit unconsciously). It also implies being able to understand and link the semantic (meaningful) relationships among sentence constituents—being able to recognize semantic agents, patients, and so on.

In psycholinguistic studies of comprehension, various techniques are used to measure the relative time subjects take to parse sentences, for example, via tracking eye movement or by using devices to measure event-related potentials. *See* **eye movements, event-related potentials (ERPs)**.

### Participants (or interlocutors)

Includes all those who take part in a conversation or speech event, for example, parents, siblings, friends, co-workers, fellow students, acquaintances, strangers, and professionals (teachers, physicians, and nurses). This includes the people and the social relationships among them. For instance, we speak differently to various people out of respect and familiarity (the roles people play in our lives), so we tend to adjust our speech when we are around English professors, ministers, parents, grandparents, teammates, and roommates. See **purpose, setting, situations of speech**.

### Passive knowledge

The type of knowledge needed to recognize a form—spoken, written, or signed. See **active knowledge, productive knowledge, receptive knowledge**.

### Pattern

Particular sequences or arrangement of forms, for example, ABC, DEF. In many modern approaches to language processing and acquisition, the fact that language patterns out in consistent and, therefore, reasonably predictable ways is an important element of theories of learnability (and teachability). If a language did not pattern out in regular ways of some kind, it would be difficult to learn.

Regarding the ability to parse language units, in most varieties of English, for instance, names for things (nouns) typically cluster with other word classes (determiners and adjectives) in patterned ways to form *noun phrases*, those structures that can be the subject of a sentence. The ordering is often *article + adjective + noun*, as in the noun phrase, *A brown cow*. The only elements necessary for noun phrases are types of nouns or pronouns (or a word or phrase that functions like a noun). By becoming familiar with such a pattern, the location of the noun becomes predictable, therefore, learnable. In various neo-Piagetian (interactive) approaches to language, children are seen as pattern makers; that is, they seem to be able to perceive patterns in the speech of caregivers, and remember those patterns, both necessary steps in the acquisition of language. See **Language Acquisition Device (LAD), Language-Making Capacity (LMC), operating principles (OPs)**.

### Pedagogical (or teaching) grammar

Any approach to language teaching that is designed to aid in the learning process.

In many countries, teachers are responsible to teach prescriptively (e.g., according to a text) to prepare their students for the demands of education and academic registers of speech. Those involved in classes devoted to English instruction and the language arts are also expected to help students identify perhaps more colorful (and less academic) expressions that are part of popular culture—words, phrases, and sentence structures—that are not part of the standard, but common, nonetheless. In popular discourse, informal, spontaneous speech can be quite influential. It is frequent in the schoolyards, at sporting events, during musical performances, and other informal gatherings in the speech of siblings, friends, acquaintances, strangers, and even parents. Therefore, some teachers may need to take a more descriptive approach.

A pedagogical grammar, therefore, often combines aspects of both descriptive and prescriptive approaches. For students of English, it teaches correct usage (e.g., how to speak and write according to a standard in school), but it also prepares learners for what speakers actually do with their speech in informal situations. For ELLs, this means being able to understand how native speakers compress their speech (*gonna, cudja, wudja*, etc.) and use informal speech that seems to violate a lot of rules ("ain't never been there"). The skillful teacher informs students that native speakers may talk one way in informal situations and another in formal situations, and that some things people say are simply not Standard English. *See* **descriptive grammar, prescriptive grammar, Standard English**.

## Percentile

Ranking of a student's performance relative to the performance of all others who take a test for the purpose of comparison. It does not measure the percentage of correct answers. For example, a percentile ranking that places a student in the top 90 percent means that he or she scored as well as or better than 90 percent of the test takers irrespective of actual right or wrong answers.

Many educators are critical of this type of ranking system, especially when applied to bilingual students. First, it does not seem fair to compare native speakers with either nonnative speakers or with speakers of nonstandard varieties. Native speakers of standard varieties typically have an advantage in the area of vocabulary knowledge. One may also question the validity of tests that are culturally based, that require a depth of cultural literacy, and that consequently blur distinctions between (a) academic achievement and (b) proficiency in a language variety. Ironically, a student may get a high percentage of the answers correct on a test, but still score relatively low according to a percentile ranking. In addition, such tests do not measure communicative competence (how the child communicates with members of her own community). They typically miss the child's strengths because they confuse active literacy skills (performance) with his or her overall ability to communicate (his or her linguistic competence). *See* **achievement, census surveys, cultural literacy, formative testing, literacy, norm-referenced testing, self-assessment**.

## Perception

There are two sides to the issue of perception with respect to language. The first is interpreting what an object is, beyond merely sensing the presence of the object. In some views, objects such as animals are recognized according to perceptual properties such as size, shape, color, texture, and other features such as wings, feathers, beaks, fur, teeth, and legs (cf. Markman 1989: 9; Field 2002: 101). The natural world itself provides the clues for the existence of kinds of things like dogs, cats, birds, and snakes.

The other side of perception is the ability to analyze the speech stream and to isolate the word-form that is associated with the object being named, also known as the *segmentation problem*. Children must learn to pay attention to particularly salient or prominent stretches of speech, and to anticipate where and when they are likely to occur. Hence, perceptual salience is a property that can refer to particular facets of speech, for example, the presence of stressed syllables that stand out in speech. In addition, to engage in the comprehension of speech, the listener must be able to distinguish between sounds that are in many ways similar, for example, the phonemes /p/ and /b/ that are pronounced in the same place and manner with one exception, voicing (the use of the vocal cords in pronunciation). In that children appear to be particularly suited for the perception of language, many language acquisition specialists agree that this ability is innate or inborn. By looking at the evidence, researchers hope to clarify more precisely what that ability consists of. *See* **taxonomic assumption**.

## Performance

In linguistic theory, what a speaker does with language. It is actual speech, including such characteristics as pauses, unfinished utterances, occasional mistakes (slips of the tongue), and memory lapses. The term is typically contrasted with *competence*, an idealized view of one's overall knowledge (active and passive) in a language. In theory, one's competence is not subject to the limitations of performance.

Some approaches use the analogy of an actor or musician, whose competence is theoretically unlimited—once a person learns how to act or play an instrument, he or she can in principal perform a scene from any play or perform a line from any musical composition. However, on a given day, a performance may be flawed for a number of reasons, a lack of sleep, or for any number of potential distractions. Many current models of language acquisition are finding it useful to distinguish among the receptive, passive types of language knowledge required for perception (e.g., being able to decode the written word) and the productive, active types of knowledge required for performance. *See* **active knowledge, competence, passive knowledge, productive knowledge, receptive knowledge**.

## Performance analysis (PA)

The study of the progress being made by SL learners based on what they do well, and not necessarily limited to what they do poorly (errors).

Example are early morpheme studies that focused on the emergence of particular grammatical morphemes over time, and studies of children's gradually emerging syntax (in steps or stages) in the acquisition of such constructions as negative sentences and question formation (both yes-no type questions and Wh-questions). While the limited focus of error analysis (EA) is still considered useful in analyzing and tracing errors back to their possible sources, it gave way to longitudinal approaches that measured incremental progress in naturally occurring speech (Larsen-Freeman and Long 1991: 62–69). *See* **contrastive analysis (CA), Contrastive Analysis Hypothesis (CAH), developmental sequences, error analysis (EA), morpheme studies**.

## Personality

A collection of traits or characteristics that makes up an individual person. In studies of language acquisition/learning, it is a multifaceted psychological factor that influences acquisition. It includes individual characteristics such as one's self-esteem, extroversion (versus introversion), anxiety levels, risk-taking, sensitivity to rejection or failure, inhibition, and tolerance of ambiguity (a characteristic often necessary when learning a second or subsequent language). One might add that having a sense of humor can be beneficial, as well. See **aptitude, cognitive style, learning strategies**.

## Perspective

Point of view. In language acquisition studies, a child speaker's perspective may change how a person or thing is addressed. For example, a child's father may be referred to as *Mr. Jones*, or *William* by the people in the child's environment, *honey* or *husband* by a spouse or partner, and, of course, *dad* or *papa* by the child.

In earlier studies, it was believed that new terms had to be mutually exclusive; in other words, to the child, a new term had to refer to a new object or entity of some kind. If the child was familiar with the word *kitty*, for example, and heard the word *doggy*, she or he would immediately search his or her environment for an unfamiliar object (and then map that form onto the new object). This tendency is called the *mutual exclusivity assumption*. However, recent work has cast light on the fact that young children can, in fact, view the people, animals, and things in their environment from differing perspectives. So, the family dog may be known as the *dog*, *pet*, *schnauzer*, or other individual name like *Lassie* (Clark 2003: 98–100). *See* **mutual exclusivity assumption, taxonomic assumption, whole-object assumption**.

## PET (positron emission tomography) scan

A brain-imagining technique used to produce a three-dimensional picture, or "image," of a part of the body. It is similar in intent to a CT scan. A positron-emitting element (radioactive tracer) is introduced into the body that gives off gamma rays. A computer detects the emissions and reconstructs an image of the activity for the purpose of analysis. Through the computer analysis, specialists can observe activity in the body, for example, the metabolism of glucose in the brain, in order to diagnose abnormalities. *See* **brain-imaging techniques, CT (Roentgen-ray computed tomography), event-related potentials (ERPs), fMRI, MRI, neuroimaging, SPECT**.

## Phonemic awareness

The conscious awareness that phonemes are parts of words, an important step in the development of reading and writing skills; a part of phonological awareness (Hoff 2009: 333). *See* **categorical perception, phonological awareness**.

## Phonics

An approach to literacy instruction that stresses a more-or-less strict correspondence between graphemes (letters) and phonemes (sounds) and sounding out individual letters and specific letter combinations (e.g., the digraphs *ch*, *ph*, *th*, and *sh*). It requires conscious attention to form, how words are spelled, and explicit instruction in grapheme-phoneme (letter-sound) correspondences. Phonics is often associated with "back to basics" movements, and it is contrasted with *whole language* approaches to literacy instruction.

Among specialists in SLA, phonics has come under criticism because it assumes native or native-like ability in the spoken language. A native speaker is expected to know the sounds of a language by the time he/she starts to read, so it is a natural progression from mastering the grammar of a language to learning to read it. However, bilinguals, who often use one language at home and the other at school, may still be learning the phonological and lexical characteristics of their additional or second language. This increases the burden of learning for the child who is still learning the language, and who is forced to learn to read it at the same time. See **phonological awareness, whole language**.

### Phonological awareness

Conscious awareness of the sounds of a language. This includes phonemic awareness and how sounds are strung together in words. It extends to the ability to discover rhymes or to count the number of sounds or rhythmic beats (syllables) in words. Phonological awareness may be cultivated in language activities such as songs, nursery rhymes, and the reading of children's books, and may have some relationship with early reading skills (Hoff 2009: 169–170, 333). See **phonemic awareness**.

### Piaget, Jean

Twentieth-century Swiss philosopher and developmental theorist known for his work with children and stages in their cognitive development.

He identified four stages according to age: the *sensorimotor* stage (birth to age 2)—children first experience the world through their senses and movement; *preoperational* stage (2 to 7)—children develop motor skills more fully; *concrete operational* stage (7 to 12)—children begin to think logically, but concretely; and *formal operational* stage (from 12 on)—children develop abstract reasoning. It is at the second of these stages, the preoperational stage, that language begins to emerge in the child. This stage is also associated with the acquisition of motor skills.

Applied to language, it is no surprise that the child's first words are from her/his immediate environment, for example, body parts, and names for caregivers. While Piaget was not a behaviorist, his developmental approach appeared to provide a middle ground between *nativism*, which assumes innate knowledge, and *behaviorism*, which states that all knowledge is the result of experience. Piaget's ideas fit well with current theories of brain organization and neural networks, and that, as the child's brain develops anatomically, so do cognitive skills. There is a biological element, but it does not assume specific innate knowledge. See **behaviorism, Chomsky, nativism, Piagetian/Neo-Piagetian, Skinner**.

### Piagetian/Neo-Piagetian

Having to do with the developmental psychology of Jean Piaget, particularly recent theories of language development.

Neo-Piagetianism is a recent reworking of Piaget's ideas given recent advancements in technology. It is most often associated with connectionist models of language processing, although Piaget apparently proposed no specific model of the human brain (Karmiloff-Smith 1992: 180). However, ideas that link biological maturation (and a fundamentally domain general view) to the gradual socialization of the child fall in neatly with current thinking on brain architecture that neurons gradually develop in response to biological development and experience. Neo-Piagetian ideas, in general, incorporate Piaget's notions of stages of development with the emergence of cognitive abilities, particularly language. See **connectionism/connectionist models, constructivism, interactionism, Piaget**.

## Pidgin

A make-shift or reduced language that arises in a multilingual situation usually for the purposes of business or trade among groups having their own native languages. Pidgins typically have a small or restricted lexicon (vocabulary), and relatively simple grammar with no inflectional morphology. The lexicon typically comes from one language, the so-called *superstrate* and perhaps socially dominant variety, while the grammar comes from the native languages of its speakers, the underlying *substrate*. A pidgin, by definition, has no native speakers. The result of such language mixing is a variety with limited usage, though speakers can be quite fluent (Holm 1988: 4–5).

Pidgin languages have become significant in studies of language acquisition because they involve the early stages of language learning, albeit under unique social circumstances. They have also become important in general linguistics because of their possible links to theories of language origins. The processes of pidginization (emergence of a pidgin variety) are said to copy (or recapitulate) language evolution, and, by analogy, ontogeny (the origins of language) repeats phylogeny (the organization and classification of languages into families or phyla) as if they were biological species. In this scenario, a pidgin is thought to resemble the early stages of human language as it evolved into increasingly complex forms. Two flaws in this argument are that the vocabulary (words) of the pidgin originate some place (the superstrate), and the speakers already have a native language (the substrate), demonstrating a mature faculty of language. See **contact languages, creole, language evolution, mixed language, Pidginization Hypothesis**.

## Pidginization Hypothesis

A hypothesis developed by John Schumann (e.g., Schumann 1978) that likens early SLA to pidginization.

The hypothesis developed as an offshoot of the Harvard Project (Cazden *et al.*), on oft-cited project on SLA. Schumann noted the lack of language development of one test subject, Alberto, whose *interlanguage* (IL) variety showed characteristics similar to pidgin languages. (He was learning English in untutored, naturalistic settings, without the benefit of ESL instruction.) His IL was marked by such things as a reduced lexicon (limited vocabulary), simplified forms of negatives (mostly *no + verb*), simplified interrogatives (lack of subject-auxiliary inversion), and the absence of tense endings. No claim was made that Alberto actually spoke a pidgin, only that his learners' variety showed the same types of restrictions and simplifications as do pidgin varieties. Schumann also suggested that the reduced nature of Alberto's interlanguage was a result of its reduced functions, in that he used it only for basic communicative (referential) needs.

Schumann's hypothesis has received a lot of criticism. Among the objections were that pidginization takes place among speakers of several native languages, not just one (Spanish in Alberto's case); pidginization is a group phenomenon (birth and spread of a language) while SLA is an individual phenomenon (developmental process). In addition, the underlying social conditions in pidgin communities (e.g., conditions of slavery and forced servitude) and in situations of SLA are surely distinct, so the effects of social distance will differ. Linguistically, pidgins contain a smattering of words from various native languages; ILs don't show the language admixture typical of pidgins. Importantly, pidgin varieties take on a life of their own, become targets of acquisition in their own right, and can stabilize for intergroup and intragroup communication. In contrast, interlanguages typically continue to progress until degrees of proficiency are attained in the target language (Larsen-Freeman and Long 1991: 251–266).

Despite the criticism, the term *pidginization* may still have some currency in SLA research. And, concerning the emergence of creole languages, many theorists argue that SLA does, indeed, play a role in creolization (see, for example, Field 2004). *See also* **Acculturation Model, creole, creolization, interlanguage (IL), language mixing, mixed language, pidgin**.

## Placement

The goal or outcome of some types of testing is to place students in different classes (grade levels) or programs. Such testing is typically formative and administered at the beginning of the school year or semester. It aims to find the student's level of proficiency for the purpose of placing him or her in the appropriate class. In general, school districts in the United Kingdom and the United States give such tests to find which students need remediation in skills areas, specifically in English proficiency and arithmetic. However, in specific English language programs, placement tests are given to find specific levels of language instruction.

The test is constructed to correspond with groupings in a particular program according to degrees of proficiency. These groupings can differ greatly from one school or program to the next with respect to the number of levels available to students, stretching from pre-beginner to intermediate to relatively advanced and concerning the particular skills being taught (e.g., listening, speaking, reading, and writing). Skills are often taught in pairs, for example, listening and speaking in one course, and reading and writing in another, assuming developmental links between the two. *See* **assessment, formative testing, literacy, norm-referenced testing, normative testing, summative testing**.

## Popular culture

The perspectives, attitudes, values, and behaviors (including speech, dress, and forms of body art such as piercings and tattoos) of contemporary people. It is an important distinction for teachers, particularly in multilingual and multicultural settings because of its pervasive influence on the behavior and speech of young people. It is often intimately linked to individual and group identity.

So-called pop culture is typically influenced by current trends and popular personalities in the arts and media (recording artists, authors, television and film personalities, and so on). For instance, particular personalities in hip-hop culture have a great influence over the younger generations, just as the cultural traits of rock and roll culture (followers of Elvis Presley, the Beatles, the Rolling Stones, or Bruce Springsteen) had on earlier generations. Informal, involved registers of speech can be greatly influenced by the speech, values, and cultural norms of such cultural icons. Pop culture, therefore, often stands in stark contrast to traditional Anglo Saxon culture that has ostensibly formed the basis of the cultural institutions of government, economy, education, and the standard media (conservative by nature). The registers of speech associated with education, for example, are academic registers that have been determined by academic conventions that have accrued over a good deal of time—they are not necessarily contemporary or linked to pop stars. *See* **genres, registers**.

## Positive evidence

Actual speech that is presented to a child in the process of language acquisition. It is positive evidence in the sense that the child acquires the language that he or she hears and sees demonstrated, inferring the rules of grammar according to the forms and patterns that make up his or her input/intake, and not through the negative feedback of error correction by teachers.

Positive evidence comes from the actual speech of caregivers to which the child is exposed. The evidence of how forms and structures are correctly made, therefore, is drawn from the data she/he receives as linguistic input; according to some theoretical approaches, the child's theories are constrained in some way by his or her internal LMC or LAD. The child acquirer develops his or her hypotheses, which he or she, then, tests against further evidence in the linguistic and social environment. The term *positive evidence* is usually contrasted with *negative evidence*, which is typically provided through direct instruction by teachers who want to prevent learners from making errors and making a habit out of them. *See* **hypothesis testing, input, intake, negative evidence**.

## Poverty of the stimulus

The argument that the input for acquisition is simply too weak and corrupt for a child to reconstruct the grammar of a language successfully (Cook 1988: 55, 1993: 207–208). Children hear sentence fragments, performance errors (and repairs), and other ungrammatical utterances; yet, they learn to generate all the grammatical utterances of the language they are acquiring. It is also known as "Plato's problem," given mainly by generativists in their claims of an innate, Universal Grammar (UG).

It is argued that children demonstrate knowledge of language that they could not have heard in their input, from the speech of various caretakers in their environments. (They do not repeat back what they've heard, but reconstruct an abstract grammar of their target language from the ground up.) This knowledge of language, therefore, must be innate, hardwired into the brains of children via a biological endowment (through the instructions given by their DNA). In addition, if we compare (a) what goes into the child's mind, his or her Language Acquisition Device (or LAD), now termed UG, with (b) what comes out (the knowledge that he or she demonstrates), we can determine the types of knowledge the brain supplies to the task of acquisition.

Many recent approaches reject these basic assumptions, in particular, those that try to qualify what must be innate (e.g., developmental models). Granted, the language faculty is uniquely human, and language is the sole property of human beings (as far as we know). All humans acquire language, and nonhumans don't. Nevertheless, not enough is known about the child's input to say conclusively that the child cannot possibly acquire a native language without the help of an innate grammar (UG). Children may have general learning abilities that make it possible for them to attend to the language(s) of their environments and figure it out, through interactions with speakers. They construct and test their theories and hypotheses of the nature of their target language as they develop. *See* **constructivism, developmental models, hypothesis testing, input, interaction, interactionism, Language-Making Capacity, operating principles**.

### Pragmatic knowledge

Knowing how language works as a behavior, its functions in interaction with other members of a community, and the speech norms of that community. It is part of a child's communicative competence that goes beyond merely being able to construct a well-formed sentence in a language (linguistic competence).

Children gradually acquire the ability to use language to express their intentions, from merely gesturing (or squirming) to expression in words (speech acts). For example, they learn to label things, complain, and make requests. But, they also learn the subtle ways these basic functions of speech are communicated (expressed) in their communities, through interaction (trial and error) and observing the behaviors of others. In SLA, particularly by adults, pragmatic knowledge may be transferred from the native language until it develops in the new language. In that all aspects of a native language are culturally transmitted, we should expect that language-specific behaviors also need to be learned—they may depend somewhat on social–psychological factors such as attitude and motivation. *See also* **communicative competence, cultural literacy, discourse knowledge, Piaget, sociolinguistic knowledge, social–psychological factors, speech act, transfer**.

### Prescriptive (grammar)

An approach to language instruction that gives rules for correctly forming utterances in a language; often associated with language teachers.

*Prescriptivists* are those who express strong preferences for keeping rules of correctness and who make strong judgments about proper, correct, or "educated" *usage* according to some national or international model or set of *standards*. Any form or usage that differs (or *deviates*, a term expressing distaste for a specific language behavior) from the standard is considered an error. A prescriptive approach is like the physician who writes out a *prescription*. "Take two aspirins, get plenty of rest, read this grammar book, and do plenty of exercises. Your grammar should be better in the morning. See me again in two weeks."

Concerning English, there are two sides to prescriptivism. First, there is no single, monolithic version of English that all can agree on; hence, not everyone in society speaks a standard variety. There are regional and social varieties of English the world over, some that can best be described as nonstandard. Imposing one variety on all implies a basic misunderstanding of the nature of language in society. Variation is normal. Second, prescriptivists tend to equate their own preferred forms with "good," correct, or "proper" English. They may assume that there is only one right way to speak or write. This automatically puts dialect speakers in negative light: their speech is assumed to be "bad," or wrong, and that they simply cannot speak correctly. The problem with this is that all children learn the language of their parents and caregivers. And, as with popular culture, the speech of friends, siblings, schoolmates, and other acquaintances carries strong indicators of personal and group identity. The danger is, if prescriptivists see it as their mission to fix everything that's wrong with language, that they will alienate many people with a harsh and critical attitude, away from the culture of education. *See* **descriptive grammar, dialects, language ideology, pedagogical grammar, Standard English**.

## Primary language

A person's first language according to preference or importance; the language used most often in a multilingual's repertoire to gather new information/knowledge. Also, the most important language of a community. *See* **dominant, native language**.

## Productive knowledge

The type of knowledge needed to produce utterances in a language.

In studies of the acquisition of vocabulary by language learners, this involves the active selection of a term from a potentially endless list of possible alternatives (synonyms, near synonyms, or other alternatives). It is often contrasted with *passive* or *receptive* knowledge, the minimal kind of awareness necessary to recognize a word in some kind of context. For example, a language learner may easily recognize words from a list, sign, or menu, but when called upon to construct a coherent sentence in a new language, the same learner may find a great deal of difficulty in finding the correct word or phrase. Similarly, it may seem relatively easy to understand passively what people are saying, but it is an entirely different task to create original sentences in conversation (Nation 1990: 30–49). *See* **active knowledge, passive knowledge, receptive knowledge**.

## Proficiency/proficient

A term often used to indicate general ability in a language.

A (highly) proficient speaker of English, for example, can use it for nearly every natural function of language, from informal usage in everyday speech to the formal usage necessary for academic purposes. In other words, he or she is conversant with a broad range of registers of speech. A person of limited or low proficiency has yet to develop the skills necessary for participating in a wide range of language activities. The term *proficiency* includes fluency (interacting rapidly over a broad range of topics) and accuracy (correctly, according to native- or near-native-speaker norms). In this sense, it is both a qualitative and quantitative measure. *See* **competence, performance, relative proficiencies**.

## Psycho-social factors

Factors typically discussed in studies of SLA that include *motivation* and *attitude*.

Motivation is an individual's inner drive to learn a new language. Attitude is the mental disposition or feelings of an individual toward the target language and its speakers and what they represent. When members of a linguistic minority are in contact with a linguistic majority that is culturally dominant and antagonistic to minority groups (as in the case of former colonial powers known for exploitation and racism), emotions and attitudes can be quite negative. (This may also lead to strengthened ties and a sense of solidarity among language minority members.) As a consequence, a particular individual may be highly motivated to learn a language such as English for instrumental reasons (for economic survival and to support family members locally and abroad), but also have a negative attitude toward English and its speakers, making assimilation difficult, at best, and rendering language learning slow and tedious. Entire social groups (ethnic enclaves) may have ambivalent feelings about cultural assimilation when there are unresolved conflicts (especially, regarding the after-effects of political domination and resistance). See **Acculturation Model, attitude, motivation**.

## Psycholinguistics

The study of language from a psychological viewpoint. It includes the empirical study of language acquisition in children and the everyday ability to produce and understand language (Steinberg 1982: 2). This includes investigating production (planning and producing actual speech) and understanding (perception and comprehension of the spoken and printed word) through planned experiments. One should expect the lines between psycholinguistics and neurolinguistics to be increasingly blurred. See **neurolinguistics**.

## Pull-out classes

Classes in which language minority children are removed from mainstream classes (those taught in the majority language) for the purpose of focused, remedial (or developmental) work in Standard English.

Some educators think that this type of class may be preferable to strict mainstreaming (and the possible negative effects of submersion), but it may also carry the additional side-effects of creating a second-class group of students who are viewed as incapable of mainstream education. Those pulled out of mainstream classes may be marked for their inability, though perhaps only temporarily, to succeed in the general classroom. See **dual immersion, mainstream/mainstreaming, structured immersion, submersion**.

## Purpose

The reason behind a speech act; its intended result.

In discussion of situations of speech, purpose includes the *functions* of speech, for example, apologies, requests, instructions, complaints, and compliments. One may make a request or purchase, greet a friend or acquaintance, deliver a sermon or joke, tell a story, or do a classroom assignment. The purpose of the speech act in the specific situation of speech will determine to a great degree the language forms that are used. Purpose is influenced by the intentions of the speaker and how he or she wants a particular interaction to turn out (the outcome). A favorable response (success) is usually the preferred outcome of a request for something. The forms of language that one uses with a girlfriend or boyfriend, husband or wife when expressing affection will differ when discussing taking out a loan for a home, illustrating that purpose and topic are closely tied together. *See* **genre, participants, register, setting, situation of speech**.

## Qualitative research

A type of research methodology that looks for patterns of behavior based on in-depth analysis of one (or few) subjects. It tends to be subjective and deductive based on uncontrolled, naturalistic observation. It relies on single case studies that appear to be typical (to the researcher) of a particular environment or class of subjects—for example, minority-language children in an urban environment.

Qualitative studies, though they may be documented in extreme detail, are not necessarily generalizable to larger populations, for instance, to various different age groups (children and adults may not behave in the same given similar conditions). However, this type of research can be very intuitive (matching the reader's intuitions of real situations), producing a lot of information that can be used, perhaps, in other types of research. Controlled conditions often can be found once a particular type of result is identified, for example in the morpheme-order studies that were first carried out with small groups of children that were later applied to much larger groups (Larsen-Freeman and Long 1991: 10–15). See **quantitative research**.

## Quantitative research

A type of research methodology or design that features large-scale quantitative analysis of the speech of groups of people. Rather than observing naturally occurring phenomena, a quantitative study may focus on the relative occurrence of one particular form in a large corpus of empirical data. Quantitative research paradigms tend to be completely objective, data-driven, and inductive (looking for patterns in the data). They involve controlled experiments that can be replicated (repeated with consistent results) in similar environments. Importantly, a quantitative study will produce results that can be generalized across larger populations (Larsen-Freeman and Long 1991: 10–15). See **CHILDES, qualitative research**.

## Recessive language

In bi- or multilingual or diglossic situations, it stands in opposition to culturally *dominant* language according to a (Mendelian) genetic model; a language of lesser influence. A recessive language gradually recedes (in a sense, loses ground to the dominant language variety) in domains of usage and in numbers of speakers. (It shrinks in terms of the number of domains of usage, and in terms of the size of the speech community.) Minority languages are typically recessive in one sense or the other because of the high status of English.

In almost all situations of language contact, one language takes the role of cultural or social leadership or dominance because of its association with groups of influence and power (in government, education, the economy, the media, and so on). It is, therefore, useful in a wide range of situations. The other language varieties are reduced to lesser social roles as a consequence. The imbalance results from the hierarchical social relationships among cultural and ethnic groups, a process known as *social stratification*. By association, the language varieties that belong to groups variously ranked are also socially stratified, with varieties ranked according to the range and depth of their influence. In such situations, speakers of recessive languages in the process of shift, because of their receding influence, may choose to change over to the culturally dominant variety. *See* **attrition, contact, diglossia, dominant language, High-Low language status, language maintenance, shift.**

## Recipient

A language variety into which borrowed items are adopted. It is the borrowing language system. *See* **borrowing, contact phenomena, and donor.**

## Recognition point

*See* **cohort model.**

## Regional dialect

The variety of speech associated with a particular region, for example, the Southern American dialect spoken throughout the American South. Regional differences of speech have long been recognized by linguists, so, the idea of regional dialects or varieties has been around for some time.

In the study of regional varieties of English in England, numerous dialect areas have been identified. A shortlisting would include the modern dialects of the North, divided into Northern (e.g., Newcastle, Lancashire) and Central (York); Midlands, for example, Merseyside (Liverpool), Northwest (Manchester), Central (Nottingham), and West (Birmingham); and the South, divided between Southwest

(Bristol, Exeter) and East (Norwich, London) (Trudgill 1991: 66–67). In the United States similar names have been given to various regions of the North, divided into the Northeast (Boston) and Midwest (Chicago, Detroit); Midlands (Philadelphia, Pittsburgh), which is further divided by some sociolinguists into Lower North and Upper South; the South, including areas of the Upper and Lower South (Richmond, Atlanta); and West (Los Angeles, Portland) (Wolfram and Schilling-Estes 1998: 103–105, 135–137). New York appears to encompass a dialect in its own right, including Metropolitan New York City.

Dialect boundaries are seldom absolute, so one might expect gradual changes from one place to the next. It is evident, also, that particular regional dialects have, in fact, become independent languages, for example, the Romance varieties that spread throughout much of Western Europe that were originally dialects of Latin. Regional dialects are often contrasted with other types of dialect, for example, social dialect. *See* **dialect, dialect continuum, social dialect**.

### Register

The lexical and grammatical patterns of speech appropriate to a particular speech event or *situation of speech*. These patterns of speech are determined by functional (e.g., purpose) and situational (setting, participants) factors.

For example, a conversation in a classroom setting will require a particular choice of words appropriate to the topic of discussion and take in to consideration the participants, for example, the teacher and students in a classroom setting. The grammatical characteristics are expected to be as close to Standard English as possible (i.e., academic registers of speech). In contrast, a conversation in the school yard at lunch among peers may require completely different vocabulary, pronunciation characteristics, and grammatical style, often reflecting a nonstandard variety of English. (The effects of popular culture are felt most in casual, informal conversations.) Topics related to school necessitate certain word choices, and those that pertain to popular culture bring out quite another. Some teachers may have as much difficulty interacting with students on the playground as their students have interacting in a classroom.

Registers are typically described in terms of a *continuum* (or continua) of linguistic characteristics. For example, a *formal* register of speech may be characterized by a higher frequency of *complex* and *passive* sentences than informal registers, which have a correspondingly higher frequency of *simple sentences*. Formal registers are also characterized by *the lack* of sentence-final prepositions, contractions, and colloquialisms (slang and vulgar expressions), those features that some students frequently use in speech but are discouraged from using in formal written papers, exams, and classroom assignments. Importantly, there are steps in between, for example, interactions with an employer, clients/customers, co-workers, acquaintances, best friends/family members, characterized by degrees of formality/informality (on a sliding scale) along a continuum of speech events and corresponding registers. *See* **informal, informational, involved, registers, situations of speech**.

### Relational relativity hypothesis

A theory of why verb meanings must be learned from usage, while nouns require more simple form-to-meaning mappings (according to the natural partitions hypothesis) in explaining why classes of nouns are apparently learned before verbs and why nouns greatly outnumber verbs and other word classes in children's vocabularies.

While noun meanings seem to emerge the world around us (e.g., *table, chair, dog*), verb meanings appear to vary from language to language, for example, how stative and active verbs are treated syntactically, how transitive and intransitive mark subjects and objects, how verbs of motion are realized, and how active and passive (or middle) voice are expressed. Typically, nouns more often have direct translations from one language to the next, but verbs require explanation and instruction in usage. *See* **natural partitions hypothesis**.

## Relative proficiencies

Degrees of proficiency in each language of a multilingual's linguistic repertoire will vary, from relatively low to relatively high.

In a bilingual community, there will be those who are proficient in the ancestral (traditional or heritage) language and are also proficient in the language of the dominant culture. However, in the community at large, there will be those who are stronger in one language or the other; in fact, there will be those monolinguals who speak only one language. In many immigrant communities, there may be households in which three generations (or more) live under the same roof. The oldest generation may speak only the heritage language and have little or no ability (e.g., only a degree of passive or receptive knowledge) in the language of their newly adopted homeland. Conversely, the youngest generation may only know the new, dominant language of their environment; they may have only a passive knowledge of the ancestral language (or none at all). This helps account for what is seen in many bilingual communities, where extended families are the rule: a member of the oldest generation—an apparent grandmother or grandfather—speaks one language to a child (grandson or granddaughter), while the child speaks back in a completely different language. This type of cross-linguistic phenomenon occurs in the home and such places like supermarkets and malls, particularly when the oldest generation participates in child care. *See* **diglossia, linguistic repertoire, three generation rule**.

## Rememberers

Languages on the verge of extinction may shrink or contract (recede) to the extent that there are no more fluent speakers of the language. The only remaining members of the speech community are those who only remember a few words and phrases (hence, rememberers) and that an ancestral language was spoken by members of the community at a point in time (Campbell and Muntzel 1989: 181–184).

They may recall specific culturally important words, for example, names for foods and expressions for traditional celebrations and events, greetings, salutations, or other congratulatory comments. In so-called "token" code-switching, rememberers may sprinkle such terms in their speech that give the impression of a greater degree of competence in the ancestral language. In communities where personal and group identity survive language attrition, the ancestral terms demonstrate ethnic (or regional) pride, and the occasional term interspersed in speech in the culturally dominant language serves as a token of that pride and as symbols of closeness, familiarity, and solidarity; they may also serve as discourse markers for various purposes (Mertz 1989: 113–114). *See* **attrition, language death, language maintenance**.

### Restricted code
A highly controversial term used to describe relatively simple speech patterns that can, perhaps, be associated with undereducated people, used in informal situations, and characterized by gesturing and context-bound deictic expressions. The term contrasts with *elaborated code*; both expressions reflect cultural stereotypes and concepts of social class.

The terms *elaborated* and *restricted* code were developed by the late sociologist Basil Bernstein whose work focused on the links between language and processes of socialization, particularly the effects of culture and social class. The terms and concepts have been subject to a lot of criticism from linguists and other language specialists, though they have also been thought of by some educators as insightful descriptions of language usage in many classrooms.

Many linguists find his distinctions both subjective and biased. For example, he described restricted code as characteristic of the speech of members of lower social classes. It contains short, simple sentences, fragments, poor syntactic form, and much repetition; and, according to Bernstein, it is less logical than its counterpart, elaborated code used by the upper, more educated classes (cf. Wardhaugh 2006: 326–332). He claimed that elaborated code uses accurate grammatical order and syntax, complex sentences, propositions to show logical relationships, and a wide range of adjectives and adverbs. Needless to say, terms such as "accurate," "poor," and "logical" appeal to the biases of educators, but they are not based in objective fact. For instance, the term *accurate* confuses *standard* with accuracy. In addition, many of his descriptions are at odds with the work of sociolinguists who write of the *logic* (systematic variation) of nonstandard varieties, for example, in the work of William Labov (Labov 1972). While it may be possible to link socioeconomic class with lack of success in school, it is not possible to link a particular language variety with inherent intellectual capacities, despite one's prejudices. One should anticipate that his approach will be applied to the perceived deficits of SL learners. *See* **BICS, CALP, code, deficit model, dialect, difference model, elaborated code, linguistic relativity, register, standard**.

### Rule
A set of procedures on how to do something (e.g., how to form an utterance or language structure). In any case, language rules are not inviolable; many are simply ignored or replaced by other rules. For instance, *subject-verb agreement* is a rule in the "how to" sense, but not every variety of English is subject to that rule in the same or identical way. Consequently, we see patterns of usage that may vary considerably from individual to individual and from group to group (e.g., in regional or social dialects) because different groups may simply follow different sets of rules. Another perspective on rules suggests that *patterns* of speech exist in different communities, and these patterns are acquired natively by children within a specific community. When linguists sit down to describe these patterns, they

may indeed describe them as predictive rules. Nevertheless, speakers of one variety of English, for example, may have a rule that says, "Put an –s on a verb in the present tense when its subject is 3$^{rd}$ person, singular," and another dialect simply has a different one (it is not obligatory to put the –s on the verb). There is also variation within social groups, where patterns exist only in a statistical sense. *See* **descriptive grammar, prescriptive grammar, rule-governed, variation**.

## Rule-governed

While there is considerable disagreement among linguists on what exactly constitutes rules, it is axiomatic that language is a rule-governed behavior. That is, the patterns that we see in language can be stated as principles or laws that are predictive: they can be stated as laws in the sense of "how to do something" and not in the sense of "break this rule and you will receive a penalty" of some sort (according to a sports analogy).

Some approaches to grammar, notably the generative approach, see rules as determining what is allowable in a language. There are phonological rules (a set of instructions on how words are to be pronounced), morphological rules (how words are formed), and syntactic rules (the linear ordering of words in a language and the grammatical relationships among elements, for example, regarding the placement of verbs and types of nouns). Rules, therefore, are like principles of nature, akin to biological, physical, and chemical laws that limit the possible interactions among elements, and that require some kind of mental computation. Evidence to illustrate such a conclusion are grammatical mistakes (which cause native speakers to cringe). However, it should be noted that many such rules or patterns are language specific; it is quite a different task to state universal laws of language, a task that generativists have long dealt with. Another view, a developmental approach, is that language-specific patterns of usage can vary from community to community and from individual to individual. Young children, as pattern makers, observe these patterns and internalize them in the course of language development (perhaps as rules). *See* **hypothesis testing, Language Acquisition Device, Language-Making Capacity, Universal Grammar (UG), universalism**.

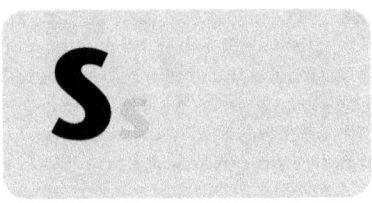

### Sapir–Whorf Hypothesis

A hypothesis of the influence of language on thought attributed to the American anthropological linguist Edward Sapir and his student, Benjamin Whorf (based on their observations of Native American languages and cultures). Sapir's conclusion was that we are all influenced by how our individual languages encode our thoughts, that we all look at the world according to the words and grammatical categories of our native language. Language and thought (assumed to be culturally influenced) are so deeply intertwined that each language also carries with it its own characteristic worldview. As a consequence, the English language is automatically linked to an Anglo-Saxon worldview. By implication, native acquisition of English would seem to ensure the acquisition of Anglo-Saxon culture. Whorf, however, carried it further to its strongest form, *linguistic determinism*, in which language is claimed to determine our thought processes, not merely influence them.

The first issue is bilingualism, itself. Some bilinguals may indeed be bicultural and able to "think" as monolinguals in each language. However, a bilingual person is not merely two monolinguals in one body (Grosjean 1995: 259). Each is a unique individual with specific linguistic abilities and sets of skills. In essence, a bilingual is one speaker with two languages. True binguality and biculturalism are most likely associated with the relatively rare minority of balanced bilinguals who have acquired their languages simultaneously. The ability to *translate* from one language to the other also points to the facility with which many fluent bilinguals can represent their thoughts in each of their languages. It's difficult to envision that a bilingual "thinks" one way in one language and another entirely different way in another, although biculturalism implies behaving in appropriate ways according to the norms of two distinct cultures.

It can be argued, too, that cultural elements of speech can be teased away from language, and that more than one culture can be represented by one language—for example, African American or British West Indian (Caribbean) culture as it is expressed via the medium of English. Current work in the analysis of literate, academic discourse, nonetheless, looks at rhetorical strategies that can be linked to various cultures in the area of *contrastive rhetoric*. See **Contrastive Analysis Theory (CAH), contrastive rhetoric, linguistic determinism, linguistic relativity**.

### Scaffolding

A term derived from the concept of a scaffold, a temporary platform used to support workers as they repair or construct a building (Cazden 1983: 6). By analogy, it involves providing support or a model for learning by demonstrating similar structures. In interactionist approaches, it is believed that teacher–student social interaction is important for the presentation of new ideas to ensure that they are understood by the child based on her prior knowledge. Therefore, scaffolding, as a technique to facilitate learning, features comprehensible input, the use of analogies, the teacher's direct intervention and encouragement, and the gradual increase of the amount and type of information that the child receives until the child can solve the problem himself or herself without adult help. *See* **comprehensible input, SDAIE, sheltered**.

## SDAIE (Specially designed academic instruction in English)

A type of sheltered English instruction for English language learners. It is also known as Sheltered English and Sheltered Content Instruction.

It is "sheltered" in the sense that minority-language students are taught according to a specially designed curriculum to teach content areas such as language arts, math, science, and social studies. Teachers use a simplified form of English (basic vocabulary) and specific methods involving cooperative learning techniques (students interact with other students), visual aids (e.g., realia) and demonstrations, hands-on experiences, and frequent checks by teachers of student comprehension (Baker 2006: 220). Texts are progressively more demanding, gradually introducing academic vocabulary items. Nevertheless, all instruction is in English, and the goals seem to be socialization (into language and culture) and *subtractive bilingualism*.

Sheltered instruction frequently involves pull-out classes in which students are segregated from their mainstream counterparts. The advantages to segregated classrooms is that ELLs are with other students who may have similar strengths and problems. However, by being set apart, they are less likely to interact with peers who are native speakers of English. And, the curriculum they are presented with may be simplified and less challenging with respect to academics. Some see this as "dumbing down" their course work, in a sense, and holding them to lower standards. To critics of such programs, it is another example of giving ELLs language instruction in the place of an education, masking deep-seated biases against language-minority students (Baker 2006: 217–221). *See* **achievement, achievement gap, bilingual education, biliteracy, literacy, pull-out classes, sheltered**.

## Second/subsequent language (SL)

A language learned nonnatively, for example, learned as an adult.

Many experts in education feel that either term focuses more on what the child does not know. They often become stigmatized because of their association with a remedial type of education (e.g., ESL) in which students achieve below age and grade level in academic studies because of the overemphasis on language learning. Another term is *additional* language, which places a greater emphasis on the proficiency already achieved in a native/heritage language.

Moreover, the term *second language* may be somewhat misleading. The ordinal number "second" implies some kind of chronological order, or that a person learns a first language as a child and a second one later on. But, many people around the world learn more than one "first" language; a "second" language may actually be an individual's third or fourth. Therefore, the acronym SL is usually used to represent a *subsequent language*, that is, one that is *not* learned natively. It is contrasted with *native language* (*NL*), referring to a "first" language—a. k. a. *mother tongue*. See **Bilingual First Language Acquisition (BFLA), subsequent language, second/subsequent language acquisition (SLA)**.

### Second/subsequent language acquisition (SLA)

The learning of a language nonnatively, in addition to a native language (hence, subsequent) often by conscious study. In some approaches, the term is associated with the ways adults learn languages later in life (second-language learning), for example, in classroom situations featuring structured lessons and rote learning. Naturalistic processes of acquisition obviously can occur in and outside the school environment, particularly in the environment of younger learners who interact with other speakers of the target language.

The acronym SLA originally referred only to "second" language acquisition/learning, but it did not take into account that many children learn two (or more) languages from birth. A portion of almost every bilingual community is composed of native bilinguals, those who acquire simultaneously both (or all) languages used in that community. In addition, the order in which languages are learned (one and then the other, or both at the same time) can have an affect on the outcome, whether one language is stronger or weaker than the other(s). See **acquisition, Bilingual First Language Acquisition (BFLA), native-language acquisition (NLA), sequential bilingual acquisition, simultaneous bilingual acquisition**.

### Segmentation problem

Represents the task that the child faces in isolating significant portions of speech when acquiring vocabulary items (words) and other grammatical information (e.g., inflectional and derivational morphemes) in his or her native language.

Words in every human language consist of individual sound segments or phonemes. For example, the word *cat* in English consists of three sounds, [k], [æ], and [t]. Essentially, segmentation is a part of the *mapping problem*, being able to associate a form or word with its appropriate word meanings (people, things, actions, etc.). The child must divide up the speech stream into relevant stretches of speech, that is, individual phonemes or combinations of phonemes that could possibly be a word or other meaningful unit (morpheme) or expression (phrase). See **map, mapping problem, phonemic awareness, phonological awareness, speech stream**.

### Self-assessment/rating

One's own personal and, therefore, subjective evaluation of proficiency levels in a language.

Such assessments are notoriously unreliable because of the tendency of some individuals to overestimate for reasons of identity and status (proficiency in a prestigious language is important for social status), or to underestimate abilities in a minority, low-prestige language. Some people (perhaps functional bilinguals) may rank themselves as fluent because they can talk fast (but on a limited range of topics). They may overestimate their abilities, while others who tend to be more self-deprecating will rate themselves lower than native speakers would rate them. It is likely that cultural factors influence self-assessments. In a culture where humility, politeness, and group loyalty are overtly expressed, people may choose labels that deemphasize personal achievement. In the absence of institutional and objective testing, it may be impossible to interpret what one intends by such ambiguous terms as "understand" or "speak" when proficiency is obviously gradient (Baker 2006: 26–27). See **assessment, testing**.

### Semantic loan

In the case of a semantic loan, a *meaning* or concept is borrowed from a donor language but without its accompanying form. It takes its form from its own native lexicon, pouring the new meaning into an old form (Field 2002: 8). For example, the English word *superman* comes from the German *Übermensch* (literally, "over, above"—in the sense of *superior* + "human being, man"). In linguistic borrowing, when a word is borrowed, usually the form and the meaning (the entire form-meaning set) gets borrowed from the donor language. See **borrowing, calque, host**.

### Semilingual (or double semilingual)

A highly controversial term that refers to an ostensibly bilingual person who is not proficient in either of his/her languages. It is associated with negative views of bilingualism.

The term originated in a serious of studies of Finnish immigrant children in Sweden (e.g., Skutnabb-Kangas and Toukomaa 1976) that suggested that their bilingualism was to blame for their poor academic progress because their acquisition of Swedish (the only language medium of instruction) was slow, delayed, or "retarded" (Romaine 1995: 260–273). This type of labeling is also controversial because it suggests that a child may have no language at all. It implies a type of cultural isolation reminiscent of stories of the last speakers of native American languages, whose physical isolation led to the gradual death of their native languages, and little exposure to English, which in turn led to limited abilities in both languages (Hoffman 1991: 27–28).

The term has been tempered somewhat by including the word "double" (so-called double semilinguals), that the child is merely deficient in *two* languages, not that she has no language at all. But, it is still implicit that bilingualism is to blame for the slow development of a child's academic skills. Discussions of semilingualism (by various names) have arisen regarding the language skills of ethnic minorities (Romaine 1995: 261); educators must be aware of the influence of ethnic stereotypes. There are a host of social (e.g., individual and group identity), economic (poverty, lack of educational background), and psychological (attitude, motivation) factors that can influence cultural assimilation. See **achievement, achievement gap, bilingual, formative testing, normative testing, testing, Thresholds Theory**.

### Separate Development Hypothesis

The hypothesis that each of a bilingual's languages develops independently of the other.

The Separate Development Hypothesis (De Houwer 2005) suggests that "... in learning to speak, children raised with two separate languages from birth approach their languages as two distinct, closed sets" (30). Consequently, for native bilinguals, learning a "second" language does not cause confusion or influence the acquisition of the "first" language—and the reverse, the first language does not interfere with the acquisition of the second. The importance of this is that they do not get confused, and their languages do not randomly interfere with each other. Children may mix their languages in various ways (e.g., in code-switching), but this is not necessarily a result of their lack of control. It is more likely a result of their input and the language mixing behaviors of other members of their community.

What seems to be at issue is to what degree bilingual children develop separate language systems for each language. Past studies have produced ambiguous results. In view of language mixing behaviors and transfer phenomena, there has been some debate about how language systems are represented in the mind of the bilingual, whether the bilingual child has one unitary language system, or two separate systems, one for each language. The answer to this question could account for much cross-linguistic influence. Earlier studies suggested that the child basically formed one general language system and only gradually learned to differentiate them, teasing them apart in a three-step process. First, the child begins to (a) develop separate lexical systems, and then (b) develops a single, unitary grammatical system (e.g., word order, inflectional affixes) that encompasses both lexicons, moving on to (c) eventually separate language systems. The theoretical question remains on how the child teases apart two separate grammatical systems. *See* **one system (or two)**.

### Sequence

A type of ordering, but generally restricted to the step-by-step acquisition of grammatical structures (processes). A sequence in the acquisition of structures suggests that patterns gradually change in the speech of language learners from simple, easy-to-perform basic structures to more complex, adult/native-speaker versions of the structures.

For example, question formation is learned in a *developmental sequence*. The child's grammar gradually evolves into adultlike language structures, for example, with a rising intonation on the last word to indicate a question ("You love me?") to the reordering of elements ("Do you love me?"). Negative sentences usually start out in child speech with a *no* in front of the verb ("I no like broccoli!") and develop into more adultlike constructions with the contraction *don't* ("I don't like broccoli!"). There are stages or developmental sequences evident in every known human language. *See* **developmental sequences, morpheme studies**.

### Sequential bilingual acquisition

When a bi- or multilingual person acquires one language (the L2) after the other (L1); also called consecutive language acquisition. Often, sequential bilingual acquisition is linked to additive bilingualism, when a person or speaker adds to her/his linguistic repertoire. The term is often used in contrast to simultaneous bilingual acquisition or BFLA, when bilinguals learn their languages at the same time. *See* **additive bilingualism, Bilingual First Language Acquisition (BFLA), consecutive language acquisition, linguistic repertoire, simultaneous bilingual acquisition, subtractive bilingualism**.

## Setting

One of the factors determining the situation of speech and, consequently, the register of speech. The setting, much like in a play, includes the physical setting/location (e.g., a classroom, school cafeteria or gymnasium, home, church), the *scene*, the emotional or psychological setting, often involving culturally determined behaviors and displays of emotion (joyful, introspective, sad), and, in some views, the topic (social science, sports, pop culture) (Hymes 1974: 55–56).

For instance, a funeral is usually at the grave site or in a church or chapel and the emotions tend to be sad or grieving. Topics of conversation are generally reminiscences of the deceased. Most parties are happy, noisy occasions in various types of physical locations, when people tell jokes or stories and talk about work or personal relationships. A class meeting at a school includes the physical location, and (one hopes) a degree of seriousness and attentiveness. Classroom topics center on the course curriculum (though teachers are known to digress). The physical setting itself may cause anxiety. Put together unfamiliar participants (authority figures) and the purposes of testing situations (to measure achievement or proficiency in a language for the purpose of advancement or graduation), and it is not surprising that some children feel anxious in testing situations. *See* **formal, informal, informational, involved, register, situation of speech**.

## Sheltered

A class or program that provides language minority students with special curriculum and content to protect them (figuratively) from being overwhelmed by an unfamiliar language and environment and school work that might be too difficult for them.

Sheltered classes often emphasize gesturing and visual aids to assist the learning of concepts. There is frequent repetition and summaries of the main points. Vocabulary is basic, and the syntax is simple, with no long, complex sentences. The teacher's speech is slow and careful, and she often checks the students for feedback regarding their understanding. However, the classes are typically closed and students have little interaction with native speakers (NSs). They also feature a lot of language instruction and classroom materials that are simplified in content areas of study. While this may facilitate learning in some respects, language-minority students may lag behind their mainstream counterparts as a consequence. Simplified curricula can be interpreted as "dumbing down" instruction and not holding language learners to the same high standards as all other students. In some cases, such programs have been criticized for appealing to the lowest common denominator in the attempt to raise academic achievement levels equally for all the members of a class. While overall test scores may go up, the more advanced students may not see any discernable improvement. *See* **bilingual education, SDAIE (specially designed academic instruction in English)**.

## Shift

When a community changes over to a new language, for example, when it chooses a culturally dominant or prestige language in place of a traditional, ancestral language.

For example, speakers of a minority language may shift to English as their principal (primary) language and abandon their native/heritage language. The new language may symbolize modernity, technology, and socioeconomic progress (opportunity), while the heritage language may represent outdated traditions, backwardness, and the so-called "old country." Shift has obviously had a profound impact on the indigenous (Amerindian) languages of the Americas and aboriginal languages of Australia leading to attrition and the extinction of many languages. Shift also regularly occurs with immigrant languages as in-migrants assimilate into a new language and culture. *See* **diglossia, domains of usage, endangered language, heritage language, language attrition, language death, registers**.

### Silent period

Believed to be a stage in the language-acquisition process in which learners are silent for a period as they build up competence in the target language.

As part of the Input Hypothesis, it was suggested that acquirers/learners go through a time when they do not speak and only listen to the language that they are acquiring. This was reported to occur in both native and second language acquisition. For example, children will go through a period of silence in the first few months of any type of language acquisition, indicating that they are attending to and comprehending speech addressed to them.

While this sounds intuitive (as do many of Krashen's hypotheses), the assertion has been questioned. According to Larsen-Freeman and Long (1991: 140–141), not every learner goes through a silent period (children are active participants in the acquisition process). Evidently, there is considerable variation among children in this respect. In fact, silence might indicate lack of comprehension at first, and, in some cases, indicate that the child is withdrawing psychologically rather than actively processing input. Nevertheless, some evidence appears to support Krashen's Input Hypothesis and his preference for input-based approaches (e.g., immersion programs that stress comprehensible input) rather than production-based programs (e.g., the Audio-lingual method which stresses repetition and oral practice). *See also* **acquisition, Input Hypothesis, Krashen, second/subsequent language acquisition**.

### Simultaneous bilingual acquisition

When a bi- or multilingual person acquires both (or all) languages at the same time. This term is of particular importance if/when children are native speakers of both languages, for example, in BFLA. At issue is the age at which the bilingual child is exposed to each language and language acquisition begins.

A child may be exposed to two languages almost from birth but not necessarily acquire them to the exact same extent. Some may resist acquiring one for sociocultural reasons, or the heritage language may stop being used because the number of domains in which it is used cease to exist outside the home (language attrition). For example, languages are typically assigned to domains of usage and compartmentalized: one language for use in the home and the other elsewhere in public domains, a situation referred to as *diglossia*. In that event, the linguistic character of the heritage language may be affected, too, as forms and structures are no longer available for acquisition because of shift and resultant attrition—including the loss of the numbers of native speakers and the loss of forms and structures. Children do not necessarily acquire a language merely because they are exposed to it (Myers-Scotton 2006: 327): exposure is not sufficient though it is a necessary step. *See* **attrition, Bilingual First Language Acquisition (BFLA), consecutive language acquisition, diglossia, native-language acquisition (NLA), shift, sequential bilingual acquisition**.

## Situation of speech

The physical and psychological circumstances of speech, or of a speech event. It is determined by such variables as the *setting* (the physical location, emotional background, and topic of conversation), the *purpose* (e.g., a request, complaint, or monetary transaction), and the *participants* (or interlocutors), including all people involved in a social interaction and the social relationships among them (see Hymes 1974: 51–62).

These three factors interact in dynamic ways. For example, in the typical student–teacher relationship, a classroom situation calls for particular accepted behaviors that may change according to the topic (discussing an academic topic versus a sporting event), purpose (a lecture versus pleading for a better grade or mark), and participants (conversational pairings of professor and student vs. two students from similar cultural backgrounds). For instance, in many US classrooms, one preferred behavior is for a student to raise his/her hand to ask a question. The teacher, as a social superior in this particular situation, has the privilege to recognize which student will speak next.

The topic of discussion will also influence the word choices. A discussion in a social studies class will call forth particular lexical patterns, for example, names and the terms typically associated with a military battle (*Charlemagne*, *invasion*, *resist*). A discussion of voting rights may use many of the same terms, but will also include others (*Susan B. Anthony*, *suffrage*, *register*). However, if any of the three basic variables change, then one would expect the forms of language to change somewhat, too. Say, the student and teacher see each other at the supermarket, a restaurant, or a theme park. (For many very young students, this can be an uncomfortable situation because they may not know how to engage in conversation with a teacher outside the classroom.) Or, when a student and a teacher talk about a particular sports or entertainment star. Their speech may be quite spontaneous, informal, and perhaps colorful when such topics are brought up. (And, teachers, particularly younger ones, may try to appear informal and approachable to their students.) Finally, when classmates meet outside of the classroom, the topics can be quite different from those in the classroom. And, one might guess, academic topics will not be a high priority. *See* **dialect, formal, register, informational**.

## Skills areas

Generally refers to the difference between content areas (academic subjects such as history, the language arts, and social studies) and skills areas that include everything from time management to basic interpersonal skills.

Regarding language, there are four types of skills: listening, speaking, reading, and writing. There are many assumed links between the oral skills (listening and speaking) and written skills (reading and writing), but there is not a lot of agreement about the true development of literacy skills, which evidently require considerable socialization and educational experience. While all normal children (those not born with some sort of genetic anomaly or other impairments) will learn a spoken (or signed) language, not all children will learn to read and write with equal ease and levels of skill and comprehension. *See* **biliteracy, critical literacy, cultural literacy, language skills, literacy.**

### Skinner, B. F.

One of the chief proponents of behaviorism (behavioral psychology). He viewed the language learner as having no specific ability to acquire language; rather, his view of language learning was that it was no different from any other kind of learning, and achieved through conditioned responses (based on experience). His behaviorist views were similar to the philosophical views of John Locke and the Empiricist school of psychology. His view is typically contrasted with that of Noam Chomsky, who assumes that all children are born with innate knowledge of (or mechanisms for acquiring) language. Chomsky's 1959 critique of Skinner's book, Verbal Behavior (1957), in which Chomsky challenged the behaviorist approaches, was perhaps a defining moment in the eventual development of the so-called cognitive revolution and the cognitive sciences, which sounded the "death knell" of behaviorism.

Language teaching methods based on behaviorist approaches (e.g., the Audiolingual method—ALM) view language along structuralist lines. As a consequence, particular aspects of grammar (e.g., nominal categories of case and number and verbal categories of tense, voice, and mood) are taught in sequence. The more words and structures one knows in a language, the better one's ability to use it. This is based on the concept that the ideal learner (e.g., children) learns the words and structures of their native language one by one. Behaviorist approaches also focus on habit formation, so curricula are based on practice and rote learning. This is in direct contrast to generative approaches that see children as specially gifted language acquirers that are helped along in the acquisition process by an innate (preprogrammed) language faculty (an LAD or Universal Grammar—UG). Children only need to be exposed to quality input for the acquisition process to succeed. *See* **Audio-lingual method (ALM), behaviorism, empiricism, Locke, nature versus nurture, structuralism, Universal Grammar.**

### Social dialect

A specific version or dialect of a language associated with a particular social group, for example, the cockney dialect of London (Trudgill 1999: 46–47) or African American Vernacular English (AAVE) (Rickford and Rickford 2000: 169).

All languages have dialects, various versions of the language based on region (regional dialects) or social grouping (social dialects). For centuries, linguists and philologists have accepted regional dialects as legitimate varieties; some have become independent languages according to the family tree model of language genesis (e.g., languages such as Spanish, French, and Italian that descended from Latin of the Roman Empire).

A language variety that is associated with a particular region or part of a country is called a *regional dialect*. A social dialect, by analogy, is a language variety that is associated with a particular social group, for example, an ethnic group. For example, AAVE, also known as Ebonics, is considered a social dialect. As a language variety, it is typically associated with African Americans irrespective of a particular region of the country. It is important to note that it is a language variety, not a racial characteristic: Not all African Americans speak AAVE, and not all speakers of AAVE are African Americans. *See* **bidialectal, dialect, difference model, language, nonstandard, regional dialect, sociolect, standard**.

## Social stratification

The tendency of society to organize itself hierarchically into levels or strata. The social stratification of language is the response of society to language usage and the unconscious association of speech with social rankings. At the heart of the issue is language variation across situations of usage and among social groups.

Varieties can be evaluated in different ways. As it is often noted, proficient speakers of a language can often quite accurately associate the speech of an individual with her/his social circumstances—occupation, sex, education, and so on. (Wolfram and Fasold 1974: 1–2). It can be evaluated upwardly, with prestige groups, or downwardly toward stigmatized groups. A prestige variety, therefore, is typically linked to upper socioeconomic strata, and a stigmatized variety is linked to levels of society that are considered unfavorable, lower class, and perhaps to some kind of perceived cultural or social deprivation. Technically, a stigma is neutral and merely a mark of some kind. The term, however, has taken on negative connotations so that it is customary to consider stigmatized varieties as those belonging to the lower classes or undesirable social groupings (cf. Wolfram and Fasold 1974: 15–17). The often-cited work of Labov (1966) that looked at the relative prestige of /r/ in postvocalic position in New York City showed conclusively how even one linguistic feature can be associated with social strata. *See* **deficit model, dialect, difference model, nonstandard, standard, variation**.

## Societal bilingualism

When two or more languages are used in a society. The term is often used in contrast to individual bilingualism (or bilinguality).

This society can be created in two ways. The first occurs when a conquering or colonial power comes into a locale, establishes its social and cultural dominance, and promotes the use of its language over that of all other (socially subordinate) languages. Obviously, this comes as a result of an imbalance of power (politically, militarily, and culturally), creating asymmetrical social relationships among groups. The reverse situation occurs when an immigrant group comes into an area already established by a dominant one, either temporarily or permanently. In either case, the nondominant (or recessive) group typically begins to learn the language of the dominant group for utilitarian reasons (for economic reasons), and then perhaps for deeper reasons of social integration as social ties become more lasting.

Individuals become bilingual one at a time, and the nondominant community, therefore, becomes increasingly bilingual as more and more members become bilingual (the dominant language spreads to other speakers of the less powerful language). The development of bilingual contact phenomena such as borrowing and code-switching typically develop as a result of asymmetrical social relationships, as members of the nondominant group borrow words from the dominant language (more than the reverse direction) and switch back and forth from language to language (for a variety of social purposes). The degree of linguistic contact usually corresponds to the degree of social and cultural contact. See **bilingual, bilingualism, contact, contact phenomena, shift, relative proficiencies.**

### Society
A term that refers to how people organize themselves into groups, sometimes used synonymously with community. It can refer to an official society of people united by common interests, for example, the *Linguistic Society of America* (a community of linguists), and it may refer to the larger, overarching society within which individual communities/societies exist. In this latter sense, it can refer to *American*, *British*, or *European* society, or other general characteristics, for example, *an industrial society*. Sociolinguists study the connections between society at large, and language usage, particularly how language correlates with social groups. See **cultural literacy, social stratification.**

### Sociolect
A *lect* or language variety associated with a particular social group—a social dialect. See **dialect, idiolect, lect, social dialect.**

### Sociolinguistic knowledge
In studies of NLA, a type of knowledge that children must acquire in addition to linguistic competence (the ability to generate well-formed sentences in a language).

In recent years, much research has been devoted to how children are socialized into their speech communities. Many language specialists have noted the daunting task that the child faces in learning to use a language according to native-speaker norms. In this view, the knowledge of language involves much more than just a mechanical ability to construct grammatically correct (or acceptable) utterances. Sociolinguistic knowledge includes an awareness of how usage varies according to social variables like status (which may include professional and other societal roles), gender (acceptable ways males and females interract), and cultural variables of respect (e.g., how one deals with elders in the community). See **discourse, communicative competence, discourse knowledge, linguistic competence, pragmatic knowledge, sociolinguistic knowledge.**

### SPECT (single photon emission computed tomography)
A sophisticated method of scanning the brain to measure blood flow, similar in intent to fMRI procedures. Unlike an X-ray, which can only take a two-dimensional image of what an organ looks like, the SPECT scan uses a special (gamma) camera that can construct a three-dimensional image, or projection, that (when rotated) can show how the organ is working.

When a test subject is given a task, particular regions of the brain become activated. When areas of the brain are activated, there is an increase in the flow of blood to the area in which the task is processed (where the event takes place). When particular radiopharmaceutical compounds are injected in very light, tracer amounts, their photon (a unit of light or electromagnetic radiation) emissions can be detected much like X-rays in a CT scan. The images that a scan detects represent places at which the specific, labeled compound accumulates. The compound may reflect the concentration of, for example, blood flow, oxygen or glucose metabolism, or dopamine transporter (a neurotransmitter that is known to play a significant role in cognition). Often these images are displayed with a color scale, providing researchers with important information about the chemical activities of the brain. *See* **brain-imaging techniques, CT (Roentgen-ray computed tomography), event-related potentials (ERPs), fMRI, neuroimaging**.

## Speech

Language as it is used, particularly when spoken or signed. In a restricted sense, it may refer to technical aspects of pronunciation. For instance, in the areas of articulatory phonetics and phonology, linguists study how speech sounds (phonemes) are articulated.

The term *speech* can also be used in a more general sense to refer to actual spoken/signed language, in contrast to language in an idealized sense. When discussing speech communities and speech acts, the focus is on speech in this latter sense. It refers to all facets of performance, from phonetics to semantics and the construction of meaning in discourse. Consequently, in areas of sociolinguistic and discourse analysis, all data comes from naturally occurring speech. It corresponds to the term *parole* in a Saussurean sense. *See* **generative grammar, ideal speaker, performance, speech act, speech community, speech stream**.

## Speech act

An instance of speech in which there is a specific effect (an anticipated response).

It is clear that human speech does more than state logical propositions or communicate facts. We also do things with the words that we use. A speech act is, therefore, speech that accomplishes something. For example, we make requests, promises, claims, pleas, inquiries, and so on. We curse, cajole, and criticize. The actual words that we use to do these things are called performatives, for example, "I bet you," when making a bet, or "I promise to..." when expressing solemn vows during a wedding. Another example is saying "I do!" during a wedding ceremony (by the correct person at the appropriate time). In written form, a signature "seals the deal," thereby becoming a performative when signing a check, loan document, or contract.

One way of analyzing speech acts (which has been adapted to the development of intentionality, expressing intention and will in children) is to divide them into three parts: (a) the form of the utterance (locution); (b) the intended function (illocution); and (c) its effect or desired outcome (perlocution). Children appear to go through phases in their development that correspond to these three fundamental distinctions. The first is the perlocutionary phase, in which children influence the people around them, but the behaviors that appear to have an affect are not necessarily directed to the listener (they may squirm or reach for something). The second is the illocutionary phase, when children become aware that they can signal their intentions to others in order to get their help in obtaining something they want. The third is the locutionary phase, as children learn to use language forms to expresses their likes and dislikes (Hoff 2009: 90–92). *See* **communicative competence, Piaget, speech**.

## Speech community

A group of people who share a language and perhaps a culture and history.

The concept of speech community has been controversial. Community boundaries can be particularly difficult to define, and the same types of problems arise as in definitions of *language* and *dialect* (See Wardhaugh 116f). Nevertheless, one can certainly speak at least of a hypothetical speech community, a social unit that shares a language, culture, history, and so on. Thus, one may speak of all those who speak, comprehend, and use English as a language as constituting a (rather large) speech community. But, as we should suspect, English itself is not a monolithic entity that is the same from place to place and from person to person.

Not every member of a community acts the same way all the time, so there is always variation even in the speech of an individual. Nevertheless, all members of a community typically exhibit linguistic traits or characteristics in various numbers and strengths. While members of a speech community use linguistic features to establish group identity according to sets of shared norms (and distance themselves from speakers of other varieties), they also show other cultural characteristics that are social (socioeconomic), ethnic, and political, as well. Though it may be impossible to find the *ideal* member who exhibits all identifiable traits of community membership, it is possible to find a representative sample. For example, a community of professors will have advanced academic degrees (usually doctorates) and jobs at a university (with various titles). Not all, however, will have identical duties. Some may teach, some not; some may hold office hours, some not; some may belong to learned societies, be on committees, participate in administration, and some not. Then, too, there may be other individuals who have some of the traits common to professors, but not belong to that community.

This type of definition of speech community stands in stark contrast to the concept of an ideal, homogeneous speech community proposed by those working within the generative tradition (for the purpose of establishing native-speaker intuitions of grammaticality). However, the generative definition is admittedly an ideal one that may not truly exist in the real world. See **community, community bilingualism, language ideology, ideal speaker, standard.**

## Speech event

The occurrence of language as a social event. In branches of sociolinguistics, it is a basic unit for the study of spoken intercourse, with particular attention paid to the interactions among participants and their roles in creating verbal (spoken or signed) interchanges. See **genre, register, situation of speech, speech, speech act.**

## Speech stream

Refers to language (speech) as it comes out of the mouths or from the hands of actual speakers/signers in a continuous stream, not as discrete words on a printed page.

For instance, in spoken English, there is a continuous stream of words, so much so that it may be difficult for nonnatives or learners who are not yet proficient to grasp where one word ends and the next one begins. This steady stream of speech is what infants and children hear as everyday speech, whether directed to them or not. Consequently, what a child hears from parents, siblings, and other caretakers in informal speech may be far from the kind of language one finds in a book; there are no "spaces" between words or punctuation marks to indicate phrase and sentence boundaries or intonational contours. See also **compressed speech, infant-directed speech, mapping problem, motherese, segmentation problem.**

### Split languages

A mixed language. A split language is a single language variety that has a split character (Myers-Scotton 2002: 246). It is typically split between the lexicon (primarily the content items) of one language and the grammar (and system morphemes) of the other. An often-cited example is Media Lengua, a language spoken in the highlands of Ecuador, which has the lexicon of Spanish intertwined with Quechua grammar (see also Muysken 1981, 1997). See **contact languages, mixed languages.**

### Split-brain studies

Specific studies of patients who have undergone surgery to sever their corpus callosum to a degree. Such studies have provided valuable information on how the two hemispheres of the brain function (see Hoff 2009: 47).

Some of the earliest split-brain research was carried out by Roger Sperry (later joined by Michael Gazzaniga). Sperry tested ten patients (with otherwise healthy brains) who had undergone a surgical procedure (originally performed in 1940) to treat epileptics with severe and uncontrollable *grand mal* seizures. It involved severing the corpus callosum, the specific part of the brain that transfers signals between the right and left hemispheres, in hopes of reducing the severity of the symptoms. Sperry and his colleagues tested these patients with tasks that were thought to depend on specific hemispheres and demonstrated that the two halves of the brain operate independently (Gur, Levy, Gur 1977: 125–129).

The brain is constructed in such a way that the primary connections from the body to the brain go from one side of the body to the opposite hemisphere of the brain (contralaterally). So, what the left ear hears (or what the left eye sees) goes to the right side of the brain, and the reverse, what the right ear hears (or right eye sees) goes to the left side of the brain, where the language center is on most (right-handed) people. When a split-brain subject was presented with an object or image in his or her left visual field, he/she was unable to name what was seen. (Those with the speech control center in the right side will experience similar symptoms when an image is presented in the right visual field.) Fortunately researchers have devised other techniques to locate brain functions. In recent decades, significant advances in technology have opened up new ways to see (metaphorically) into the brain. See also **brain imaging, contralateral connections, corpus callosum, dichotic listening tasks, functional magnetic resonance imaging (fMRI), functional architecture, hemispheric specialization.**

### Spread

Occurs as a particular form or feature moves from one group of speakers or language variety to another. For example, the characteristic r-lessness of New York

City is a result of its spread from the New England states and its cultural center, Boston. New York was originally r-ful (also known by the technical term *rhotic*).

The term *spread* can also refer to a language, as it moves from its original speech community to members of other communities by virtue of its cultural dominance (Edwards 1994: 104–118). English has spread to all parts of the United Kingdom, for example, to Cornwall, Scotland, and Wales, where Gaelic speakers were once a majority; in the process of shift, these different groups adopted English to varying degrees. The history of English in the United States is also one of cultural and political dominance. It first spread to speakers of indigenous languages but also gradually to speakers of other immigrant or "foreign" languages (e.g., German, Swedish, Italian, Polish, and Spanish). (One can just as easily say that English was an immigrant language as the colonists brought Anglo Saxon culture and language to North America.) *See* **dialect, shift**.

## Standard

Refers to a variety of a language against which other varieties are measured. Standard languages are also typically the "official" language of a nation, and the language of government, education, commerce, and the media.

The features of standard languages are typically determined by influential groups of people, for example, according to the speech of (a) an influential city or region, or (b) a specific elite or prestigious group (a culturally dominant group). For instance, standard French, Italian, and German are based on the speech of particular cities or regions, Parisian French, Florentine Italian, and High German, respectively. In China, the national language is Mandarin ostensibly based on the Beijing Dialect, considered to be the official language of government, commerce, and the media.

In Latin America, what people call Spanish is only one of the languages spoken in Spain, *castellano*, the language of Castile, a region and former kingdom within modern-day Spain, as a result of its political role in the Conquest and establishment of the Spanish Empire. Standards of Spanish are, therefore, based on the speech of European-origin settlers with ties to Spain and direct and indirect links between education and the Royal Academy of Spanish, in Madrid. The Academy is an official group of scholars and language experts, founded in 1713 to oversee all matters associated with the Spanish language. Members are responsible for establishing correct forms, spellings, and so on. Such an academy is also in charge of publishing an official dictionary. Members decide if/when a new word comes into the language, and typically reject or, at least, resist loanwords from other languages. There has never been an English academy, though proposals for one have popped up.

One language variety, therefore, becomes politically institutionalized (and enforced) as the language of education, therefore, the *educated*, making it the language of business and all official discourse, hence, the power associated with money. By association, the language varieties of influential people become the idealized, preferred ways of speaking and writing, containing the forms and structures that compete on a daily basis with forms and structures of other lesser (or minority) dialects and/or languages. *See* **dialect, nonstandard, standardization**.

## Standard English

The ideal or model against which speakers of varieties of English measure their speech for accuracy and elegance. It is the variety of English that is ostensibly established as the speech of the most educated and literate members of society. However, what exactly the standard is depends on time and place. For example, the English of 16th-century London certainly differs from that of 21st-century Los Angeles. What counts as English in the United Kingdom and the United States differ, and what one considers "Standard English" in both nations has evolved in the past 400 years or so. In addition, the discussion of standard language may be particularly relevant to bilingual studies in that language learners often struggle to learn a range of usages that encompass informal as well as formal registers of speech.

Standards are often associated with "official" languages. However, England has never had an official language or a national academy that determines standard usage. For England and its colonies, it hasn't seemed necessary to state explicitly that English citizens speak English, and a certain way. English is, however, the *de facto* national language of both nations. Instead of reflecting the pronouncements of an academy, standards are arrived at by a consensus of sorts of those speakers in positions of influence, for example, in government, the media, and especially education (teachers, textbook authors, and dictionary writers). It should be evident that Standard American English, for example, is not modeled after the speech of a particular city or region. One could argue, though, that it is patterned after the speech of the ethnic group traditionally with the greatest influence in politics (diplomacy and international relations), the economy (distribution of land and wealth), and education (how children are socialized into American culture) with a good deal of regional and individual variation. This influential group happens to be the Anglo Saxon founders from England and the masters of a vast colonial empire.

While most people recognize the utility of a unifying language (on the national level) and the establishment of a set of rules that apply to society, in general, there are dissenting voices to be sure, particularly concerning speakers of nonstandard, vernacular varieties. According to some language specialists, so-called standard usage is based on faulty assumptions of the nature of language, "to justify judgments that have more to do with race, national origin, regional affiliation, ethnicity, and religion than with human language and communication" (Lippi-Green 2004: 292). It follows, then, that the notion of a national language is based on an ideology, a belief in the existence of a single, monolithic (unified), unchanging, and almost mythological language called English. Ideas of Standard English can be entirely subjective based on what one has been taught in school, and opinions (prejudices) of how an educated person behaves linguistically. But, it must be pointed out that English, as a living language, is not static; it is always changing and growing. Most of us change the ways we speak as we are exposed to new forms and new social contexts. So, changes are typically unconscious; we merely opt for the form that fits the situation at hand. An example of this is the ever-changing usage of slang terms, which can become old and outdated in a very short time. *See* **formal, language ideology, nonstandard, registers, vernacular, standard, standardization, vernacular.**

## Standardization

Entails institutionalizing language forms and making one particular variety or set of norms the official and socially preferred variety. It usually comes from "above," implying that it is the variety that is used by particularly influential groups, upper classes or higher levels of society. Some forms and structures may also come from "below," from surrounding dialects and vernaculars associated with the lower classes as forms are adopted into broader usage. It involves codifying all levels of grammar plus, in the case of written languages, mechanical facets of language such as spelling, punctuation, and capitalization in formal situations of usage, for example, in the media, government, and education.

Regardless, the speech habits of all social groups change over time, as they have with American, Canadian, Australian, New Zealand, and British varieties (and dialects thereof) and in other nations where English is an official language. Conservative elements in government and education may want to slow down the processes of change, but they cannot bring change to a halt—it isn't possible. For example, schools may prohibit words or structures that they consider undesirable or less than standard (hence, substandard)—words like *ain't* and so-called *double negatives*. But, they can't eliminate such forms from popular usage. Such words and expressions come from vernacular speakers (below) linked to the lower socioeconomic levels of society, but they have a way of surfacing in a variety of settings. They are, nonetheless, frowned upon by those whose opinions apparently count. Thus, a child may grow up with consistent exposure to a relatively standard variety in the home, and, as a consequence of upbringing (the *where* and by *whom*), may have relative command of the language of school. However, another child from a different social group or part of the country may grow up speaking a nonstandard variety. And, as a consequence of his or her upbringing, he or she may have to learn the standard language in school. This is a particularly gnawing problem for vernacular speakers, when the language that is learned in the home is held in such low esteem that it has no place in the classroom. *See* **dialect, dialect awareness, nonstandard, standard**.

## Stigmatized

A variety that is marked in some way, usually in a negative sense. A stigma is some kind of marking; the term itself comes from the ancient practice of burning a mark into a person's flesh indicating that he/she was a slave or convict. Therefore, any language variety that is stigmatized generally is considered inferior in some way. This type of value judgment is obviously a subjective reaction to speech that is merely different, reflecting a sense of superiority that the person making the judgment reserves for himself/herself. Regardless of the informed opinions of language specialists, stereotypes and subjective judgments linger in relatively educated parts of society. *See* **nonstandard, social stratification, standard, Standard English**.

## Stroop test

A test developed in 1935 by John Ridley Stroop to observe the connections between perception and production in speech and whether or not external, perceptual clues effect word choice. When applied to bilingual situations, it demonstrates that, evidently, bilinguals can't ignore (completely deactivate or turn off) the language that is being spoken to them. Evidence comes from the Stroop test, one of a number of tests used to observe the levels of activation of each language during bilingual processing tasks.

Test subjects are given color terms printed in a color that does not always match the color referred to by the word. For example, the word *blue* might be printed in yellow ink, creating a mismatch. In a monolingual version, the subject names the color that the color term is printed in. When the word and color of ink are the same, of course, there is no problem. When they differ, the task is to name the color of the ink. However, they cannot completely disregard the meaning of the term itself; they cannot gate (filter) it out. Their reaction time is slower, and their responses are prone to mistakes (the Stroop effect). The bilingual version adds a slight twist. The task involves naming the color of ink in one language or the other, depending on the prompt. Results of the test show that bilinguals can't completely block out the other language. They have difficulty when the response is in either language. The test contains different types of words, but test subjects have more difficulty when the word is a color term. Most of the studies, however, have found that the task is easier when the color terms and the responses are in different languages, suggesting that bilinguals can, indeed, concentrate on only one of their languages. That is, they can focus on naming the color of the ink in one language without being influenced by the color term in the other (Romaine 1995: 95–96; Grosjean 2006: 51).

## Structuralism

A philosophical (intellectual) movement in the early 20th century that led to the first major school of psychology.

Structuralism argues that there is a "third order" of things separate from reality and the imagination based on the structures that organize human experience. For example, family structures determine the ways we behave, and the structures of capitalism determine economic behavior—as ideologies of a sort. Language, as proposed by such linguists as Roman Jakobsen, was seen as an ideal example (an *analog*); various linguistic systems comprised the structures of language. So, because the structures of languages are unique, the ways that different people groups express their thoughts are also obviously unique. Structuralism, as a school of thought and branch of psychology eventually gave way to different forms of functionalism, and then to behaviorism in the 1950s. *See* **structural linguistics**.

## Structural linguistics

Also referred to as structuralism. An approach to the analysis of language that focuses on the description of linguistic features in terms of their structure, particularly how such features constitute systems and subsystems. In a more narrow sense (e.g., in American linguistics), it is associated with the work of American anthropological linguist Leonard Bloomfield in the early half of the 20th century.

Inspired by discoveries of the languages and language families of the so-called New World, Bloomfield's approach paid careful attention to the analysis of words and structures into their component parts—as presented in his classic introductory text, *Language* (1933). In doing so, it has been a constant resource for field linguists charged with the descriptions of previously undocumented languages. However, it has been this same attention to the structural characteristics of language that may have brought so much criticism to structuralism by generativists, from the new ways of viewing language that emerged during the so-called cognitive revolution led by another American linguist, Noam Chomsky. Bloomfield's work was full of the wonder of linguistic diversity; this, plus his emphasis on linguistics as a natural science, contrasted with Chomsky's universalism and theories of innateness (Hocket 1984: ix–xiv; cf. Campbell 1997: 27–28). Description, however, is a necessary step toward theory.

Some form of structuralism in a general sense has been incorporated into many approaches to language learning, particularly by behaviorist approaches such as the ALM. It also forms much of the basis for CA in which the structures of languages are compared. Structural descriptions developed by Sapir (1921) and later Comrie (1989) have also contributed much to theories of grammaticalization, language processing (i.e., of different types of morphemes), and borrowing (see Field 2002: 25–40). *See* **Audio-lingual method (ALM), behaviorism, Chomsky, cognitivism, contrastive analysis (CA), generative approaches**.

### Structured immersion (programs)

So-called *structured immersion* programs are very weak forms of bilingual education. For example, in programs centered on teaching English as a second/subsequent language, they use a simplified form of English while allowing for some use of a native language or L1 in the very beginning. However, there is no L1 (heritage language) support, no books, lessons, or sustained effort from the teacher that make content available to the students outside the medium of English. The desired outcome is cultural *assimilation*, and the approach is *subtractive*, meaning that acquisition-learning of the dominant language is at the expense (neglect) of the culturally recessive, minority language.

In stark contrast, *two-way/dual language* and *dual immersion programs*, sometimes called developmental bilingual education (DBE), both languages are used as media of instruction. Language minority and majority students meet together in integrated classrooms where two cultures are typically represented, as well. Nonnative speakers of English, therefore, are in continual contact with native speakers who serve as models for majority language learning and classroom behaviors (the reverse is obviously also true). Each class period in the day is reserved for only one language, so languages are kept separate, while the proficiency levels of the students are taken into consideration. Classroom work is designed to be challenging and not merely to appeal to the lowest common denominator. Students who may lag behind have bilingual teachers to assist them. The goal of two-way immersion programs is typically cultural pluralism, additive bilingualism, and biliteracy. One obvious drawback is the expense of finding qualified bilingual teachers. Another is the hegemony of English in predominantly English-speaking countries. *See* **dual immersion, two-way/dual language, submersion**.

## Style shifting

Typically associated with the study of *African American Vernacular English* (AAVE), a social dialect of American English. In this sense, the term refers to the alternation of *dialects* (assumed to be personal manners of expression), from AAVE to a standard variety (and back) (see Smitherman 1977: 3; Baugh 2000: 105). For example, a speaker of AAVE may switch from AAVE to Standard American English based on perceived characteristics of a participant in the situation of speech. A style, in this context, can also be a group phenomenon, assuming that AAVE and Standard English are merely different ways of speaking the same language (a point that dialect specialists would dispute).

The term *style*, however, can refer to a number of different aspects of speech. It can refer to an individual writer's personal style (in a literary sense), or the speech mannerisms of a particular speaker (Wardhaugh 2006: 48–49), for example, the particular writing style of Hemingway in fiction. For instance, one speaker may choose to use a lot of slang, colloquialisms, and informal speech, and another may prefer a more formal, academic, or poetic style. In this sense, to shift styles may be a strategy used by an author to indicate a change from the development of a plot or story line by a (fictional) narrator to the informal dialogue among characters to capture the characteristics of spoken language (intentionally, for stylistic purposes). To avoid the confusion of terms, some linguists prefer to use the term *dialect shifting* when referring to the switching from one dialect of English to another, while others prefer *code-switching* (in that the switch is from one linguistic system to another). See **code-switching, dialect, register**.

## Submersion

Also known as "sink or swim," this is a term applied to an approach to language instruction characterized by placing language minority children into a classroom with mainstream students, with curriculum and instruction only in the culturally dominant language. The desired outcome is cultural *assimilation*, and *subtractive*—the acquisition-learning of the dominant language is at the expense of the culturally recessive, minority language.

It has the connotation of tossing a child into a river or lake, or into the deep end of a swimming pool where she or he can't touch the bottom and expecting him or her to learn to swim without the help of a raft, flotation devices, lifeguard, or swimming coach (Baker 2006: 216). *Structured immersion* is one example. The instructor may use a simplified form of English at first. However, there is no L1 support, no books, lessons, or sustained effort from the teacher to make content available to the students outside the medium of English. The desired outcome is complete and rapid cultural assimilation. See **immersion, structured immersion**.

## Subordinate bilingual (Type C)

A type of bilingual individual according to a classification scheme proposed by Uriel Weinreich (Weinreich 1953: 3–5, 9–11; Field 2002: 10).

Subordinate bilinguals, or Type C bilinguals, are those who have learned their languages in such a way that forms in a weaker language can only be accessed through the stronger language (one language is subordinate to the other). For example, the subordinate bilingual learning Classical Latin or Hebrew in school through written texts (without interaction with native speakers) must translate a text word by word in order to comprehend it. The obvious problem with this term is that it is difficult to call learning to read a language via constant translation language acquisition, even the minimum type of language learning necessary to produce a speaker who can function meaningfully in both languages (functional bilingual). Nevertheless, in the case of SLA, learners may pass through a stage in which the term *subordinate* seems applicable. *See* **bilingualism, coordinate bilingual (Type A), compound bilingual (Type B), semilingual, sequential bilingual acquisition**.

### Subsequent language (SL)
A language learned later in life, as an adult or adolescent, nonnatively, and subsequent (after) a native language or languages. This term often replaces the term *second language* because it avoids the problem implicit in the term *second*, that one learns one language than the other (that all acquisition is consecutive). It takes into account the fact that many in the world learn more than one native language. *See* **second/subsequent language**.

### Substrate
In a creole, pidgin, or other relatively mixed language, the language variety that provides the underlying grammatical system. In a community that has undergone language shift, the original language of the community may leave residual effects, for example, in pronunciation, vocabulary, or other particular grammatical characteristics (e.g., in syntax or discourse-level phenomena). These characteristics that can be traced back to a heritage language and culture are often referred to as substrate, or substratum (singular), as well. *See* **shift, superstrate**.

### Subtractive bilingualism
A situation in which competence in a second or subsequent language is accomplished at the expense of the native language. For example, instruction in a majority, prestige, or culturally dominant language may be emphasized to such an extent (with a sense of urgency) that a minority, stigmatized, or culturally recessive language is completely neglected, particularly in situations of language shift.

Bilingualism in such language minority communities is characterized by a broad range of proficiencies in either or both languages and the gradual loss of the traditional/heritage language. The process is hastened by the fact that educational programs do not foster bilingualism of any kind; they are essentially monolingual programs designed to teach only the culturally dominant language. While such programs are often well-intentioned, children are subjected to pressure to perform in a new and unfamiliar language and culture, and to abandon old, culturally bound behaviors. The term *subtractive* in nations where English is the dominant language has been applied to educational systems that ignore the language (language rights) and culture of minority peoples, that heavily stress cultural assimilation to Anglo Saxon norms by both indigenous and immigrant population. The term is typically used in opposition to additive bilingualism, which is essentially adding proficiency in an additional language to that of a heritage language. *See* **additive, attrition, bilingual education, immersion, mainstream/mainstreaming, SDAIE, sheltered, shift, stigmatized, structured immersion, submersion, three-generation rule, tracks.**

## Summative testing

A type of testing that summarizes students' attainment. This type of testing is generally given at the end of a semester of school year to gauge the progress that has been made in the four language skills, to measure the effectiveness of a particular program or approach, or to judge a particular teacher's effectiveness. Achievement tests in individual skills areas are also designed to measure a student's current productive/performance level on some scale (e.g., percentile). *See* **census surveys, formative testing, normative testing, self-assessment.**

## Superstrate

In the genesis of a pidgin or creole language, the language system that provides the lexicon. It is typically the language of a colonial or politically dominant group, so, in a sense, it is higher in terms of cultural or social influence (not necessarily linguistically superior). As a term, it is typically used in opposition to *substrate*. Because many analogies have been proposed between pidginization or creolization and language learning, terms such as *substrate* and *superstrate* are relevant to any study of bilingualism or language contact. *See* **substrate, donor.**

## System morpheme

A term similar in meaning to *function word* (or functional category) but inclusive of function words (with the exception of some pronouns and prepositions) and inflectional affixes.

According to the 4-M model of code-switching proposed by Myers-Scotton (2002, 2006) (also used to account for the results of language contact), system morphemes can be divided into two basic types, early-system and late-system morphemes. Early-system morphemes, similar to content morphemes, are selected for the meanings they express (i.e., conceptually activated), for example, plural forms that are included in the underlying representations of words—or, lemmas.

Late-system morphemes are thought to be activated at a later stage of production than early-system morphemes; they are required in the construction of a well-formed utterance. They can be further divided into (a) bridge and (b) outsider morphemes. Bridge morphemes are said to provide bridges; they link elements into larger constituents. For example, in English, the preposition *of* links noun phrases (e.g., "picture of my mother") as does the possessive *'s* ("my mother's picture). Outsiders depend on grammatical information that comes from outside the element that they accompany/mark; examples are agreement markers, for instance, the verbal *-s* in English that indicates that the subject of the sentence is third-person, singular in the present tense (e.g., "Fred hates cheese"). Other examples are case markers that express abstract relationships. *See* **4-M model, content morpheme, function word/item, Matrix Language-Frame Model, Matrix Language Hypothesis (MLH).**

### Tadpole-frog problem

An analogy used to describe how a baby's grammar develops from semantically based to syntactically based.

Evidently, the child's first internal representation of grammar is based on words and their meanings (semantics)—the tadpole. This grammar later develops into one that is like adult grammars, abstract and based on syntactic categories of subject, predicate, noun, verb, and so on—the frog. The problem is understanding how this development proceeds, whether it is a gradual process of increasing complexity (essentially, there are no tadpoles, only frogs), or whether it is discontinuous—that there is a point at which it changes from one type of system to the other, however gradual it may appear (Hoff 2009: 265–266). *See* **continuity-discontinuity, continuity assumption, discontinuous**.

### Target language (or TL)

The language being acquired or learned; the target of acquisition. The target can be the first language in NLA, or the second one in SLA. In the case of BFLA, in its true sense, the emerging bilingual has two targets. *See* **acquisition, Bilingual First Language Acquisition (BFLA), native-language acquisition, second/subsequent language acquisition, sequential bilingual acquisition, simultaneous bilingual acquisition**.

### Taxonomic assumption

The assumption that a new word in a child's vocabulary refers to a kind or type of object, and not necessarily the specific object itself. It is associated with theories of NLA and the early acquisition of word meanings.

Because the mapping problem seems so formidable for very young children (the possibilities of linking words and their referents seem endless), many researchers believe that children must have ways to restrict possible word meanings. They appear to do this by having basic assumptions about how speakers use words. For instance, when a child first hears the word *doggy*, he or she assumes that the term refers to a particular *kind* or category of animal. There are other similar animals that can be lumped into this category based on perceptual features (physical characteristics such as size, hair/fur, wings or legs, claws, and other aspects of appearance) (Clark 2003: 132–135). Language itself appears to be designed hierarchically into word families representing categories of objects. Word families such as terms for animals (e.g., the hyperonym dog) consists of family members (the hyponyms *schnauzer, poodle*, etc.). *See* **mapping problem, mutual exclusivity assumption, overextension, underextension, whole-object assumption.**

## Teaching English as a foreign language (TEFL)
Teaching English as a second or additional language to nonnatives, specifically in a non-English-speaking nation (where English does not have legal status as an official language). *See* **English as a foreign language (EFL), English as a second/subsequent language (ESL), English language development (ELD).**

## Teaching English as a second/subsequent language (TESL)
The field of teaching English as a second or additional language. It involves the methods and practices of teaching English to nonnatives, typically to immigrants (or indigenous groups) in the United States, United Kingdom, Canada, and Australia or other nation in which English is learned natively or has official status, a so-called English-speaking country. *See* **English as a second/subsequent language (ESL), English for academic purposes (EAP), English language development (ELD).**

## Teaching English to speakers of other languages (TESOL)
A rewording of TESL, typically to include TEFL. Hence, TESOL includes teaching English to immigrants in the United States, Canada, Australia, United Kingdom, and so on, and teaching it to speakers of other languages in countries where English is not an official language, for example, in Germany, Korea, Egypt, or the Russian Federation. *See* **English as a foreign language (EFL), English as a second/subsequent language (ESL).**

## Technique
Formal manner by which one practices an art (e.g., correct bowing technique for playing the violin). Extended to pedagogical practices, it involves a particular classroom activity that follows from a methodology. For instance, in the Natural Approach, a particular method known as Total Physical Response (TPR) involves acting out and pointing to individual body parts and objects to facilitate learning of vocabulary items in second language acquisition. *See* **approach, method, Natural Approach.**

## Telegraphic speech
A term used to describe a stage in the development of speech characterized mostly by the production of content items (e.g., nouns, verbs, and adjectives) and few, if any, function words (e.g., prepositions and conjunctions).

Children typically proceed from holophrastic speech (the one-word stage) to the two-word stage, and then begin stringing more and more content items together while they are still sorting out the function words that link expressions in ever-longer chunks of discourse (e.g., pronouns, determiners, prepositions, conjunctions, and so on). Telegraphic speech is similar to composing a telegram in which a person is charged by the word: leave out those words that are not absolutely necessary for communication. For instance, "Send money fast" may express a very complex set of ideas including desperation, need, calamity, emergency, or just plain begging. When a child says, "Me fall down," her meaning is quite transparent. *See* **holophrastic speech, two-word stage**.

## Testing

The evaluation and assessment of a student's abilities, either in academic topics or in language proficiency. Problems come from (a) the aims and goals of testing—what the tests are designed to measure and (b) methodology—how they propose to measure the results of whatever data they may produce. A particular problem occurs when goals are mixed, for example, when tests of academic skills are mixed with those that measure language proficiency.

One type of testing is designed to pinpoint problem areas that a student might be experiencing that can enable educators to intervene and help the student to improve. This can be divided into *formative* tests that are given at the beginning of a school term and *summative* tests given at the end of the academic year that measure how the individual has progressed. A second general type of testing is the *normative*, or *norm-referenced* test. It is designed to rank students (or groups) or to compare them with other students or groups. This type of test focuses on student performance on standardized tests.

In today's politicized educational environment, teachers' jobs and salaries often depend on measurable improvement in test scores. This presents unique challenges, particularly when comparing (a) native speakers of English against nonnative speakers; (b) mainstream, language and cultural-majority students against immigrant, ethnic and language-minority students; or (c) those from upper socioeconomic strata against those from lower socioeconomic strata. In some social environments (e.g., densely populated metropolitan areas), these three classification types can converge or overlap, increasing the likelihood of results that feed into prejudices against certain minorities. For instance, ethnic and linguistic minority status often correlate with lower socioeconomic status, giving the impression that ethnicity is a *cause* for both poverty and low academic achievement. The fact that factors correlate does not, and in fact cannot, suggest that one causes the other. *See* **achievement gap, formative testing, literacy, norm-referenced testing, normative testing, percentile, self-assessment, summative testing**.

## Theory theory

Not a misprint, a theory of theories, how children develop their own theories about the language(s) in their environment that they test and gradually refine (Gopnik 2001: 46–48). A theory, in this sense, "is an articulated set of beliefs that allow the deduction of expectations.... Indeed, conceptual development is thought of as a series of theory replacements or reconstructions, as over-simple theories are replaced with ones more adequate to the data of experience..." (Bowerman and Levinson 2001: 6).

In some recent work in NLA, one view suggests that children are born with a constrained set of theories of language (or their conceptual apparatus for learning languages is constrained somehow in the types of theories it can generate). To interpret the linguistic data they receive (the input), children develop a theory to account for its regularities and apply it to the language being acquired.

Accordingly, children go through the gradual honing of their theories (reconstructions or corrections) to account for the language phenomena they hear and see. For example, the well-known development of the regular past-tense ending *–ed* proceeds from an apparent rule (verbs get the suffix to mark past tense), a theory that eventually needs to account for counter evidence and irregular past-tense forms (*go-went*, *see-saw*, *sing-sang*). The child's theory must evolve to account for apparent exceptions. *See* **hypothesis, hypothesis testing, Language Acquisition Device (LAD), Language-Making Capacity (LMC)**.

## Three generation rule

The tendency for third-generation in-migrants to abandon their heritage language in the process of shift, stated as a "rule" (with many exceptions) that in-migrants abandon their native languages by the third generation. This apparently does not apply to speakers of some indigenous languages, particularly those groups for whom social identity is attached to proficiency in the traditional language of the community (Baker 2006: 77–78).

Generally, members of first generation of in-migrants are recent arrivals who are monolingual in a native (heritage) language. They may become bilingual as they gradually achieve proficiency in an additional language, for example, the socially dominant language of their newly adopted land. For instance, Spanish may be the native language, and a variety of English is learned nonnatively, therefore, they may speak a learner's variety of English. Members of the second generation may grow up as native bilinguals, learning simultaneously their parents' language (via normal, cultural transmission) and English, the language of the social environment of their new social networks.

The third generation typically has a choice (partly because their parents are bilingual and not restricted to the usage of one traditional, heritage language). They typically adopt the dominant, majority language, motivated by its usefulness in the vast majority of their social settings and by their individual loyalty to their newly adopted homeland. Members of the third generation are, therefore, native speakers of English (with all rights and privileges); in addition, they may have only minimal, passive skills in the language of their grandparents. This, indeed, is typically the case in the bilingual Spanish-English community in the United States, though the continuing migration of native Spanish speakers into the United States may give the appearance that Spanish is being preserved in all segments of the bilingual community. When language maintenance is a specific goal of the family or community, the process may be slowed down, but not necessarily stopped. *See* **attrition, maintenance, passive knowledge, productive knowledge, shift**.

## Thresholds Theory

States that an emerging bilingual must reach a turning point, or threshold, at which competence in both languages is developed sufficiently so that she can enjoy the cognitive advantages of balanced/proficient bilingualism, enough to handle the demands of a curriculum taught in a new or second language.

The theory is credited to the early work of Jim Cummins (1976) and Toukomaa and Skutnabb-Kangas (1977), which began with the observation that children who are still learning a second language often struggle in school settings. Critics argue that the theory is not specific enough about the types of language that must be mastered (e.g., academic registers) and that any possible deficit a bilingual child might have is most likely semantic, in the area of vocabulary development. She or he just hasn't learned the terms and concepts necessary for academic success, not that she or he cannot learn them. The problems that bilingual children may have in school are most likely attributable to relatively low socioeconomic status (SES) and the lack of preparation (exposure to reading in the home) and opportunity—middle-class children often have more resources and a greater amount of parental involvement in their education.

One aspect of Thresholds Theory proposes that higher levels of abstract thinking are only available to those bilingual children who are highly proficient in both their languages, presumably a native language, and then one learned non-natively. This neglects to consider the existence of native bilinguals. The main problem, as many language specialists see it, is precisely identifying proficiency levels and teasing out the much more general effects of schooling (e.g., in a child's native language), or the lack thereof. This is a highly debated topic in the English-speaking world regarding ELLs. There are two distinct issues: (1) overall proficiency in formal, written English and (2) the types of knowledge one gets from going to school. Though usually not included in the discussion is the likelihood that there are indeed many children who are educated in a native language (other than English) who would be able to transfer prior academic knowledge. Through the transfer of literacy skills, they can reduce the time necessary to acquire formal registers of English because they are familiar with academic concepts and the kinds of adjustments student writers need to make in written registers.

As an outgrowth of this theory were claims by Cummins in the early 1980s of two different kinds of language skills, *BICS* and *CALP*, the first obviously associated with informal, spoken language, and the other with highly literate, written forms. This distinction has appealed to the intuitions of teachers, who see their bilingual students struggle with an English-based school curriculum. But, such theories are open to a lot of criticism because they apparently (1) fail to consider a child's semantic and pragmatic competence while looking only at surface grammatical performance (e.g., on standardized tests); (2) they lack empirical evidence in the form of well-constructed research; (3) they are full of implicit, subjective judgments about language and supposed links to intelligence, and oversimplifications of the true nature of language acquisition; and (4) they typically understate the complex relationships among a child's language development, cognitive development, social environment, and experience in the classroom (Hoffman 1991: 127–128, 130–135; Romaine 1995: 265–273; Baker 2006: 170–180). *See* **achievement, basic interpersonal communication skills (BICS), cognitive/academic language proficiency (CALP, elaborated code), literacy, restricted code, testing**.

## Top-down

Approaches to language teaching that focus on meaning, deemphasizing attention to form. In the beginning stages of language instruction, the goal is for students to get the gist of the meaning of actual speech or when processing reading material, to recognize forms gradually, and to infer grammatical principles based on (positive) evidence, much as a child acquires his or her native language. It features interaction with native speakers and the unconscious processes of acquisition. (cf. Morley 1991: 87–88). *See* **bottom-up, comprehensible input, phonics, interaction/interactive**.

## Tracks (streams)

Blocks of classes that are reserved for particular types of students—harking back to the time when such practices were thought to be based on scientific approaches (and the philosophy of John Dewey) and along evolutionary lines.

In general, there are two kinds of tracks (terminology may vary) in the United States. For example, there are college-prep tracks (or streams) for those bright students that are considered university bound, and vocational tracks for those who seem destined to fill blue-collar jobs. One of the criteria for placement may be the ability to use Standard English; proficiency in nonstandard varieties of English and/or languages other than English are not measured, and consequently, do not count in assessing a student's overall ability to succeed.

Language skills do not equal intelligence—there are many successful scientists worldwide who speak no English at all. Despite this, many educators are biased against language varieties other than Standard English. And, because such factors as socioeconomic class, ethnic and/or language minority status, and access to academic resources and preparation may correlate in particular locales, one consequence is that social factors such as these figure prominently in assessment and placement in tracks. And, once one is placed into a vocational track, it may be difficult to "advance" to a college-prep track. The end result is that many students are unprepared for post-secondary education, that is, the community college or state college classes in which they eventually enroll. *See* **bilingual education, mainstream/mainstreaming**.

## Transfer

In SLA, transfer refers to influence of the mother tongue—the general tendency of SL learners to apply aspects of their first language to the *target* of acquisition (Gass and Selinker 1993b: 1–17; Sharwood Smith 1994: 13). It is perhaps most noticeable in pronunciation in the form of a "foreign" accent. A native language, however, can influence the acquisition of a second language in more than one way. It may involve syntax (word order and the knowledge of inflectional categories such as tense, number, gender, and so on) and in more pragmatic aspects of language usage. It accounts for "accented writing" through the use of characteristic native-language syntactic or discourse patterns.

Transfer has often been viewed as a barrier of sorts to acquisition in that it appears to impede or interfere with progress in a new language. It has also been linked negatively to outdated behaviorist views of language acquisition, and, for this reason, alternative terms are frequently used (e.g., cross-linguistic influence). However, transfer was preferred over the earlier term *interference* because interference implied random, uncontrollable effects of a native language in the head of a bilingual. It is now accepted that the influence of the native language can be quite systematic, though its effects are not always completely predictable. Moreover, transfer is not always negative. In a positive sense, SL learners appear to use prior linguistic knowledge and apply this knowledge to the target language, which allows them to use the language while still learning it. In addition, transfer can be positive in the transference of literacy skills from a native language to a second language. See **acquisition, contrastive analysis (CA), contrastive rhetoric, error (CR), fossilization, interference, language mixing, language skills, second/subsequent language acquisition, sequential bilingual acquisition**.

### Transitional bilingual education (TBE)

An ostensibly bilingual program in which the primary goal is to transition, or shift the child from instruction in a native, minority (heritage) language to instruction only in a culturally dominant, majority language. Transitional programs are associated with weak forms of bilingual education where proficient, balanced bilingualism is not the goal. The outcome is typically cultural and linguistic assimilation and, therefore, it is subtractive.

In some programs, for example, students are initially allowed to use their native languages for a while until they are transitioned into mainstream classes. Such programs are typically divided into two types, *early exit* (two years maximum of native-language instruction) and *late exit* (which allows a percentage of instruction in the native language until perhaps the sixth grade). Older ELLs in middle or high school may also enroll in transitional classes when available. Students run the risk of being labeled "second-class" citizens, "foreigners," or other pejoratives when they enroll in any type of remedial class, and ESL courses can be viewed as such. As one might expect, this can lead to cultural resistance by some ethnic minorities and the perpetuation of class distinctions based on level of education, socioeconomic status, and cultural characteristics. See **assimilation, bilingual education, English as a second/subsequent language (ESL), immersion, subtractive bilingualism, tracks**.

### Two-way/dual language programs

Sometimes referred to as *developmental bilingual education* (DBE). Both languages are used as media of instruction. Because there are two targets for acquisition, this has the effect of emphasizing the languages. Language minority and majority students meet together in integrated classrooms where there are typically two cultures represented as well through decorations, posters, announced meetings and cultural events, and the observance of special days. See **bilingual programs, dual immersion, heritage language bilingual education, structured immersion, submersion**.

### Two-word stage

A stage in the emergence of children's production of speech in which they progress from holophrastic speech (the one-word stage), to putting words together into short phrases, something significantly more complex linguistically.

For example, a child acquiring English may produce a noun-like expression (or nominal as subject/agent) followed by some sort of verb or predicate-like expression (or functor). Importantly, the order of two words is not random; it approximates the word order of adult speech (SVO in English). The child appears to be reconstructing the language from the ground up, so word order will never be random or the "word salad." Thus, an expression like, "Mommy up!" most likely is an expression, "Mother, would you please pick me up?" "Daddy shoe" may mean, "This is Daddy's shoe." It is important to realize that a baby's grammar is not adult grammar, *yet*. So, his or her grammar cannot be described in textbook terms. To baby, *up* is like a verb, and it is the name of an action or process. In Standard English, *up* is either a preposition, verb particle, or adverb of some kind. *See* **holophrastic speech, telegraphic speech.**

## Typological classification
Applied to languages, one of two ways to classify languages. The other is the genealogical/genetic classification (according to a family tree model). The intent of typological classification is to classify languages according to structural characteristics, for example, according to their phonological, morphological, or syntactic systems. Reflecting the nature of human languages, types, however, are not rigid or categorical in an absolute sense; they involve degrees (scales, hierarchies) or shadings of types. The goal is to uncover those characteristics that are common to all languages, language universals (Greenberg 1974; Comrie 1989). *See* **formal grammar, language typology, language universals, structuralism, typology**.

## Typology
Arranging and classifying items according to sets of characteristics. Applied to languages, the term refers to a method of classifying languages into types (representative kinds), for example, according to morphological types (language-specific ways words are formed) (Greenberg 1974). *See* **language typology, typological classification**.

### Underextension
Used to compare a child's word usage and the adult equivalent. In underextension, the child's word refers to a narrower range of applications or meanings than its adult equivalent, for example, when the word *kitty* refers to only one cat, or *dog* refers to collies and spaniels but not to Chihuahuas (Hoff 2009: 191). See **overextension, taxonomic assumption**.

### Unilingual/unilingualism
Having and using strictly one language, for example, a unilingual book or unilingual person. The term is typically used as a synonym for monolingual, and in opposition to bilingual or multilingual. Unilingualism refers to the state or condition of being unilingual, and the practice of monolingualism. For example, the goal of many educational programs is the skilled usage of one, politically and socially dominant language (subtractive bilingualism). See **bilingual, bilingual programs, bilingualism, monolingual/monolingualism**.

### Uniqueness point
See **cohort model**.

### Universal
A universal is a property thought to be common to all languages. It is often implied that the existence of true universals demonstrates that human beings are born with certain innate abilities and the knowledge of language.

There are a number of ways of looking at universals. For instance, in generative linguistics, there are two general kinds of knowledge represented by formal and substantive universals. Formal universals are the abstract principles governing, for example, ordering and movement rules. Substantive universals are the structural elements (primitives) without which analysis would not be possible, for example, nouns, verbs, subjects, and objects (Larsen-Freeman and Long 1991: 227). In typological and functional approaches to language universals, there are statistical universals based on the frequency and relationships of particular structures. For instance, statistically, in most languages of the world, the subject precedes the main verb (Hawkins 1994: 329). Implicational universals, in contrast, are arranged conditionally (as if…then propositions). That is, if a language has a particular property (P), then it will have some other property (Q)(Hawkins 1983: 19–22). Due to differing approaches and perspectives, some linguists also refer to absolute universals, properties that all languages have without exception (say, words or sounds/gestures), and relative universals, general tendencies in language.

See **generative grammar, language universals, typological classification, typology, Universal Grammar (UG)**.

## Universal Grammar (UG)

According to generative approaches, children are born with innate knowledge of language known as Universal Grammar (UG). Its main concern is cognition, the internal structure of the human mind.

Current conceptualizations of UG, however, need to be understood in the context of evolving and expanding generative theory. In the literature, terms may depend on the age (copyright date) of the text. For example, some definitions reflect Government and Binding (GB) theory, while earlier ones may reflect the version known as Principles and Parameters. At this writing, the current version is known as Optimality Theory (or OT), which is ostensibly more generalized (and abstract). As a consequence, terms and the nature of the claims have evolved, as well.

The original conceptualization of an UG was based on the assertion that children should not be able to acquire language based on the deficient and poor quality of the input data they receive (the *poverty of the stimulus argument*). Their input is deficient in two respects. First, they hear *performance* errors (mistakes, slips of the tongue, false starts, and ungrammaticality due to the effects of online, real-time communication), so it is "degenerate" as a result. Second, it is grossly underspecified (insufficient or meager) in that all the child essentially hears is *positive evidence*, with little or no corrective feedback. The child must come up with an internalized grammar that is capable of generating an infinite number of possibilities (to handle novel utterances) from a limited number of elements (words and rules). Positing the existence of UG is an attempt to explain how they acquire their native language(s) so quickly, efficiently, effortlessly, and in a predictable order, without the aid of overt instruction. Because knowledge of the universal characteristics is innate, native-language acquisition is merely learning which particular aspects of this underlying, Universal Grammar apply to the specific language being acquired.

This view of an innate, UG, however, has come under a lot of criticism. One is of the nature of the input—a vast majority of the child's input consists of well-formed sentences (Larsen-Freeman and Long 1991: 228). Another is, perhaps, more general: If all people share the same knowledge or underlying principles of language, then, why are languages not more alike? There is also ongoing controversy about the nature of the human mind/brain and whether language acquisition is a result of a general learning capacity. Because of its near ubiquitous role in language studies in the1960s, 1970s, and later, generative linguistics (or grammars) are typically included in discussions of bilingual acquisition, in spite of its perceived flaws and association with nativist views of language (see, e.g., Larsen-Freeman and Long 1991: 114–116; Hoff 2009: 25–27). *See* **domain, generative grammar, Language Acquisition Device (LAD), performance, positive evidence, poverty of the stimulus**.

## Universalism

The philosophical view that all human beings have deep, underlying similarities or universals; that all human beings have shared, universal capacities based on their shared humanity (encoded in human DNA), and especially the faculty of language. This has been the dominant view in linguistics since the late 1950s and the development of the cognitive sciences (and Chomskyan linguistics). It is typically used in opposition to *linguistic relativity*, which emphasizes the incredible diversity among human beings and their languages. *See* **linguistic relativity, Sapir–Whorf Hypothesis**.

## Usage

How *language* (or speech) actually occurs as a social behavior; language out there "in the world," so to speak. The term *common usage* often refers to the colloquial way a term is used, or according to *vernacular* usage. This contrasts with the way in which a technical term is used, for instance, the ways linguists use common words according to highly specialized definitions. For example, the term *accent* usually means the way a people sound when they speak, a French accent or Brooklyn accent; its technical usage refers to *stress* (how loudly a particular syllable is pronounced), or to a diacritic applied to written forms (Spanish *está*, indicating stress on last syllable). *See* **dialect, genre, speech, variation, vernacular**.

## Utterance

A neutral term used to describe units of speech larger than the individual word due to the many conflicting and/or vague definitions of such terms as phrase or (complete) sentence.

Because of the inability to classify the speech of children according to the formal characteristics of adult speech, the things that a child says cannot always be described as complete sentences, clauses, or even according to specific types of phrases. At particular stages of acquisition, one word may be like a sentence in adult speech (i.e., the one-word stage, or holophrastic speech). The neutral term *utterance*, therefore, includes single words and larger groupings of words. *See* **mean length of utterance (MLU)**.

## Variation

The variable usage of forms in the performance of speech in such areas as pronunciation, lexicon, and grammar. Variation can depend on situations of usage, for example, *registers* of speech, and on the circumstances of acquisition, for example, in the acquisition/learning of regional and social *dialects* of a language. There is also individual variation in the sense that we do not speak the same way in every single personal encounter; our speech will vary according to the *genre*. And, we would not expect a person born and raised in Los Angeles, California, to speak in the same identical ways as one born and raised in Ipswich, Suffolk County. Their speech will differ (vary) in pronunciation, lexicon, and syntax (to perhaps a lesser degree), even without having to consider genre, though they both might consider themselves quite correct. See **dialect, genre, register, speech**.

## Vernacular

A locally based speech variety, particularly the variety of language learned natively in the home and based on a *regional* or *social dialect*.

All varieties of English share most of their linguistic features with each other. The core remains intact, particularly concerning the larger issues of grammar and vocabulary. Most differences are relative; there may be subtle differences in pronunciation (e.g., whether or how one pronounces the "r" sound in words like *car*) or the choice of a few different words. There may be noticeable differences between American and British varieties, but few that block understanding. When looking at the differences among national standards, the differences will seem especially minimal, but this is usually by design. The similarities are intentional to preserve continuity and to provide access to a shared literature.

Vernaculars, in contrast, may diverge considerably. Wald (1984) distinguishes the term *standard* from *vernacular*, noting that a national standard of English is not ostensibly modeled after the speech of a particular group of people or locale. It is supposed to represent the ideal form of linguistic communication that all members of a nation or society are to use in public discourse. The variety of a language that is learned in the home as a native language, however, is typically the dialect of a locally based speech community, with its own community standards of behavior and individual demographic (ethnic and socioeconomic) makeup. From a strictly linguistic point of view, the standard is no less a dialect than any other. Vernaculars, however, tend to differ from each other in pronunciation and vocabulary, and to a lesser extent in grammar (syntax and morphology). The fact that differences are minimal, despite our subjective reactions and biases, gives credibility and a unity to the concept of English, bringing together national varieties such as American, British, and Australian English and all the dialects thereof (Wald 1984: 17). So, we all learn a vernacular from caregivers, parents, siblings, and other members of our immediate social environment. One may *think* that it is (relatively) standard, but that depends on factors not under personal control (e.g., the circumstances of birth). *See* **deficit model, dialect, difference model, nonstandard, standard, Standard English**.

### Wernicke's aphasia (also known as sensory aphasia, syntactic aphasia)

A brain disorder (aphasia) with a set of symptoms associated with an injury to *Wernicke's area*.

Patients with Wernicke's aphasia have no trouble speaking; they are quite fluent. Their speech, however, tends to be full of strange word choices and somewhat scrambled syntax. In the most severe cases, the output may consist of a type of paraphasia (disordered speech) filled with nonsense words (words that sound made up), or neologistic jargon (Goodglass 210). Comprehension is poor even concerning common words, and more so with sentences. Lexical access is very limited; while speech may be very rapid, it appears empty of meaning. In contrast to Broca's aphasics, Wernicke's patients are unaware of their many errors. Syntactically, their utterances have standard noun and verb morphology, function words, and word order, but phrasal chunks (expressions) will appear farfetched. In other words, an English-speaking Wernicke's aphasic will sound as if she is speaking English, but it will be almost totally incomprehensible—called *jargon aphasia* in severe forms (Goodglass 1993: 210–211). *See* **aphasia, bilingual aphasias, Broca's aphasia, CT, fMRI, MRI, neuroimaging, Wernicke's aphasia**.

### Wernicke's area

An area of the brain located in the left hemisphere in the lower posterior portion of the first temporal gyrus. It was named after Carl Wernicke, who in 1874 wrote of a region of the brain responsible for comprehension of auditory (hearing) messages. Wernicke helped develop a model of brain organization when he proposed that this posterior region was connected to the anterior portion (Broca's area). Hence, an injury to this region would produce a disorder in which the articulatory processes and auditory comprehension are left intact, but access to the lexicon (word retrieval) is blocked (Goodglass 1993: 18–19, 40–42). The work of Wernicke and others such as Broca have formed the basis for connectionist models of brain organization. *See* **aphasia, Broca's aphasia, Broca's area, connectionism/connectionist models, fMRI, MRI, Wernicke's aphasia, Wernicke's area**.

### Whole language

A philosophical approach to literacy instruction that does not divide language into its elements (sounds, sound patterns, words, and grammatical characteristics such as tense on verbs, countability on nouns, and so on), but looks at language as a whole as it occurs naturally in context. It is typically associated with top-down teaching methodologies, and its focus is on meaning (as opposed to form as in a bottom-up approaches like *phonics*).

It is usually linked to researchers such as Stephen Krashen who was greatly influenced by cognitivism and a reaction to behaviorist methods. Its focus is on meaning, minimizing attention to form and the specifics of language. A central idea is that children will acquire literacy skills as they acquire a language and that they will eventually and successfully infer grammatical principles by exposure to quality input. In some specific programs, teachers were discouraged from error correction (no red ink, please) because criticism may slow down the acquisition process due to increased attention to form and increasing the so-called affective filter. (Children may become worried about making mistakes.) It has not been without its critics. Many reading specialists prefer an eclectic type of approach that includes some phonics-based instruction. *See* **bottom-up, interaction/interactive, phonics, top-down**.

### Whole-object assumption

In some theories of NLA and the early acquisition of word meanings, it is the assumption that a child has that a new word refers to the entire object being named, not to a part or a group of similar objects.

Because, in theory, the possibilities of linking words and their referents seem endless (the mapping problem), many researchers believe that children must have certain strategies to restrict possible word meanings. They appear to have basic assumptions about how people use words that constrain the number of possible referents. The whole-object assumption is one of a set of presuppositions that young children apparently have. It suggests that a child assumes (a "built-in" bias) that the adult is selecting an object as the intended referent when saying (or signing) an unfamiliar word (Clark 2003: 132–134). For example, when a child sees his mother point to something and utter a word, he/she assumes that the mother is referring to (or naming) an object. The word being introduced refers to the whole thing and not characteristics (like color or size), individual parts (like tails or noses), or clusters of objects in a particular area. For instance, the word *doggy* refers to the entire animal, not just its nose or tail or to a group of animals (dogs and cats). *See* **mapping problem, mutual exclusivity assumption, overextension, taxonomic assumption, underextension**.

### Word

A unit of meaning, often thought to be the smallest unit of meaning in a language (by non-linguists). However, there are many definitions depending on perspective.

Words typically consist of smaller units called morphemes. For example, a single word like *biology* consists of two units, *bio-* (meaning "life") and *-logy* (meaning "study of"). Importantly, words are formed differently in different languages. What is considered a "word" in one language may not be a word in another. For example, in languages like Russian and, to a lesser extent, English (so-called synthetic languages), words can consist of one to many morphemes. In contrast, in languages like Vietnamese or Mandarin (isolating languages), words consist mostly of only one morpheme. As a result, there is much discussion of word status (is *the* a word?) and word boundaries. How a language constructs words (its morphology) can also complicate descriptions of language acquisition. In highly synthetic languages, for example, in the Inuit (Eskimo) languages, one word can consist of many morphemes, with entire portions of a sentence incorporated into the verb. So, while it is relatively simple to describe the *one-* or *two-word* stage of acquisition in languages like English, the development of syntax in an Inuit variety most likely requires a completely different terminology.

In addition, a word as a grammatical unit (part of speech) is a word in an abstract sense. Therefore, a *grammatical word* is distinguished by its contrastive and combinatorial properties (e.g., an adjective goes with a noun) (Lyons 1968: 68–70). An *orthographic* word is one that occurs in print with a space immediately before and after it. But, what do we do with words like *flying squirrel*? What about compounds (e.g., *strongbox*)? Is *four-leaf clover* one, two, or three words? And, what about contractions? Is the word *don't* one word? A *phonological word*, in contrast, is a word in speech, especially where spelling has remained static for centuries while pronunciation has changed. For example, *wanna* is apparently a word (a contraction of "want to"): it is a unit, and it is understood as a word in speech. Similar observations are made for *gonna*. But, what about phonological contractions of *could you*, *would you*, *should you*, *used to*, and *have to*? There are also colloquialisms such as *ain't* whose legitimacy as words is questioned (by non-linguists). *See* **nonstandard, register, standard, standardization**.

### Word class
A classification scheme that organizes grammatical words into classes, for example, classes of noun, verb, adjective, and adverb. The traditional classification system for European languages generally is adapted from the word "classes" of classical Greek. Such classification systems are typically language specific. *See* **content word/item, function word/item, word**.

# References

Aitcheson, J. 2000. *The Seeds of Speech: Language Origin and Evolution*. Cambridge: Cambridge University Press.

Arends, J. 1995. "The socio-historical background of creoles." In *Pidgin and Creoles: An Introduction*, J. Arends, P. Muysken, and N. Smith (eds), 15–24. Amsterdam/Philadelphia: John Benjamins.

Baker, C. 2006. *Foundations of Bilingual Education and Bilingualism*. Bristol, PA: Multilingual Matters.

Bakker, P. 1995. "Pidgins." In *Pidgin and Creoles: An Introduction*, J. Arends, P. Muysken, and N. Smith (eds), 25–39. Amsterdam/Philadelphia: John Benjamins.

Bakker, P. 1997. *A Language of Our Own: The Genesis of Michif, the Mixed Cree-French Language of the Canadian Métis*. Oxford: Oxford University Press.

Bakker, P. and M. Mous (eds). 1994. *Mixed Languages: 15 Case Studies in Language Intertwining*. Amsterdam: IFOTT.

Bardovi-Harlig, K. 1995. "The interaction of pedagogy and natural sequences in the acquisition of tense and aspect." In *Second Language Acquisition Theory and Pedagogy*, F. Eckman, D. Highland, P. Lee, J. Mileham, and R. Rutkowski Weber (eds), 151–178. Mahway, NJ: Erlbaum.

Baugh, J. 2000. *Beyond Ebonics: Linguistic Pride and Racial Prejudice*. New York: Oxford University Press.

Bialystok, E. 2005. "Consequences of bilingualism for cognitive development." In *Handbook of Bilingualism: Psycholinguistic Approaches*, J. Kroll, and A. De Groot (eds), 417–432. Oxford: Oxford University Press.

Biber, D. 1988. *Variation across Speech and Writing*. New York: Cambridge University Press.

Bloomfield, L. 1933. *Language*. Reprinted (1984), Chicago, IL: University of Chicago Press.

Bowerman, M. 1985. "What shapes children's grammars?" In *The Crosslinguistic Study of Language Acquisition. Volume 2: Theoretical Issues*, D. I. Slobin (ed.), 1257–1319. Hillsdale, NJ: Lawrence Erlbaum.

Bowerman, M. and S. C. Levinson. 2001. "Introduction." In *Language Acquisition and Conceptual Development*, M. Bowerman and S. C. Levinson (eds), 1–16. New York: Cambridge University Press.

Brown, R. 1973. *A First Language: The Early Stages*. Cambridge, MA: Harvard University Press.

Burt, M. K., H. C. Dulay, and E. Hernández-Chavez. 1976. *Bilingual Syntax Measure I (BSM)*. New York: Harcourt Brace Jovanovich.

Campbell, L. 1997. *American Indian Languages: The Historical Linguistics of Native America*. Oxford: Oxford University Press.

Campbell, L. and M. C. Muntzel. 1989. "The structural consequences of language death." In *Investigating Obsolescence: Studies in Language Contraction and Death*, N. C. Dorian (ed.), 197–210. Cambridge: Cambridge University Press.

Cazden, C. 1983. "Adult assistance to language development: Scaffolds, models, and direct instruction." In *Developing Literacy: Young Children's Use of Language*, R. P. Parker and F. A. Davis (eds), 3–17. Newark, DE: International Reading Association.

Cazden, C., E. Cancino, E. Rosansky, and J. Schumann. 1975. *Second Language Acquisition Sequences in Children, Adolescents and Adults*. Final report submitted to the National Institute of Education, Washington, DC.

Celce-Murcia, M. 1991. "Language teaching approaches: An overview." In *Teaching English as a Second or Foreign Language*, Second Edition. M. Celce-Murcia (ed.), 3–10. Boston, MA: Heinle and Heinle.
Chambers, J. K. and P. Trudgill. 1980. *Dialectology*. New York: Cambridge University Press.
Chomsky, N. 1965. *Aspects of the Theory of Syntax*. Cambridge, MA: MIT Press.
Chomsky, N. 1966. *Cartesian Linguistics: A Chapter in the History of Rationalist Thought*. New York: Harper and Row.
Clark, E. V. 2003. *First Language Acquisition*. Cambridge: Cambridge University Press.
Clyne, M. G. 1967. *Transference and Triggering*. The Hague: Nijhoff.
Comrie, B. 1989. *Language Universals and Linguistic Typology*. Chicago: University of Chicago Press.
Connor, U. 1996. *Contrastive Rhetoric: Cross-cultural Aspects of Second Language Writing*. Cambridge: Cambridge University Press.
Connor, U. 2002. "New directions in contrastive rhetoric." *TESOL Quarterly, 36*: 493–510.
Cook, V. 1993. *Linguistics and Second Language Acquisition*. New York: St. Martin's Press.
Cook, V. 1988. *Chomsky's Universal Grammar: An Introduction*. Oxford: Blackwell Publishers.
Corbett, G. 1991. *Gender*. New York: Cambridge University Press.
Corder, S. P. 1993. "A Role for the Mother Tongue." In *Language Transfer in Language Learning*, S. M. Gass and L. Selinker (eds), 18–31. Amsterdam/Philadelphia: John Benjamins.
Crawford, J. 1995. *Bilingual Education: History, Politics, Theory, and Practice*. Los Angeles, CA: BEA.
Crystal, D. 2000. *Language Death*. Cambridge: Cambridge University Press.
Cummins, J. 1976. "The influence of bilingualism on cognitive growth: A synthesis of research findings and explanatory hypotheses." In *Working Papers on Bilingualism*. Ontario Institute for Studies in Education, 1: 1–43.
Cummins, J. 1984. *Bilingualism and Special Education: Issues in Assessment and Pedagogy*. Clevedon: Multilingual Matters.
Dale, P. 1976. *Language Development: Structure and Function*, Second edition. New York: Holt, Rinhart, and Winston.
De Bot, K. and R. Schreuder. 1993. "Word production in the bilingual lexicon." In *The Bilingual Lexicon*, R. Schreuder and B. Weltens (eds), 191–214. Amsterdam/Philadelphia: John Benjamins.
De Houwer, A. 2005. "Early bilingual acquisition: focus on morphosyntax and the Separate Development Hypothesis." In *Handbook of Bilingualism: Psycholinguistic Approaches*, J. Kroll and A. M. De Groot (eds), 30–48. Oxford: Oxford University Press.
De Houwer, A. 2009. *Bilingual First Language Acquisition*. Buffalo, NY: Multilingual Matters.
De Villiers, J. and P. De Villiers. 1973. "A cross-sectional study of the acquisition of grammatical morphemes in child speech." *Journal of Psycholinguistic Research, 2*(3): 235–252.
DeGraff. M. 1999. "Creolization, language change, and language acquisition: A prolegomenon." In *Language Creation and Language Change: Creolization, Diachrony, and Development*, M. DeGraff (ed.), 1–46. Cambridge, MA: MIT Press.
Dennett, D. 1991. *Consciousness Explained*. Boston: Little, Brown and Company.
Dijkstra, A. and W. Van Heuven. 1998. "The BIA model and bilingual word recognition." In *Localist Connectionist Approaches to Human Cognition*, J. Grainger and A. M. Jacobs (eds), 189–225. Mahwah, NJ: Erlbaum.
Dijkstra, T. 2005. "Bilingual visual word recognition and lexical access." In *Handbook of Bilingualism: Psycholinguistic Approaches*, J. Kroll and A. De Groot (eds), 179–201. Oxford: Oxford University Press.

Dillard, J. L. 1972. *Black English: Its History and Usage in the United States*. New York: Random House.
Dorian, N. C. 1989. "Introduction." In *Investigating Obsolescence: Studies in Language Contraction and Death*, N. C. Dorian (ed.), 1–10. Cambridge: Cambridge University Press.
Dorian, N. C. 1993. "Internally and externally motivated change in language contact settings: doubts about dichotomy." In *Historical Linguistics: Problems and Perspectives*, C. Jones (ed.), 131–155. London and New York: Longman.
Dulay, H. and M. Burt. 1973. "Should we teach our children syntax?" *Language Learning*, 23(2): 245–258.
Dulay, H. and M. Burt. 1974. "Natural sequences in child second language acquisition." *Language Learning*, 24: 37–53.
Edwards, J. 1994. *Multilingualism*. London: Penguin Books.
Elliot, A. J. 1981. *Child Language*. Cambridge: Cambridge University Press.
Eubank, L., L. Selinker, and M. Sharwood Smith. 1995. *The Current State of Interlanguage*. Amsterdam/Philadelphia: John Benjamins.
Felix, S. 1995. "Universal grammar in L2 acquisition: Some thoughts on Schachter's Incompleteness Hypothesis." In *The Current State of Interlanguage: Studies in Honor of William E. Rutherford*, L. Eubank, L. Selinker, and M. S. Smith (eds), Amsterdam and Philadelphia: John Benjamins.
Fennell, B. 2001. *A History of English: A Sociolinguistic Approach*. Oxford: Blackwell Publishers.
Fergusson, C. A. 1959. "Diglossia." *Word*, 15: 325–40. Reprinted in Giglioli (1972) and Hymes (1964).
Field, F. 2002. *Linguistic Borrowing in Bilingual Contexts*. Philadelphia and Amsterdam: John Benjamins.
Field, F. 2004. "Second language acquisition in creole genesis: The role of processability." In *Creoles, Contact and Language Change: Linguistics and Social Implications*, G. Escure and A. Schwegler (eds), 127–160. Amsterdam: John Benjamins.
Field, F. 2011. *Bilingualism in the USA: The Case of the Chicano-Latino Community*. Amsterdam/Philadelphia: John Benjamins.
Finegan, E. 2008. *Language: Its Structure and Use*, 5th ed. Boston, MA: Thomson Wadsworth.
Fishman, J. 1989. *Language and Ethnicity in Minority Sociolinguistic Perspective*. Clevedon/Philadelphia: Multilingual Matters.
Fitch, W. T., M. Hauser, N. Chomsky. 2005. "The evolution of the language faculty: Clarifications and implications." *Cognition*, 97(2): 179–210.
Fodor, J. A. 1983. *The Modularity of Mind: An Essay on Faculty Psychology*. Cambridge, MA: The MIT Press.
Francis, W. "Bilingual semantic and conceptual representation." In *Handbook of Bilingualism: Psycholinguistic Approaches*, J. Kroll and A. M. De Groot (eds), 251–281. Oxford: Oxford University Press.
Gardner, R. C. 2001 "Integrative motivation and second language acquisition." In *Motivation and Second Language Acquisition*, Zoltán Dörnei and Richard Schmidt (eds), 1–19. Mānoa, HI: Second Language Teaching & Curriculum Center, University of Hawaii.
Gardner, R. C. and W. E. Lambert. 1972. *Attitudes and Motivation in Second-Language Learning*. Rowley, MA: Newbury House.
Gass, S. M. and L. Selinker. 1993a. "Afterword." In *Language Transfer in Language Learning*, S. M. Gass and L. Selinker (eds), 233–236. Amsterdam/Philadelphia: John Benjamins.
Gass, S. M. and L. Selinker. 1993b. "Introduction." In *Language Transfer in Language Learning*, S. M. Gass and L. Selinker (eds), 1–17. Amsterdam/Philadelphia: John Benjamins.
Gee, J. P. 1992. *The Social Mind: Language, Ideology, and Social Practice*. New York: Bergin and Garvey.

Gee, J. P. 1996. *Social Linguistics and Literacies: Ideology in Discourses*. Bristol, PA: Falmer Press.
Goodglass, H. 1993. *Understanding Aphasia*. San Diego, CA: Academic Press.
Gopnik, A. 2001. "Theories, language, and culture: Whorf without wincing." In *Language Acquisition and Conceptual Development*, M. Bowerman and S. C. Levinson (eds), 45–69. New York: Cambridge University Press.
Greenberg, J. H. 1974. *Language Typology: A Historical and Analytic Overview*. The Hague: Mouton.
Grosjean, F. 1995. "A psycholinguistic approach to code-switching: the recognition of guest words by bilinguals." In *One Speaker, Two Languages: Cross-disciplinary Perspectives on Code-switching*, L. Milroy and P. Muysken (eds), 259–275. New York: Cambridge University Press.
Grosjean, F. 1997. "Processing mixed languages: Issues, findings, and models." In *Tutorials in Bilingualism: Psycholinguistic Perspectives*, A. M. B. de Groot and J. F. Kroll (eds), 225–254. Mahway, NJ: Erlbaum.
Grosjean, F. 1998 (2004). "Studying bilinguals: Methodological and conceptual issues." *Bilingualism: Language and Cognition*, 1, 131–149. Cambridge: Cambridge University Press; In *The Handbook of Bilingualism*, T. K. Bhatia and W. C. Ritchie (eds), 32–63. Oxford: Blackwell Publishers.
Grosjean, F. 2006. "Studying bilinguals: methodological and conceptual issues." In *The Handbook of Bilingualism*, T. K. Bhatia and W. C. Ritchie (eds), 32–63. Malden, MA: Blackwell Publishing.
Gumperz, J. 1982. *Discourse Strategies*. New York: Cambridge University Press.
Gumperz, J. and S. Levinson. 1996. *Rethinking Linguistic Relativity*. New York: Cambridge University Press.
Gunderson, L. 2009. *ESL (ELL) Literacy Instruction: A Guidebook to Theory and Practice*. New York: Routledge.
Gur, R. E., J. Levy, and R. C. Gur. 1977. "Clinical studies of brain organization and behavior." In *Biological Bases of Psychiatric Disorders*, A. Frazer and A. Winokur (eds), 115–137. New York: Spectrum Publications.
Haegeman, L. M. V. 1994. *Introduction to Government and Binding Theory*. Malden, MA: Blackwell Publishing.
Hakuta, K. 1986. *Mirror of Language: The Debate on Bilingualism*. New York: Basic Books.
Hauser, M., N. Chomsky, and W. T. Fitch. 2002. "The language faculty: What is it, who has it, and how did it evolve?" *Science*, 298: 1569–1579.
Hawkins, J. A. 1983. *Word Order Universals*. Philadelphia, PA.: John Benjamins.
Hawkins, J. A. 1994. *A Performance Theory of Order and Constituency*. Cambridge: Cambridge University Press.
Heredia, R. R. and J. M. Brown. 2006. "Bilingual memory." In *The Handbook of Bilingualism*, T. K. Bhatia and W. C. Ritchie (eds), 225–249. Malden, MA: Blackwell Publishing.
Hill, J. H. and K. Hill. 1986. *Speaking Mexicano: Dynamics of Syncretic Language in Central Mexico*. Tucson: University of Arizona Press.
Hinkel, E. 2002. *Second Language Writers' Text: Linguistic and Rhetorical Features*. Mahwah, NJ: Lawrence Erlbaum Associates.
Hocket, C. F. 1984. "Foreword." In *Language*, L. Bloomfield (ed.), (first published in 1933), ix–xiv. Chicago, IL: University of Chicago Press.
Hoff, E. 2009. *Language Development*, Fourth edition. Belmont CA: Wadsworth Cengage Learning.
Hoffmann, C. 1991. *An Introduction to Bilingualism*. London and New York: Longman.
Holm, J. 1988. *Pidgins and Creoles, Volume 1: Theory and Structure*. Cambridge: Cambridge University Press.

Hymes, D. 1974. *Foundations in Sociolinguistics: An Ethnographic Approach*. Philadelphia, PA: University of Pennsylvania Press.
Jackendoff, R. and S. Pinker. 2005. "The nature of the language faculty and its implications for evolution of language (Reply to Fitch, Hauser, and Chomsky)." *Cognition, 97*(2): 211–225.
Kaplan, R. 1966. "Cultural thought patterns in intercultural education." *Language Learning, 16*: 1–20.
Karmiloff-Smith, A. 1992. *Beyond Modularity: A Developmental Perspective on Cognitive Science*. Cambridge, MA: The MIT Press.
Kimura, D. 1967. "Functional asymmetry of the brain in dichotic listening." *Cortex, 3*: 163–178.
Krashen, S. 1985. *The Input Hypothesis: Issues and Implications*. London: Longman.
Krashen, S. and T. Terrell. 1983. *The Natural Approach: Language Acquisition in the Classroom*. Hayward, CA: Alemany Press.
Labov, W. 1966. *The Social Stratification of English in New York City*. Washington, DC: Center for Applied Linguistics.
Labov, W. 1972. *Sociolinguistic Patterns*. Philadelphia, PA: University of Pennsylvania Press.
Lado, R. 1957. *Linguistics Across Cultures*. Ann Arbor, MI: University of Michigan Press.
Lambert, R. and B. Freed. 1982. *The Loss of Language Skills*, Rowley, MA: Newbury House.
Lakoff, R. 1975. *Language and Woman's Place*. New York: Harper and Row.
Larsen-Freeman, D. and M. H. Long. 1991. *An Introduction to Second Language Acquisition Research*. New York: Longman.
Levelt, W. J. M. 1989. *Speaking: From Intention to Articulation*. Cambridge, MA: The MIT Press.
Lippi-Green, R. 2004. "Language ideology and language prejudice." In *Language in the USA: Themes for the Twenty-first Century*, E. Finegan and J. Rickford (eds), 289–304. New York: Cambridge University Press.
Lyons, J. 1968. *Introduction to Theoretical Linguistics*. New York: Cambridge University Press.
Markman, E. M. 1989. *Categorization and Naming in Children: Problems of Induction*. Cambridge, MA: The MIT Press.
McClelland, J. L. and D. E. Rumelhart (eds) 1986. *Parallel Distributed Processing: Explorations in the Microstructure of Cognition. Volume 2: Psychological and Biological Models*. Cambridge, MA: MIT Press.
McClelland, J. L. and D. E. Rumelhart. 1981. "An interactive activation model of context effects in letter perception. Part 1: An account of basic findings." *Psychological Review, 88*: 373–405.
McClelland, J. L. and J. Elman. 1986. "The TRACE model of speech perception." *Cognitive Psychology, 18*: 1–86.
McLaughlin, B. 1978. *Second Language Acquisition in Childhood*, Hillsdale, NJ: Lawrence Erlbaum.
Meillet, A. 1928. *La méthode comparative en linguistique historique* (*The Comparative Method in Historical Linguistics*, translated by Gordon B. Ford, Jr, 1966). Paris: Librairie Honoré Champion.
Mertz, E. 1989. "Sociolinguistic creativity: Cape Breton Gaelic's linguistic 'tip'." In *Investigating Obsolescence: Studies in Language Contraction and Death*, N. C. Dorian (ed.), 117–137. Cambridge: Cambridge University Press.
Michael, E. and T. Gollan. 2005. "Being and becoming bilingual: Individual differences and consequences for language production." In *Handbook of Bilingualism: Psycholinguistic Approaches*, J. Kroll and A. De Groot (eds), 389–407. Oxford: Oxford University Press.

Miller, G. A. 2003. "The cognitive revolution: a historical perspective." *TRENDS in Cognitive Sciences, 7*(3), 141–144.
Morley, J. 1991. "Listening comprehension in second/foreign language instruction." In *Teaching English as a Second or Foreign Language*, Second Edition. M. Celce-Murcia (ed.), 81–106. Boston, MA: Heinle and Heinle.
Mous, M. 2003. *The Making of a Mixed Language: The Case of Ma'a/Mbugu.* Amsterdam/Philadelphia: John Benjamins.
Murre, J. M. J. 2005. "Models of monolingual and bilingual language acquisition. In *Handbook of Bilingualism: Psycholinguistic Approaches*, J. Kroll and A. De Groot (eds), 154–169. Oxford: Oxford University Press.
Muysken, P. 1981. "Halfway between Quechua and Spanish: the case for relexification." In *Historicity and Variation in Creole Studies*, A. Valdman and A. Highfield (eds), 52–78. Ann Arbor, MI: Karoma.
Muysken, P. 1997. "Media Lengua." In *Contact Languages: A Wider Perspective*, S. G. Thomason (ed.), 365–426. New York and Amsterdam: John Benjamins.
Muysken, P. 2000. *Bilingual Speech: A Typology of Code-Mixing.* Cambridge: Cambridge University Press.
Myers-Scotton, C. 1993a. *Duelling Languages: Grammatical Structure in Codeswitching.* New York: Oxford University Press.
Myers-Scotton, C. 1993b. *Social Motivations for Codeswitching.* New York: Oxford University Press.
Myers-Scotton, C. 2002. *Contact Linguistics: Bilingual Encounters and Grammatical Outcomes.* Oxford: Oxford University Press.
Myers-Scotton, C. 2006. *Multiple Voices: An Introduction to Bilingualism.* Oxford: Blackwell.
Nation, I. S. P. 1990. *Teaching and Learning Vocabulary.* Boston, MA: Heinle and Heinle.
Paradis, M. 2004. *A Neurolinguistic Theory of Bilingualism.* Philadelphia/Amsterdam: John Benjamins.
Paradis, M. 2005. "Introduction to Part IV: Aspects and implications of bilingualism." In *Handbook of Bilingualism: Psycholinguistic Approaches*, 411–416. Oxford and New York: Oxford University Press.
Pfaff, C. W. 1979. "Constraints on language mixing." *Language, 55*(2): 291–318.
Pinker, S. 1994. *The Language Instinct.* New York: Harper Collins.
Pinker, S. 1996. *Language Learnability and Language Development.* Cambridge, MA: Harvard University Press.
Pinker, S. and R. Jackendoff. 2005. "The faculty of language: What's special about it?" *Cognition, 95*(2): 201–236.
Poplack, S. 1982. "Sometimes I'll start a sentence in Spanish y termino en español": toward a typology of code-switching. In *Spanish in the United States*, J. Amastae and L. Elías-Olivares (eds), 230–263. New York: Cambridge University Press.
Radford, A. 1988. *Transformational Grammar.* New York: Cambridge University Press.
Reinecke, J. E. 1937. *Marginal Languages: A Sociological Survey of the Creole Languages and Trade Jargons.* Ph.D. dissertation, Yale University. Ann Arbor, MI: Microfilms International.
Resnick, D. P. and L. B. Resnick. 1988. "The nature of literacy: A historical exploration." In *Perspectives on Literacy*, E. R. Kintgen, B. M. Kroll, and M. Rose (eds), 190–203. Carbondale: Southern Illinois University Press.
Rickford, J. R. and R. J. Rickford. 2000. *Spoken Soul: The Story of Black English.* New York: John Wiley & Son.
Romaine, S. 1995. *Bilingualism*, 2nd Edition. [Language in Society 13.] Cambridge, MA: Blackwell.
Rumelhart, D. E. and J. L. McClelland. 1986. "A general framework for parallel distributed processing." In *Parallel Distributed Processing: Explorations in the Microstructure*

of Cognition. Volume 2: Psychological and Biological Models, J. L. McClelland and D. E. Rumelhart (eds), 45–76. Cambridge, MA: MIT Press.

Sapir, E. 1921. *Language: An Introduction to the Study of Speech*. New York: Harcourt Brace Jovanovich.

Schumann, J. 1975. "Affective factors and the problem of age in second language acquisition." *Language Learning, 25*: 209–235.

Schumann, J. 1978. *The Pidginization Process: A Model for Second Language Acquisition*. Rowley, MA: Newbury House.

Seelye, H. N. 1994. *Teaching Culture: Strategies for Intercultural Communication*. Lincolnwood, IL: National Textbook Company.

Selinker, L. 1972. "Interlanguage." *International Review of Applied Linguistics, 10*: 209–231.

Shaffer, D. 1977. "The place of code-switching in linguistic contact." In *Aspects of Bilingualism*, M. Paradis (ed.), 265–274. Columbia, SC: Hornbeam Press.

Sharwood Smith, M. 1994. *Second Language Learning: Theoretical Foundations*. London and New York: Longman.

Silva-Corvalán, C. 1994. *Language Contact and Change: Spanish in Los Angeles*. New York: Oxford University Press.

Singler, J. V. 1993. "African influence upon Afro-American language varieties: A consideration of sociohistorical facts." In *Africanisms in Afro-American Language Varieties*, S. S. Mufwene (ed.), 235–253. Athens, GA.: University of Georgia Press.

Skutnabb-Kangas, T. and Toukomaa, P. 1976. *Teaching Migrant Children's Mother Tongue and Learning the Language of the Host Country in the Context of the Sociocultural Situation of the Migrant Family*. Helsinki: Finnish National Commission for UNESCO.

Slobin, D. I. 1985. "Crosslinguistic evidence for the language-making capacity." In *The Crosslinguistic Study of Language Acquisition. Volume 2: Theoretical Issues*, D. I. Slobin (ed.), 1157–1256. Hillsdale, NJ: Lawrence Erlbaum.

Smitherman. G. 1977. *Talkin and Testifyin: The Language of Black America*. Detroit: Wayne State University Press.

Steinberg, D. D. 1982. *Psycholinguistics: Language, Mind and World*. London/New York: Longman.

Tannen, D. 1994. *Gender and Discourse*. New York: Oxford University Press.

Thomas, C. L. (ed.) 1989. *Taber's Cyclopedic Medical Dictionary*. Philadelphia, PA: F. A. Davis Company.

Thomason, S. G. 1997. "Introduction." In *Contact Languages: A Wider Perspective*, S. G. Thomason (ed.), 1–8. New York and Amsterdam: John Benjamins.

Thomason, S. G. and T. Kaufman. 1988. *Language Contact, Creolization, and Genetic Linguistics*. Berkeley: University of California Press.

Timm, L. 1975. "Spanish-English code-switching: *El porque y how-not-to*." *Romance Philology, 28*: 473–482.

Toukomaa, P. and T. Skutnabb-Kangas. 1977. *The Intensive Teaching of the Mother Tongue to Migrant Children at Pre-school Age (Research Report No. 26)*. Department of Sociology and Social Psychology, University of Tampere.

Trudgill, P. 1999. *The Dialects of England*. Oxford: Blackwell.

Wald, B. 1984. "The status of Chicano English as a dialect of American English." In *Form and Function in Chicano English*, J. Ornstein-Galicia (ed.), 14–31. Malabar, FL: Robert E. Krieger Publishing.

Wardhaugh, R. 1970. "The contrastive analysis hypothesis." Reprinted in *Second Language Learning: Contrastive Analysis, Error Analysis, and Related Aspects* (1983), 6–14. Ann Arbor, MI: The University of Michigan Press.

Wardhaugh, R. 2006. *An Introduction to Sociolinguistics*. New York: Blackwell.

Weinreich, U. 1953 (reprinted in 1968). *Languages in Contact*. The Hague: Mouton.

Wiley, Terrence G. 2005. *Literacy and Language Diversity in the United States*. Washington, DC: Center for Applied Linguistics.
Wiley, T. G. 2007. "Immigrant language minorities in the United States." In *Handbooks of Applied Linguistics, Vol. 9: Language and Communication: Diversity and Change*. Berlin/New York: Mouton de Gruyter.
Wolfram, W. and N. Schilling-Estes. 1998. *American English: Dialects and Variation*. Malden, MA: Blackwell Publishing.
Wolfram, W. and R. Fasold. 1974. *The Study of Social Dialects in American English*. Englewood Cliffs, NJ: Prentice-Hall.
Yip, V. and S. Matthews. 2007. *The Bilingual Child: Early Development and Language Contact*. Cambridge: Cambridge University Press.

# Index

Note: Page numbers in **bold** indicate definitions.

access, **1**, 19, 20, 109
Acculturation Model, **1–2**
accuracy, **2**, 145
achievement, **2–3**, 3–4, 27, 178
achievement gap, **3–4**
acoustic phonetics, **4**
acquisition, **4**, 5, 96
Acquisition-Learning Hypothesis, **4–5**, 96
activation, **5**, 19, 20, 36–7, 135
active knowledge, **5**, 138, 145
additive bilingualism, **5–6**, 158
Affective Filter Hypothesis, **6**, 96
African American Vernacular English (AAVE), 16, 50–1, 162–3, 173
age, **6–7**, 46
age of arrival, **7**
ambilingual, **7**, 15
Amerindian, **7**, 10
aphasia, **8**, 26, 189
approach, **8–9**, 118, 125
aptitude, **9**, 124
articulatory phonetics, **9–10**
assessment, **10**, 22, 178
assimilation, **10–11**
asymmetry, **11**
attainment, 6, **11**
attitude, 2, **12**, 144
attrition, **12–13**, 59, 82, 99–100, 132
Audio-lingual method (ALM), **13**, 118, 171–2
autobiographical memory, **13–14**

babbling, **14**, 28, 128
babbling drift, **14**, 62
balanced bilingual, **14–15**
behaviorism/behaviorist, **15**, 62, 118, 140, 162
BICS (basic interpersonal communication skills), **15**, 49, 180
bidialectal, **16**, 55
bilingual, 7, 14–15, **16**, 21, 22, 23, 35, 43, 173–4
bilingual contact languages, 38
bilingual education, **16–17**, 21

bilingual families, **17–18**
Bilingual First Language Acquisition (BFLA), **19**, 69, 123
bilingual interactive activation (BIA), 5, **19**
bilingual interactive model of lexical access (BIMOLA), **20**
bilingual language phenomena, **20**, 24, 88, 101
bilingual lexicon, **20–1**
bilingual programs, **21**, 82, 87–8, 172, 182
Bilingual Syntax Measure (BSM), **22**
bilingualism, **22–3**, 88, 121
bilinguality, **23**, 163
biliterate/biliteracy, **23**
biologically transmitted (biological transmission), **23–4**
bootstrapping, **24**
borderlands, **24**
borrowing, 20, **25**, 38
bottom-up, **25**, 50, 190
brain-imaging technique, **26**, 47, 70–1, 121, 139, 164–5
Broca's aphasia, 8, **26**
Broca's area, **26**

CALP (cognitive/academic language proficiency), 15, **27**, 49, 180
calque, 20, **28**, 157
canonical babbling, 14, **28**
caretaker speech, **28**
Cartesian linguistics, 8, **28**, 32, 62, 125
categorical perception, **28–9**
census surveys, **29**
cerebral cortex, **29**
charter school, **29–30**
child-directed speech, **30**, 121
CHILDES (Child Language Data Exchange System), **30**
Chomsky, Noam, 28, **30**, 78
code, **30**, 50, 60, 63, 152
code-switching, 25, **30–1**, 38, 93, 116, 151
code-switching constraints, **31**

cognition, **31**, 77
cognitive development, 15–16, 140, 180
cognitive revolution, **32**, 162, 172
cognitive science(s), 30, **32**, 44, 96, 99
cognitive style, 9, **32**, 138–9
cognitivism, **32–3**
cohort model, **33**
communicative competence, **33**, 48, 56, 137, 144
communicative language testing, **33**
communication theory, **34**
community, **34**, 166
community bilingualism, **34**, 88, 164–4
community of practice (CoP), **34–5**
competence, **35**, 138
compound bilingual (Type B), **35**
comprehensible input, 4, **36**, 90, 118, 155, 160
compressed speech, **36**, 63, 109
computational modeling, **36**
connectionism/connectionist models, 5, **36–7**, 135
consecutive language acquisition, 5–6, **37**, 140–1, 158–9
constructivism, **37**
contact, **37–8**, 101
contact language (or variety), **38**, 44, 141
contact linguistics, **38**
contact phenomena, **38**, 163
content word/item, **39**
content-based ESL, **39**
continuity assumption, **39**
continuity-discontinuity, **39–40**
continuum, **40**, 183
contralateral connections, **40**, 167
contrastive analysis (CA), **40–1**, 42–3, 67, 171–2
Contrastive Analysis Hypothesis (CAH), 41–2
contrastive rhetoric (CR), **42–3**
conversational code-switching, **43**, 93
cooing, **43**
coordinate bilingual (Type A), **43**
corpus callosum, **43–4**, 167
creole, **44**
creolistics, **44**
creolization, **44–5**
criterion-based testing, **45**
critical literacy, **45–6**, 112–13
critical (or sensitive) period, **46**

Critical Period Hypothesis (CPH), **46**
cross-cultural communication, **47**
cross-linguistic influence, 181
CT (Roentgen-ray computed tomography) 26, **47**, 68, 71, 139
cultural literacy, **47–8**, 112–13
cultural pluralism, **48**
culturally transmitted (cultural transmission), **48–9**
culture, 43, **49**
Cummins, James (Jim), 15, 27, **49**, 179–180

dead languages, **50**, 63, 101
decode, 30, **50**
deficit model, **50–1**, 55
Descartes, René, 28, **51**
descriptive grammar, **51–2**
developmental approach, **52**, 106, 140, 153
developmental English, **52**
developmental models/perspective, **52**
developmental sequences, **52–3**, 67, 158
dialect, 16, 30, **53**, 80, 96, 113, 124, 142, 173
dialect awareness, **53–4**
dialect continuum, 40, **54**
dichotic listening tasks, 43–4, **54–5**
difference model, 50–1, **55**
diglossia, 20, 31, 38, 43, **55–6**, 83, 96, 101
discontinuous, 39–40, **56**
discourse knowledge, **56–7**, 164
dishabituation, **57**, 80, 83
domain, **57**
  general, **57**
  of language usage, **57**
  specific, **57**
dominance/balance measures, **57–8**
dominant, 2, **58**, 80–1
dominant language switch hypothesis, **58**
donor, **58**, 175
drift, 59
dual immersion, 17, **59**, 87, 172

early exit program, **60**, 182
early-system morpheme, 175
echolalia or echolalic speech, **60**
elaborated code, 30, **60–1**, 152

embedded language (EL), **61**, 94
emergence of speech sounds, **61–2**
emergentism, **62**
emerging bilingual, 27, **62**, 176, 179
empiricism, 8, **62–3**, 113, 126
encode, **63**, 126, 154
endangered language, 50, **63**, 82
English
  as a foreign language (EFL), **63–4**
  as a second/subsequent language (ESL), **64**
  for academic purposes (EAD), **64–5**
  for specific purposes (ESP), **65**
  language development (ELD), **65**
  language learner (ELL), **65–6**
equipotentiality, **66**, 81
error, **66–7**, 127, 138, 143
error analysis, **67**, 72, 138
even-related potentials (ERPs), **67–8**
explicit knowledge, 96
eye movement(s), **68**

faculty of language (language faculty), 23, 28, **69**, 144, 186
family tree model, **69**, 183
first language, **69–70**, 120, 123–4, 145
fluent English proficiency (FEP), **70**
fluent/fluency, 2, **70**, 145
fMRI (functional magnetic resonance imaging), 8, **70–1**
form, **71**
formal grammar, **71–2**
formative (testing), **72**, 142, 178
fossilization, **72**
fossilized variation, **72–3**
function word/item, **73**, 109, 117, 120
function, **73**
functional approach, **74**
functional architecture, **74**
functional asymmetry, **74**
functional bilingual, **74–5**
functional literacy, 45–6, **75**, 112–13
functional magnetic resonance imaging, 70–1
functionalism, **75**
functions of speech, **75–6**, 144, 146

gender, 56, **77**, 87, 105, 164, 181
generative approaches/linguistics, 28, 35, 72, **77–8**, 84, 86, 105, 125, 132, 153, 185

generative grammar, **78**, 98
genre, 57, 77, **78**, 187
grammatical, 72, **78–9**, 86, 96, 98, 120, 124, 129, 132
grammatical morphemes, 22, **79**, 120, 125
guest (language), **79**

habituation, 57, **80**, 82
head-turn technique, **80**
hegemony, 58, **80–1**, 102, 172
hemispheric specialization, 66, 74, **81**
heritage language, 16, 17, 20, 21, 34, 59, 63, **81**, 82, 87, 99, 102, 132, 159–60, 174, 179
heritage language bilingual education, **82**
high-amplitude sucking (HAS) technique, **82–3**
High-Low language status, **83**
holophrastic speech, **83**
host (language), 28, **83–4**
hypothesis, **84**
hypothesis testing, **84–5**, 134

ideal speaker, 35, **86**
identity, 81, **86–7**, 88, 142, 166, 179
idiolect, **87**
immersion, 59, **87–8**
in-between group, 44, **88**
incipient bilingual, 27, 65, **88**
incipient bilingualism, **88**
individual bilingualism, 34, **88–9**, 163
infant-directed speech, **89**, 121
informal, 15, 27, 36, **89**, 94, 136
  registers, 14, 71, 94
  situations, 36, 137
  speech, 71, 89, 137. 167, 173
  usage, 54, 146
informational, 71, **89–90**, 94
innate, 46, **90**
input, **90**
Input Hypothesis, **90–1**
instrumental motivation, **91**, 121
intake, **91**
integrative motivation, **91**, 121
interaction/interactive, 4, 34, 37, 39, 52, 89, **91–2**, 94, 105, 118, 131, 144, 159
interactionism, **92**
interference, **92**

interlanguage (IL), **92-3**
interlocutor, 135
intersentential code-switching, **93**
intrasentential code-switching, **93**
invariance hypothesis, 81
involvement, 71, 89, **94**
ipsilateral, 55, **94**
islands, **94**, 116

joint attention/gaze, **95**

knowledge (of language), 15, 28, 30, 32, 77, **96**, 143, 164
    innate, 8, 32, 39-40, 126, 185
Krashen, Stephen, 4-5, **96**, 108, 119, 125

L1, L2, **98**
language, **98**, 165
Language Acquisition Device (LAD), 46, **98-9**
language
    attrition, 12-13, **99-100**
    background scales, **100**
    change, **100**
    choice, **100**
    contact, 11, 24, 36, 37-8, 59, **101**, 149
    contact phenomena, **101**
    death, 12, **101**, 102
    evolution, 74, 75, **101**, 119, 141
    ideology, **101-2**
    loyalty, **102**
    maintenance, 10, 21, 82, 100, **102**, 179
    mixing, 19, 31, 38, 44, 88, **103**, 141
    minority/linguistic minority (LM), 49, **103**, 146
    modes, 71, **103**
    processing, 5, 36, **103-4**, 109, 127, 136, 140
    skills, 7, 15, 19, 29, 45, **104-5**, 152, 175, 180, 181
    socialization, 27, 56, 60, **105**, 162
    typology, **105**
    universals, **105**
    use surveys, 100, **105-6**
    variety, **106**, 149
Language-Making Capacity (LMC), **106**, 143
late-exit program, **106**

late-system morpheme, 175
lateralization, 46, 55, **106-7**
Lau v. Nichols, **107**
learnability, **107**
learnability theory, **107-8**
learner's variety, **108**
learning, **108**
learning strategies, 106, **108**
lect (-lect), **108**
lemma, **108**
length of residence, 7
lesion method, **108-9**
lexeme, **109**
lexical
    access, **109**
    category, **109**
    item, **109**
lexicon, **109-10**
limited English proficiency (LEP), **110**
linguistic
    competence, 10, 33, **110**
    determinism, **110-11**
    diversity, **111**
    relativity, **111**
    repertoire, **111-12**
literacy myth, 23, **112**
literate/literacy, 23, **112-13**
loanword, 59, 79, 84, **113**, 168
Locke, John, **113-14**, 126, 162

magnetic resonance imaging, 5, 121
mainstream/mainstreaming, 21, **115**, 146
maintenance, 10, 21, 81-2, 100, 115, 128, 192
map (mapping), **115**
mapping problem, **115**
matrix language (ML), 94, **116**
Matrix Language-Frame (MLF) model, **116**
Matrix Language Hypothesis (MLH), **116**
mean length of utterance (MLU), **117**
mentalism/mentalist, 99, **117**
metalinguistic awareness, **117**
method, 8-9, 13, **118**
mixed language, **118-19**
mode (of communication), **119**
4-M model, **1**, 116. 175
modularity, 37, **119**

monitor theory, **119**
monolingual/monolingualism, **120**
morpheme studies, **120**, 125, 148
mother tongue (maternal language), 69, 92, **120**, 123, 181
motherese, **121**
motivation, 2, 9, 12, 91, **121**, 146
MRI (magnetic resonance imaging), **121**
multilingual/multilingualism, **121**
mutual exclusivity assumption, **122**
mutual intelligibility, **122**

naming insight, **123**
native bilingual, 19, 20, **123**, 156, 179–80
native language (NL), **123**–4
native language acquisition (NLA), 5, 13, 19, 22, 43, 77, 90, **124**, 164, 190
native speaker (NS), **124**
native-like control, **124**
native-speaker intuition, **124**–5
nativism/nativist, **125**
Natural Approach, **125**
Natural Order Hypothesis, **125**
Natural Partitions hypothesis, **125**–6
nature vs. nurture, **126**
negative evidence, **127**
neural circuit, 67, **127**
neural networks, **127**, 140
neuroimaging, 8, 47, 70, **127**–8
neurolinguistics, **128**
No Child Left Behind (NCLB), **128**
Nonnative speaker (NNS), **128**
nonreduplicated babbling, **128**
nonstandard, 2, 3, 10, 16, 50–1, 53, 83, 89, 112, **129**, 137, 146, 150, 152, 181
norm, **129**–30
norm-referenced testing, 72, **130**, 178
normative, 10, 72, **130**, 178
norms of interaction, **130**–1
norms of interpretation, **131**

obsolescence/obsolete, **132**
one system (or two), **132**
operating principles (OPs), **132**–3
order of acquisition, 53, **133**
overextension, **133**
overgeneralization, 133, **134**

parallel distributed processing (PDP), **135**
parental involvement, **135**, 180
parse, 68, **135**, 136
participants (or interlocutors), **135**, 161
passive knowledge, 35, **136**
pattern, **135**
pedagogical (or teaching) grammar, **135**–6
percentile, 130, **137**, 175
perception, 31, 32, 80, 99, **137**–8, 170
perceptual salience, 137–8
performance, **138**
performance analysis (PA), 67, 73, **138**
personality, 9, **138**–9
perspective, **139**
PET (positron emission tomography) scan, **139**
phonemic awareness, **139**
phonics, **139**–40
phonological awareness, 139, **140**
Piaget, Jean, 37, 92, 136, **140**
Piagetian/Neo-Piagetian, 13, **140**–1
pidgin, **141**
Pidginization Hypothesis, **141**–2
placement, 10, 45, **142**, 181
popular culture, 136, **142**–3, 145, 150
positive evidence, 127, **143**, 185
poverty of the stimulus, **143**–4, 185
pragmatic knowledge, 33, **144**
prescriptive (grammar), 51–2, 136–7, **144**–5
primary language, 99, 123–4, **145**
productive knowledge, **145**
proficiency/proficient, **145**
psycho-social factors, 9, 144, **146**
psycholinguistics, **146**
pull-out classes, **146**, 155
purpose, **146**–7

qualitative research, **148**
quantitative research, **148**

recessive language, 17, 55, **149**, 174
receptive knowledge, 145, 151
recipient, 58, 79, 83, 116, **149**
recognition point, 33, 149
reduplicated babbling, 62
regional dialect, 53, 54, **149**–**50**, 162
register, 31, 106, **150**, 159

relational relativity hypothesis, **150–1**
relative proficiencies, 93, **151**
rememberers, **151–2**
restricted code, 30, 60–1, **152**
rule, 12, 32, 45, 71–2, 78, 84, 89, 99, 125, **152–3**
rule-governed, 67, **153**

Sapir-Whorf Hypothesis, **154**
scaffolding, **154–5**
SDAIE (specially designed academic instruction in English), 39, **155**
second/subsequent language (SL), 62, 72, 137, **155–6**
second/subsequent language acquisition (SLA), 1, 5, 6, 23, **156**
segmentation problem, 137, **156**
self-assessment/rating, **156–7**
semantic loan, 25, 28, **157**
semilingual (or double semi-lingual), **157**
Separate Development Hypothesis, **157–8**
sequence, 52–3, 67, **158**
sequential bilingual acquisition, **158–9**
setting, **159**
sheltered, 21, 39, 155, **159**
shift, 13, 63, **159–60**
silent period, **160**
simultaneous bilingual acquisition, **160–1**
situation of speech, 100, 146, 159, **161**
skills areas, **161–2**
Skinner, B. F., **162**
social dialect, 51, 53, 56, 111, 150, **162–3**, 173, 187
social stratification, **163**
societal bilingualism, 101, **163–4**
society, **164**
sociolect, **164**
sociolinguistic knowledge, 33, **164**
SPECT (single photon emission computed tomography), **164–5**
speech, **165**, 186
  act, 91, 144, 146, **165**
  community, 33, 59, 86, 98, 149, 151, **166**, 187
  event, 56, 89, 136, 150, 161, **166**
  stream, 33, 115, 137, 156, **166–7**
split languages, 38, **167**
split-brain studies, 44, **167**

spread, 11, 18, 88, 142, 150, 163, **167–8**
standard, 102, **168**, 169
Standard English, 10, 65, 83, 129, 137, 146, 150, **169**, 181, 183
standardization, 130, **170**
stigmatized, 50, 54, 56, 65, 163, **170**, 174
Stroop test, **170–1**
structuralism, **171**, 172
structural linguistics, **171–2**
structured immersion (programs), 17, 21, 59, 87, **172**
style shifting, **173**
submersion, 21, 59, 87, 146, **173**
subordinate bilingual (type C), **173–4**
subsequent language (SL), **174**
substrate, **174**
subtractive bilingualism, 6, 17, **174–5**, 184
summative testing, **175**
superstrate, **175**
system morpheme, 1, 116, **175**

tacit knowledge, 96
tadpole-frog problem, **176**
target language (TL), 2, 5, 7, 9, 13, 25, 27, 40, 59, 87, 90, 91, 108, 118, 121, **176**, 182
taxonomic assumption, **176–7**
teachability, 136
teaching English as a foreign language (TEFL), **177**
  as a second/subsequent language (TESL), **177**
  to speakers of other languages (TESOL), **177**
technique, 8, 118, **177**
telegraphic speech, **177–8**
testing, 33, 130, 142, 175, **178**
theory theory, **178–9**
three generation rule, 151, **179**
Thresholds Theory, **179–80**
top-down, 25, **180–1**, 189
tracks (streams), **181**
transfer, 23, 41, 42, 66, 79, 82, 92, 103, 104, 144, 180, **181**
transitional bilingual education (TBE), 21, 60, **181**
two-way/dual language programs, 17, 21, 172, **182**

two-word stage, 146, 177, **182–3, 191**
typological classification, **183**
typology, **183**

underextension, 133, **184**
ungrammatical, 72, 78, 143
unilingual/unilngualism, **184**
uniqueness point, 33, 184
universal, **184–5**
Universal Grammar (UG), 52, 77, 143, **185**
universalism, **185–6**
usage, **186**, 187
utterance, **186**

variation, 50, 53, 55, 129, 145, 153, 163, 166, 167, **187**
vernacular, 16, 30, 89, 129, 169, 186, **187–8**

Wernicke's aphasia (also known as sensory aphasia, syntactic aphasia), **189**
Wernicke's area, **189**
whole language, 8, 139, **189–90**
whole-object assumption, **190**
word, **190–1**
word class, 39, 73, **191**

www.ingramcontent.com/pod-product-compliance
Lightning Source LLC
Chambersburg PA
CBHW070830300426
44111CB00014B/2505